The History and Memories of the Whit Walks

In and around Manchester

Photograph courtesy of Stuart Coleman Photography

With Banners and Bands

by
Canon Jim Burns

This Book is for Isabelle Rose Burns, my first grandchild,
who took part in her first Whit Procession in 2012!

The Author.

First Published 2013 by Countyvise Ltd
14 Appin Road, Birkenhead, CH41 9HH

Copyright © 2013 Canon Jim Burns

The right of Canon Jim Burns to be identified as the author of this work has been asserted by him in accordance with the Copyright, Design and Patents Act 1988.

British Library Cataloguing in Publication Data.
A catalogue record for this book is available from the British Library.

ISBN 978 1 906823 84 9

All rights reserved. No part of this publication may be reproduced, stored in a retrieval system, or transmitted, in any other form, or by any other means, electronic, chemical, mechanic, photograph copying, recording or otherwise, without the prior permission of the publisher.

CONTENTS

Whit Walk Quotations

Foreword: The Bishop of Manchester 2002-2012 – The Rt. Rev. N. McCulloch

Introduction: The Author

PART ONE

The History the Memories and the Churches of the Whit Monday Procession.

Chapter 1   The Procession 1801 – 1901

Chapter 2   The Procession 1901 – 1951

Chapter 3   The Procession 1951 – 2013

Chapter 4   The Memories of the Procession

Chapter 5   The Churches and Communities of the Procession

PART TWO

Chapter 6   Whit Walks in Manchester Suburbs

Chapter 7   The History and Memories of the Manchester R.C. Procession

Chapter 8   Whit Walks in the Towns and Villages around Manchester

Chapter 9   Epilogue – The Future of Whit Walks

Whit Walks – Quotations

The Whit Monday Procession in Manchester

William Temple, then Bishop of Manchester, later Archbishop of Canterbury, in a letter to his brother in May 1921, wrote:

"There is a marvellous event here in Manchester at Whitsuntide. On Whit Monday thousands of children from Church of England Sunday Schools gather at the Town Hall in Albert Square for a service. Then off they go, led by many bands, in a procession to the Cathedral, which takes three and a half hours to pass any one point. The girls all wear white and carry bouquets of flowers and the boys are in smart suits and uniforms. There are swarms of banners and floral emblems, so it's a great show!"

Quoted in F.A. Iremonger's 'Life and Letters of William Temple'.

Dr. William Temple, the Bishop of Manchester, walking in the Whit Monday Procession.

Dr. Temple on his consecration as Bishop of Manchester in 1921.

The Whit Monday Procession

Dr Hewlett Johnson, Dean of Manchester, and later of Canterbury wrote in his autobiography.

'Searching for Light'

"For one day in the year Manchester's drab streets were transformed into a Fairyland of Colour by the City's famous Whit Monday Procession of Church of England Sunday Schools. Parents were up early – pavements swept and children scrubbed clean. Led by one hundred bands 50,000 walkers, from toddlers to grey-haired veterans took part in a Walk from the Town Hall to the Cathedral and then on to their own parishes.

There were smiling faces everywhere. My people would tell me how important the Procession was to them. I would stand outside the Cathedral shaking the hands of the many walkers as they passed by for the whole three and a half hours. Some businessmen attempted to make an end of the Procession, saying it interfered with business. I told them it would be over my dead body if they tried!"

Dean Hewlett Johnson greets Joan Monckton (nee Ashworth) as the Whit Monday Procession passes Manchester Cathedral in 1929.

Described in the newspaper as his "Last Walk (before becoming Dean of Canterbury) and her first Walk." - Photograph courtesy of J. Monckton.

The then Dean of Manchester – the Very Reverend H. Jones

In 1954 wrote about the Whit Monday Procession 'Why We Walk At Whitsun.'

"The streets of the City shall be full of boys and girls playing in its streets. That is not a description of the Whit Walks, but of the heavenly city as seen by the prophet Zechariah. Yet it has this in common with the Whit Walks that they testify to the fact that God is interested in the interests and joys of children, and in the fact that parents and grandparents renew their own childhood by watching the Walks. Religious people must always be aware of the tendency to think that God cares only for our devotions and not for our games, our joys and even our dresses. Yet this is not all. The Whit Walks began essentially from the laity and not from the clergy. Subconsciously they were a protest against the grimness and drabness of much of Manchester and Salford a century and a half ago. Most of the children may think more of their new dresses and suits than of the religious significance of the Walks, but it is something to have new dresses associated with a walk from the Town Hall to the Cathedral, and the majority of the children will never forget it."

The Very Revd, H Jones, Dean of Manchester, watches as the Procession passes Manchester Cathedral on the "wet" Whit Monday of 1954.
The banner is that of St. Catherine's, Collyhurst.
Photograph courtesy of Manchester Evening News and Chronicle.

The then R.C. Bishop of Salford, later Archbishop of Liverpool - the Rt. Rev. G. A. Beck

In 1962 wrote about the Whit Friday Procession in Manchester.

"The Catholic Whit Friday Procession in Manchester is always an occasion for those taking part in it to show their love for the Church. The presence of school children in the procession is a bright and attractive feature. Tastefully dressed and moving with such good discipline they are a tribute to our schools and teachers. We are proud to think that parents in this Diocese fulfil this obligation with courage and generosity."

The Whit Friday Procession: Excerpt from the Leader in the Manchester Evening Chronicle, May 1956

"They came, they walked, and they conquered the heart of the City. This was the famous Roman Catholic Whit Friday Procession which once again transformed Manchester into a breathtaking spectacle of colour."

FOREWORD

The Bishop of Manchester 2002-2012 – the Rt. Rev. Nigel McCulloch

My great-grandfather was brought up in Bengal Street at the heart of industrial Ancoats. Born in 1839, he may well have seen some of the early Walks in Manchester. They would have provided a bright interval in what must have been a dark time for most of the population.

Jim Burns has produced an intriguing and valuable overview of the significant place the Walks have had, since those early days in Manchester, in the life of local communities across the North West.

It has been a great joy to me to have taken part in Whit Walks in recent years, both at the centre and in other parts of the diocese – and, in some places, to have seen a resurgence of interest in keeping the tradition.

I would be sad to see the Walks disappear from our local calendar. So I am delighted that Jim's book will serve as a reminder of their importance in providing a public affirmation of Christian witness that, for all the richness that other faiths bring to our communities, is still at the heart of our culture.

Nigel McCulloch
Bishop of Manchester, 2002-2012

INTRODUCTION

Whitsun is the Christian Festival of the giving of the Holy Spirit. In Manchester and surrounding areas it has traditionally been celebrated in a distinctive way with outdoor processions of witness by the churches, known popularly as the 'Whit Walks'. For generations of Manchester's children, Whitsun was as exciting as Christmas. Wearing new 'Whit Week clothes' children took part in the Whit Walks, and in times when holidays away from industrial Manchester were unknown for most, many joined in Whit excursions to the seaside, or into the countryside, organised by their Sunday Schools.

My own experience of the Whit Walks is of the Church of England Whit Monday Procession in Manchester City Centre. The first Whit Monday Procession took place in 1801. It was the forerunner of Whit Walks in the suburbs, villages and towns around Manchester. In times past, the Whit Monday Procession, and the Roman Catholic Whit Friday Procession were massive events watched by thousands of spectators who lined the city streets. The Whit Walks featured in cinema newsreels, and with the coming of Independent Television they were televised live in the mid 1950s. This book begins with a history of the Whit Monday Procession, and people's memories of it. It includes, in addition, chapters on Whit Walks in the Manchester suburbs; the Manchester Whit Friday Roman Catholic Procession; and Whit Walks in towns and villages around Manchester – of which, the first 1801 Whit Monday Procession was the forerunner. Present day local history books rarely mention the Whit Walks. I hope that this book will perpetuate their memory and give this unique tradition the recognition it deserves. The Whit Walks have been a significant part of Manchester's religious and social history. In former times they were woven into the fabric of the lives of Mancunians and of their communities.

The origin of the Church of England Whit Monday Walk lay in the development of Sunday Schools in the early nineteenth century. It became a celebration for the Sunday School movement. In less affluent times Sunday Schools did much to provide education, welfare and recreation for children, and adults, in addition to teaching the Christian Faith. In areas adjacent to the city centre, which were poor in material terms, but rich in neighbourliness and community, the Whit Monday Procession became the occasion for a Festival Day, which brought relief from the monotony of working life. It was a colourful demonstration of the Spirit of Faith, and of the Spirit of Community. In its heyday, approaching 50,000 children from 45 parishes led by one hundred bands, walked in a procession which took three and a half hours to pass any point on its route. It was organised and supported, with a commitment which reflected the spirit of the times.

The Whit Friday Roman Catholic Procession in Manchester was an equally colourful demonstration of between 20,000 and 30,000 walkers from 24 parishes. It originated with the organisation of Catholic Sunday and day schools in the 19th Century.

The older-generation of Manchester people, now removed from the inner heartlands of the Whit Walks by re-housing, have fond memories of the processions. I have written this book for them, and for the departed members of my family for whom the Whit Walks meant so much.

From infancy to old age, across two centuries, Manchester people witnessed to their faith with a community spirit lost to the present generation.

On Whit Mondays Anglicans walked to Albert Square, and on to Manchester Cathedral, wearing red roses, the traditional flower of their festival day.

On Whit Fridays the Roman Catholic churches processed to Albert Square, and on to Piccadilly, their walkers wore the yellow rose.

At Whitsun, Christians, of all denominations, in and around Manchester celebrated Faith and Community in their unique Whit Walks – they walked with Banners and Bands!

Canon Jim Burns

St. Ann's Church in St. Ann's Square Manchester
from where the first Whit Walk in 1801 began.
Photograph - Manchester Libraries

PART ONE

The Whit Monday Procession:

The History, the Memories and the Churches

Chapter 1

The History Of The Whit Monday Church Of England Procession
1801 – 1901

In The Beginning...

Many people have, what they have described to the Author, as 'wonderful memories' of the Whit Walks. How did they begin and why? Dr Vanessa Toulmin in a 'Short History of Manchester' writes: "The practice of walking during Whit Week can be traced back to Manchester, with the development of the Sunday School Movement".

The strongest claim for founding the Sunday School Movement is made for Robert Raikes in Gloucester in 1780. In 1784 a Sunday School Committee for the children of all denominations was set-up in Manchester. In 1800 the Church of England formed its own committee for the development of its Sunday Schools, to provide spiritual and social care for the children of families who had moved into Manchester from the surrounding countryside to work in its cotton mills, factories and mines, during the Industrial Revolution. The Sunday Schools set out to provide a remedy for the problems of child labour and working conditions in Manchester's growing industries. A six-day working week left children free on Sundays, but many fell into the temptations of gang membership, alcohol, cock fighting and attendance at the races.

In response one of the first resolutions of the Manchester Church of England Sunday School Committee was: "That the children of the Sunday Schools be called together in Whitsun Week yearly to hear Divine Service". The original intention was that the service be held at St Ann's Church Manchester, but at the request of the Warden of the Collegiate Church (now the Cathedral) this was changed to that church. As a compromise it was decided that the children would meet at St Ann's in St Ann's Square and on Whit Monday 1801 walk in procession to the Collegiate Church, led by a military band, for Divine Service. The Whit Monday Procession was born! A tradition was begun which set the future pattern for Whit Walks in Manchester and in the surrounding areas.

Manchester Cathedral, originally the Collegiate Church. The Whit Monday Procession walked to the Collegiate Church/Manchester Cathedral from the procession's inception in 1801.

The First Procession

In 1750 Manchester and Salford had only three Church of England churches. The Collegiate Church; St Ann's Church and Sacred Trinity, Salford. Less than fifty years later there were ten churches. This is an indication of the growth in population of Manchester and Salford in those years. The Sunday Schools of those ten churches were invited to join in the first Whit Monday Procession. They were:

The Collegiate Church (The Cathedral);
St. Ann's, Manchester;
St Mary's, Parsonage, Deansgate;
St Paul's, Turner Street;
St John's, Deansgate;
St Peter's, Mosley Street;
St James, George Street;
St Michael's, Angel Meadow;
Sacred Trinity, Salford;
St Stephen's, Salford.

1,800 children took part in the first Whit Walk. The 'big' banners, which were to become a feature of the Procession in future years, were not in use on the day of the first procession. The Boroughreeve and Constables with their staves of office led the procession of children who walked six-abreast accompanied by the band of the Second Royal Dragoons. Could the organisers of that first Whit Walk, have thought, as they gathered in St Ann's Square on Whit Monday 1801, that they were starting a tradition which would continue for 212 years, and become a part of so many lives? The main purpose of the Procession was that the Sunday Schools attend Divine Service at the Collegiate Church (the Cathedral). In 1801, after the service at the Collegiate Church, every Sunday School teacher was provided with bread and cheese. In the following year they were given a dinner and a quart of ale each. This was changed for 1803, after a teacher was found drunk and disorderly in the Collegiate Church churchyard! The first procession had been a success and it was resolved to continue it annually. In its early days the route of the procession was via St Ann's Square, Exchange Street and Market Place to the Collegiate Church. The Procession would have wound its way around a very different Manchester from today. The churches taking part were all from what is now the city centre, with the exceptions of Sacred Trinity and St Stephen's, Salford, and St Michael's, Angel Meadow. St Stephen's and St Michael's walked from new suburbs, a further sign of Manchester and Salford's growth.

Cattle in Cateaton Street!

In 1801 there were still farms amongst the new mills and factories of Manchester, and the firemen and beadles were requested to form a line across Cateaton Street to keep the cattle from interfering with the Procession! As the Procession became established the service in the Collegiate Church began to attract huge congregations. Each year a children's choir led the singing. In 1807 the church was so crowded that windows had to be removed for ventilation.

By 1810 the numbers in the Procession had grown substantially, and the practice of marking out a place in St Ann's Square for each Sunday School began. A year later the organising committee asked that soldiers stationed in Manchester assist in preserving the order of the Procession.

Buns, Milk, Whit Week Clothes and Excursions

In 1812 the custom of providing the children with buns and milk was begun. The organising committee advised each Sunday School to provide buns at a cost of "no more than one penny each". The giving of buns and milk on Whit Monday continued into the late 1950s. In the 1800s buns and milk for the children would have been a significant gesture. In 1813 the Procession organisers turned their attention to the clothes to be worn by the children in the Whit Walk. They decided that 'plainness of dress be asked of all taking part'. The organisers stated that 'the girls should wear caps and tippets of plain and modest appearance, free from all finery and gaudy decoration – refraining from what is superfluous, expensive and un-becoming'. There was no advice given as to what the boys should wear! The criticism of "expensive" Whit Week clothes seems to have been made from the earliest days of the Procession. Against this it may be said that had generations of less privileged Manchester children not received new clothes for Whitsun, they wouldn't have had new clothes at any other time. In addition, Archbishop William Temple's description of Whit Monday's Procession as a "Great Show" and Dean Hewlett Johnson's portrait of the Procession as "a Fairyland of Colour" could not have been made had parents not found the means to clothe their children in Whitsun finery.

Boys and girls in their Whit Week clothes.
St. Paul's New Cross procession in the 1920s.
Photograph courtesy of members of St. Paul's Church.

As the Whit Monday Procession became a permanent part of Manchester's Whitsun, customs associated with it made for a holiday Whitsun Week for children. Whit Week excursions to the seaside or into the countryside for the children were started by Sunday Schools attached to St Paul's Church which stood in Turner Street, and was later to be replaced by St Paul's, New Cross. These Sunday Schools were, Turner Street, Spear Street, Bennett Street and German Street. David Stott of St Paul's Church and founder of Bennett Street Sunday School became an influential figure in the Sunday School Movement in Manchester. St Paul's Whitsun excursions began in 1816 with trips to Dunham Park, Kersal Moor, Flixton and Southport by canal boat – there were no railways then! Other Sunday Schools followed St Paul's lead and excursions became an important part of the Whit Week celebrations until the late 1950s. Their popularity with the children of industrial Manchester cannot be overstated.

St. Paul's New Cross ladies turn into Mosley Street – Whit Monday 1910. Photograph courtesy of Wendy Lees.

St. Paul's Bennett Street Sunday School, founded by David Stott. Their banner is carried in a 1950s Whit Monday Procession. Photograph courtesy of Wendy Lees.

A Serious Incident and the Procession's abandonment for Parish Whit Walks

In 1816 there was a serious incident in the Collegiate Church when children in the crowded congregation rushed for the exits when a window was broken. In the panic a child was killed. The Procession organisers responded by abandoning the Whit Monday Walk for two years. The Sunday Schools were encouraged to organise processions in their own parishes instead. Here lies the origin of the parish, and outer district Whit Walks, which became established in addition to the re-started Whit Monday Walk in the city centre. As the number of churches and walkers grew it became impossible for all the contingents to attend the service in the Collegiate Church. The practice of inviting a different group of parishes to attend the service each year began. This became regarded as an honour when the Collegiate Church became Manchester Cathedral and the expression "our church is in the Cathedral this year" was often heard. The question of dress was raised again in the 1820s, and again only the dress of the girls. The organisers stated: 'That strict attention should be paid to prevent any immoderate, indecorous or extravagance of dress in the females'! At this time the route of the procession was extended from St Ann's Square via King Street, York Street, Mosley Street and Market Street to the Collegiate Church. In 1822 it was decided that the Sunday Schools taking part should take their place in the Order of Procession according to the date of the consecration of their respective churches.

Growth and a Significant Part of Manchester life

The Whit Monday Procession was growing into a significant part of Manchester life by the 1830s. New suburbs were springing up in the fields around Manchester and churches and Sunday Schools were being built to serve them. These new parishes joined the Procession as they were formed. In 1830 the Procession organisers called upon adult members of church congregations to join the children of the Sunday Schools in the Whit Walk; this was a call repeatedly made over the years. Despite it the Procession remained predominantly a children's event – as adults 'watched the scholars' from the pavements.

From a Village to a Cathedral City and the Procession moves to Albert Square

In 1847 the Collegiate Church became a Cathedral as the Mother Church of the new Diocese of Manchester, and Manchester now had its own bishop. In less than a hundred years Manchester had grown from a village into a great industrial city. The Diocese of Manchester included most of Lancashire. In many of its towns and villages the Whit Monday Procession became the inspiration for their own Whit Walks and Walking Days. Ashton under Lyne, Droylsden, Oldham, Rochdale, Bury, Bolton, Wigan, the Saddleworth villages and other areas established their own distinctive processions.

Manchester Town Hall, Albert Square in 1878. The Whit Monday Procession has gathered in Albert Square since 1878.

By 1878 the Whit Monday Walk had grown from ten to forty Church of England Sunday Schools and the numbers taking part from 1,800 to 20,000 children. The organisers decided that the numbers had become too great for St Ann's Square to continue as the assembly point. A change was made to meeting at the Town Hall in Albert Square. This began an important tradition in the history of the Procession. By the 1870s each parish contingent had its own bands and was led by its 'big banner' which bore the parish's name and an illustration of a Saint or of a biblical event. Ribbons attached to these banners were held by girls in white dresses bearing bouquets of flowers. In addition to the Sunday School children, parish organisations such as the Church Lads and Church Girls' Brigade, the Scouts and Guides – and the Mothers' Union took part in the Walk. Floral emblems with a Christian message became a feature of the Procession.

With its 'big banners' colourfully dressed children, robed clergy and church choirs, floral displays and the stirring notes of uniformed bands echoing in the city streets, the Whit Monday Procession became a sight to behold. Great crowds of people lined the city streets, many waiting from 7:00 a.m., to applaud as the children passed by. Albert Square on Whit Monday became filled as the walkers gathered for a Service before moving on to the Cathedral and their own parishes.

An Eye Witness Account

In the book *'Angels from the Meadow'* telling the story of the Angel Meadow district of Manchester in the nineteenth century, James Stanhope Brown includes the account of an eye-witness of the Whit Monday Procession in Manchester on 14 May 1883: 'At half-past seven on Whit Monday morning policemen from Minshull Street were clearing people from Albert Square. At eight o'clock the Square had been transformed into a pseudo-military parade ground. Barriers were erected at strategic points in the square, with marshalls and policemen all around. Manchester was keeping a High Holiday and the strains of many bands could be heard in the distance. It was the children's Holiday Festival; long anticipated. Hope had reigned supreme as thousands of little ones had rose with the lark, donned their Whitsun best, and with their various Sunday Schools wended their way to Albert Square. No sooner had the Town Hall clock chimed 8.15 a.m., when in had marched the Strangeways Refuge Boys with their drum and fife Band and sailor boys in white uniforms.

Whit Monday 1890.
The Procession moves along Mosley Street with the former St. Peter's church in the background. Illustration courtesy of J Stanhope Brown.

After a ten minute lull a torrent of children poured into the Square, St Mary's Deansgate had been the first to arrive. The large procession of children with the big blue banner of All Souls' Ancoats had come next, followed by the first appearance of the new Church of St Clement, Broughton. Cross Street had become a surging sea; banners rippling in the breeze with each new arrival.

The Strangeways Boys' Band featured in the 19th century Whit Monday processions.

After a short Service in the packed square, and the singing of the National Anthem, the Procession began to leave for Manchester Cathedral. The robed boys of Chethams Hospital School, and the Cathedral clergy had led the way along Princess Street. It seemed that all Manchester was gathered along the route to the Cathedral. The cheers and hand clapping had become almost deafening. Not a single space was to be seen along the highway, which had become the traditional route of the Whit Walks. After what seemed an eternally long march along Princess Street, Mosley Street, Market Street and Old Millgate the tired, but happy wanderers, had arrived at the Cathedral Gates – and then went on their way to their respective schools. Some of them from Strangeways Boys' Refuge were to walk again on the late afternoon of Whit Monday in the smaller Cheetham Hill Whit Walk with St Luke's Cheetham children!'

James Stanhope Brown has this account of the progress of the Whit Monday Procession from 1801 to be a major event in the life of Manchester. In 1884 George Milner JP, Freeman of Manchester, and a figure in the Sunday School Movement from St Paul's Bennett Street Sunday School, became Chairman of the Organising Committee, a role he fulfilled until his death in 1915. During his Chairmanship he was regarded as the Whit Monday Procession personified.

The Procession had become a religious celebration of great social significance. It could be said that it was the one aspect of the life of the Church of England in Manchester that involved the mass of the population of the inner city. It provided the focus for a Holiday and Festival Week, for the industrial workers of Manchester and Salford and their children. By 1891 the Procession involved 41 Churches and 28,000 walkers, and its popularity was continuing to increase.

A Grandfather's Memories recalled

In the Local History Section of Manchester Central Library, there are copies of the Official Programmes of the Whit Monday Procession. Most of them cover the 1920s and 1930s, but a few date back to the 1900s, and one to 1893. In that year the grandfather of the author of this book, William Holt, was one of the 580 children walking in the procession from St Jude's, Ancoats. William Holt's memories of those days have remained in his family. They tell of a "magical Whitsun" for the children of the 1890s in inner-Manchester and Salford. In pre-welfare state days their lives were hard. They lived in rows of terraced houses surrounded by cotton mills and factories. Working hours for adults and young people were long, many experienced poverty, and holidays away from Manchester were unknown. There was though, good neighbourliness and a community spirit which expressed itself in preparation for, and participation in, the Whit Monday Procession. At Whitsun there was excitement amongst young and old alike. The colour, pageantry and martial music of the bands all contrasting vividly with the grind and monotony of daily life in the mills and factories.

St. Jude's Ancoats walk along Butler Street Ancoats in 1951
before the area's re-development. The St. Jude's banner is the banner which the Author's
grandfather would have walked under in 1893.
Photograph courtesy of Hilda Bennett (nee Cashinella) the first girl in line on the left.

Whit Monday would begin early. Doorsteps and pavements would be swept. Children were scrubbed clean and their new Whitsun clothes donned. Flowers to be carried in the Procession would be collected from Smithfield Market. By 6.30 a.m., children would be making their way to their respective Sunday Schools for a 7.00 a.m., start for Albert Square. In the city centre thousands of spectators, many wearing clogs and shawls would have lined the route. In Piccadilly viewing grandstands would have been erected, giving an excellent view of the Procession as it passed on its way to the Cathedral. For Mancunians, it was a great day. During the other days of Whitsun Week, the Sunday School excursions to the seaside, and into the country, would have been sheer delight for the children of industrial Manchester and Salford.

19th Century spectators watch the Whit Monday Walk.

Sunday School Celebration

By the end of the nineteenth century the Manchester Whit Monday Procession had established a one hundred year tradition and it had become the inspiration for Whit Walks elsewhere. It had begun with the Sunday Schools and it continued as an annual Sunday School Celebration. A television documentary about Sunday Schools highlighted their importance and their achievements, in times before state organised education in day schools – and afterwards, into the twentieth century. A tribute was paid to the Sunday Schools, in the 1950s, by "one acknowledged as the greatest authority on Sunday Schools in Manchester". 'The Sunday School system of Manchester began in dark times when the morals of the people were at a low ebb, and when the poor were suffering both in body and mind. There was a time when the Sunday Schools offered the hard-working poor almost the only consolation, pleasure, recreation and education they possessed in life. Work began at four o'clock in the morning and ended at about eight in the evening. Sunday Schools were, at the period, the great solace and support of the labouring poor, and without them their case would have been sad indeed. The Sunday Schools aimed at something more, and began to give the rising generation an education. To the Sunday Schools of Manchester, this generation owed all the education given in the early part of the century. Day s chool instruction hardly existed. The Sunday Schools from the beginning recognised the duty of trying to educate the poor, and this they accomplished to an extraordinary degree, considering the materials at their disposal. When the history of the Sunday Schools is written the public will be surprised to find the large number of persons holding high offices in life, who owed all their education and all they possessed in worldly terms, entirely to the Sunday Schools'. The achievements of the Sunday School Movement was worthy of celebration; and it was celebrated in great style when the Whit Monday Procession entered its second century in 1901.

In and around Manchester

St. Augustine's Monsall, an elaborate floral banner in a 1950s Walk

Christ Church Bradford confirmation banner on the 1954 wet Whit Monday.

Chapter 2

The History Of The Whit Monday Procession
1901 – 1951

Into a Second Century...

The Whit Monday Procession celebrated its centenary in May 1901. In 1801 ten Church of England Sunday Schools had taken part in the first Whit Walk with 1,800 children. At the Centenary Procession forty-five Sunday schools took part, with over 30,000 children. The Centenary Procession programme included illustrations of the various church buildings and photographs of the clergy. It listed the Sunday Schools taking part:-

1. Chethams Blue Coat School in the Cathedral Parish;
2. The Girls' Jubilee School, Bury Old Road;
3. The Strangeways Boys Refuge School;
4. The Cathedral;
5. St Saviours Mission Church in the Cathedral Parish;
6. Sacred Trinity Salford;
7. St Ann with St Mary Manchester;
8. St Thomas Ardwick;
9. Ardwick Green Industrial School;
10. St Paul Bennett Street Sunday School;
11. St John Deansgate;
12. St Peter, Mosley Street;
13. St James, George Street;
14. St Michael, Angel Meadow;
15. St Stephen's Salford;
16. St Luke's Chorlton on Medlock;
17. St George in the Fields, Oldham Road;
18. St Philip's, Salford;
19. St Matthew's, Campfield, Deansgate;
20. St Andrew's, Ancoats;
21. St Jude's, Ancoats;
22. St Thomas, Red Bank;
23. All Souls, Ancoats;
24. St Silas, Ardwick,
25. SS Simon and Jude, Granby Row;
26. St Matthias, Salford;
27. St Simon's, Salford;
28. St Barnabas, Oldham Road;
29. St Phillip's, Bradford Road and Branson Street Mission and Joynson Memorial Mission;
30. St Oswald's, Collyhurst;

31. St John's, Miles Platting;
32. St Catherine's, Collyhurst;
33. St Peter's, Oldham Road;
34. Christ Church, Bradford;
35. Albert Memorial Church, Collyhurst;
36. St James the Great, Collyhurst;
37. St Luke's, Miles Platting;
38. St Mary's, Bishop Lee Memorial Beswick;
39. St Clement's, Broughton;
40. St James the Less, Ancoats;
41. St Martin's German Street, Oldham Road;
42. St Aidan's, Bradford;
43. St Mark's, Holland Street;
44. St Augustine's, Monsall;
45. Christ Church, Harpurhey.

The Centenary Procession appears to be the only occasion on which Christ Church, Harpurhey, a considerable distance from the city centre, took part.

In *'Manchester a Short History of its Development'* an eye-witness account of the Centenary Procession is given.

1901 – An Eye Witness Account

"The scene in Albert Square this morning was one of exceptional beauty. At 8.00 a.m., the space in the Square was so arranged by the marshalls that the place of each school was indicated by a flag-staff flying the Union Jack. For the next half-hour the different schools arrived in quick succession, and the music of the bands proceeded from all corners of the Square. There was a mingling of colours – the hoods of the clergy contrasting with the costumes worn by the scholars and the Chetham Boys wearing the quaint garments of the School Order. Nathaniel Drumville unfurled his white flag to act as a baton, and to the beating of time more than 30,000 young voices sang the Old Hundreth. The schools marched out of the Square, the order being determined by the date of the consecration of their respective churches. At every point on the route great crowds of sightseers were gathered."

The Centenary Procession was marked by the wearing of commemorative ribbons and by a special Cathedral Service, but plans for a celebration gathering in Heaton Park were abandoned because the park was not available on the day required.

In its second century the Whit Monday Procession reached its heyday with estimates of the numbers taking part ranging from 30,000 to 50,000. The Whit Monday Procession programme and the Whit Monday hymn book sold thousands of copies each year. The Sunday School Movement, which the Procession celebrated, continued its outreach to communities, with societies for education, welfare, leisure, sickness, bereavement and penny bank savings.

*The Chethams Hospital Boys, in traditional uniform, led the Whit Monday Procession until 1939. Here they walk by Manchester Cathedral towards Albert Square, (where the Walk began), in the 1930s.
Photograph courtesy of Chethams School.*

The King is Dead – Long Live the King!

In 1910 the Whit Monday Procession took place on the death of King Edward VII. The banners were draped with black ribbons and the children wore black rosettes. A year later the Organising Committee resolved that on the accession to the throne of King George V special favours in the Royal Colours be worn on Whit Monday by the children, and that a telegram be sent to the King from all assembled in Albert Square.

The Great War And A Victory Procession

In 1914 as the First World War broke out, some advised that the Procession be abandoned. The Organising Committee disagreed and the Whit Walk went on with women volunteering to carry the banners! In 1916 however, the Manchester Watch Committee withdrew its permission for the Procession because of a government order cancelling the Whit Week holidays. With the War's end in 1919 the Whit Walk began again in a spirit of patriotic fervour.

Banner girls of St. Augustine's Monsall in Albert Square in the 1920s. The raised dias, from where the massed hymn-singing was conducted, can be seen behind the girls.

The theme of the 1919 Procession was "Victory in the Great War". Red, white and blue was much in evidence in the draping of banners and in the clothes worn by the children. Boys were dressed as sailors, 40 of them with St George's Oldham Road, and some with other churches. The St George's sailors marched on into the 1950s. A boy and a girl walked in the Procession dressed as John Bull and Britannia, with German Street Church of England Sunday School - a tableau which was to be ongoing. It is interesting to note that in the war-time processions of 1914 and 1915 the banner of German Street Sunday School had to have a police escort, because it bore the word "German" in the Sunday School's title! The tradition of patriotism was to be a continuing feature in the Whit Monday Procession. National flags, red, white and blue ribbons, red roses and the patriotic tunes of the bands reflected the spirit of the times. A spirit that could be encouraged in Sunday Schools, church day schools and from church pulpits. The relationship between Church and Nation was proclaimed by procession banners embroidered with the text: "Fear God, Honour the King". In the 1920s and 1930s the Procession remained a popular event, and the numbers taking part reached their highest point.

The "Victory to the Allies" theme in the 1919 Whit Monday Procession.

Girls of St. Augustine's Monsall pictured before leaving their school room for the Walk. America, Belgium, Peace, Britannia, Victory, France and Italy.

Renee Carr leaves St. Matthias Salford on an early 1920s Whit Monday Walk. Photograph courtesy R.Carr.

A Threat to the Whit Holidays and the Whit Walks

In the late 1920s Manchester businessmen raised their concerns about the local Whit Week Holiday and the Whit Walks. The Manchester Trade Organisations made a move to change the Holiday, claiming that the Procession was "interfering with the business week". The Whit Monday Procession Organising Committee responded with a resolution "deploring the action of the Manchester Chamber of Commerce, and the Royal Exchange in interfering with the time honoured custom of the Manchester Whit Walks and the Whit Holiday". Dean Hewlett Johnson was adamant that the Whit Walks should continue. Mammon retreated and the Whit Monday Procession went on!

Whit Monday 1919, girls representing the victorious allies and sailor boys leave St. Augustine's in Monsall for Albert Square.

*St Augustine Monsall photographs
- St Augustine's Ladies.*

A New King and Queen

In 1936 the death of King George V was marked in the Procession, and in 1937 the Coronation of King George VI and Queen Elizabeth was celebrated with a Procession of 37 parish Sunday Schools. The Official Programme for that year carried photographs of the new King and Queen, with features on them both. On the new King the editorial commented: "1937 will be written down in history as the year that brought to the throne, in circumstances without parallel in the history of England, the second son of the beloved George V. The thoroughfares through which the Procession passes will make a mighty blaze of colour, bunting and Coronation flags, Whit Monday coming only five days after the Coronation. When the children grow to manhood and womanhood, they will look back on this year's Procession, for in God's guidance they will see the reign of George VI brimful of great deeds. They will, it is fervently hoped, never witness the great sufferings and great perils that marked the reign of our new monarch's father". Sadly the great sufferings and perils of George V's reign were to be repeated in the Second World War in George VI's reign. On Queen Elizabeth the editorial stated: "A procession similar to that of Whit Monday would rejoice the heart of Queen Elizabeth, for she is profoundly interested in the welfare of the children of the Empire'. The 1937 Programme printed articles about the Lord Mayor of Manchester, Alderman Joseph Toole, described as "a nipper of the slums risen to First Citizen" and Councillor Peter Ashcroft, Mayor of Salford, "both of whom put Whit processions first in their enthusiasm for public pageantry".

In and around Manchester

1920s Whit Walk at All Souls' Ancoats. Note the old terraced houses now demolished.

1900s Whit Monday procession – ladies of All Souls' Ancoats.

1920s Whit Walk, All Souls' Ancoats. Photographs courtesy of C. Cumbes.

The History and Memories of the Whit Walks

In 1939, 37 Sunday Schools took part in the last pre-war Procession. The official programme included a photograph of, and a feature on, the then Bishop of Manchester, Dr Guy Warman, commenting: "Although he does not actually take part in the Whit Monday Procession, the Bishop of Manchester has nothing but praise for this annual demonstration of Faith, which cannot fail to impress the thousands and thousands of people watching it". Within months of the 1939 Procession the Second World War began, and the 1940 Procession was abandoned.

The 40 sailor boys from St. George's Oldham Road in a Whit Walk. Photograph courtesy of M.E.N.

St. Augustine's, Monsall walk to the city centre on Whit Monday 1919 at the end of the First World War. (Note the two soldiers on the pavement, to the left, behind the tram).

Walking on the same morning, in 1919 St. Augustine's Mothers' Union. (Note the spectators wearing shawls with one well-dressed lady amongst them).

In and around Manchester

*St Matthias Salford Children before
a 1920s Whit Monday Walk.*

The 1945 Post-War Procession

There were no processions from 1940 until May 1945, when the Whit Monday Walk was restarted immediately the War in Europe ended. The Procession that year showed a determined spirit. Victory in the Second World War was celebrated, but Whit Monday of May 1945 saw Whitsun outfits restricted by wartime rationing. The Procession passed through a Manchester City Centre devastated by enemy bombing. There was the continuing absence of Servicemen, and the nation was in a period of austerity. Despite these setbacks, May 1945 saw 26,000 people, young, and not so young, once again processing through Manchester on Whit Monday, with banners and bands. In the late 1940s the Procession regained much of its pre-war strength and pageantry, bringing colour into those austere post-war years.

St. Philip's Bradford Road, Rose Queen and floral banner late 1940s/early 1950s Whit Walk. (Note the mill and the long demolished shops).

An Eye-Witness View of the 1950 Procession

Writing in the 'Manchester Evening Chronicle' of Whit Monday 1950, Arthur Brooks describes the 149th Whit Walk: 'As I stand on my fifth-storey vantage point above crowd packed Market Street, I am radioing my story of this proud declaration of Faith – the 149th Whit Monday Procession from the twin cities of Manchester and Salford. Manchester in May-time and the weather is kind for all the thousands of gaily dressed children and the grown-ups walking proudly behind banners dipping in a gentle breeze. For thirty-five Church of England Sunday Schools it has meant weeks of preparation. The effort was worthwhile for today's Procession of Witness is true to its aim, looking splendid and moving with the slow grace one always associates with such an historic event. For two hours before the Procession moved off, people began to line the streets. Now they stand five-deep. In Albert Square at 7.16 a.m., a Moston boy scout, twelve years-old, looked smart in his well-pressed uniform, he was one of the first at the starting point. Chorlton on Medlock's All Saints Church, blitzed during the war and now demolished, have presented their banner to St Saviour's Chorlton on Medlock, who have taken their place in the Procession. Today, ten years after Dunkirk two veterans of the shell-torn beaches bring back a breath of All Saints' past glory when they carry the banner through Manchester in the Procession. At the head of the Procession is the tall slim figure of the Bishop of Manchester. With him is the Dean of Manchester who suffered torture at the hands of the Japanese. Here comes the leading contingent – the Cathedral and Collegiate Church, with its red and white surpliced choir and altar boys, presenting a splendid picture'.

The Procession moves along Market Street Manchester in the 1950s with the All Souls' Ancoats contingent. Photograph courtesy Cyril Cumbes.

The fifth storey vantage view of the 1950 Whit Monday Procession as it turns into Market Street from Mosley Street.

1951 – 150th Whit Monday Anniversary Procession

25,000 children took part in the 1951, 150th Anniversary Procession. As listed in the official programme, the parishes were:-

1. Manchester Cathedral;
2. Sacred Trinity, Salford;
3. St Ann, Manchester;
4. St Matthew's Mission Church Campfield in St Ann's Parish;
5. St Thomas, Ardwick;
6. St Paul's Bennett Street Sunday School;
7. St Stephen's, Salford;
8. St Luke, Chorlton on Medlock;
9. St George's in the Fields, Oldham Road;
10. St Philip, Salford;
11. St Andrew, Ancoats;
12. St Saviour, Chorlton on Medlock;
13. St Jude, Ancoats;
14. All Souls', Ancoats;
15. St Matthias with St Simon, Salford;
16. St Barnabas, Oldham Road,
17. St Philip, Bradford Road;
18. St Oswald, Collyhurst;
19. St John, Miles Platting;
20. St Catherine, Collyhurst;
21. St Peter with St James the Less Ancoats;
22. German Street Church of England Sunday School;
23. Christ Church and St Cuthberts Mission, Bradford;
24. Albert Memorial, Collyhurst;
25. St Michael, Hulme,
26. St Stephen with St Mark, Hulme,
27. St James the Great, Collyhurst;
28. St Luke, Miles Platting;
29. St Mary, Beswick;
30. St Clement, Broughton;
31. St Mark, Holland Street;
32. St Augustine, Monsall;
33. St Aidan, Bradford;
34. St Paul, Philips Park;
35. St Jerome, Ardwick.

The History and Memories of the Whit Walks

The 1951 Whit Monday Walk in Market Street, Manchester.

Barbara Wilkinson St. Augustine's Monsall Rose Queen and Attendants. Whit Monday Walk, 1956. Photograph courtesy St Augustine's Ladies.

The walkers, of whom the Author, then aged seven, was one (with several members of his family) wore commemorative ribbons. Floral emblems were carried proclaiming: "150 Years Walks of Witness". The official programme carried brief notes on "The Story of the Procession 1801-1951". The celebrations included a Service of Thanksgiving in Manchester Cathedral led by the Dean, and Salford's great parish priest Canon Peter Green. A Lord Mayor Reception for Procession Committee members, clergy, teachers and elected children was held at Manchester Town Hall. A rally was organised in Wythenshawe Park for all taking part in the Procession. At this time an Annual Pre-Whit Monday Dance for walkers was instituted at Belle Vue. The Bishop of Manchester wrote an imaginary dialogue with parents in the Anniversary Programme on the role of Sunday Schools in children being raised in the Faith.

Whit Monday 1950s – the choir boys of Manchester Cathedral.

The Bishop's Dialogue with Parents - The Rt. Rev. Dr. W.D.L. Greer

BISHOP: (To Parents) 'Do you really care for your children?'

PARENTS: 'Why, of course we do.'

BISHOP: 'Then you'll naturally want to supply their needs and equip them properly for life.'

PARENTS: 'Obviously. We like giving the kids things. You should have seen what they got for Christmas.'

BISHOP: 'Lots of presents I suppose. But did you tell them about the real meaning of Christmas?

PARENTS: 'Well, no we didn't say anything about that.'

BISHOP: 'That's just it. You parents are glad to give food and fun and toys to your children, but you forget to give them the things that matter most.'

PARENTS: 'What do you mean?'

BISHOP: 'I mean the Christian Faith. It is far more important to teach children about their duty towards God and their duty towards their neighbour; about Jesus Christ; about the Christian way of living; about the Church, and prayer and the Sacraments - infinitely more important than giving them material things.

In a few years the toys will be broken and forgotten but they'll never cease to bless you if you have provided a Christian home for them and brought them up as Christians.'

PARENTS: 'But we are not sure that we're able to teach our children all that a Christian should know.'

BISHOP: Well there are Sunday Schools. Couldn't you see that your children attend a Sunday School regularly? Any parents who neglect the spiritual education of their children will one day regret their carelessness. Our Sunday Schools have done great work in the past and it's up to parents to support them and help the teachers who give so generously of their time and interest.'

+ William Manchester

The Bishop of Manchester, the Rt. Reverend W. D. L. Greer, and his family in the 1950s procession on Whit Monday.

Evening Chronicle 1951 Report

An Evening Chronicle reporter described features of the 1951 Procession. He wrote: 'Bradford and Beswick folk like their music martial and vigorous – walkers from St Paul's Philips Park, and St Mary's Bishop Lee Memorial, Beswick had the most impressive musical turn-outs of the day. Third-oldest church in Manchester, St Thomas, Ardwick, had 350 walkers, the youngest girls carried novel and exquisite floral umbrellas. St Matthew's Mission Church, Deansgate, in St Ann's Parish carried three richly decorated images of Christ and a fourth of the nativity scene at Bethlehem. A member of St Michael's, Hulme, a veteran walker, said the Procession was one of the best in the ninety year history of the church. The rector of St Jerome's, Ardwick, the Reverend. J. Duncan Glover led his parish procession for the twenty-seventh time.'

The 1951 Procession was a memorable one, and it was the last to mark a significant anniversary of the Whit Monday Walk with special and fitting celebrations. As the 1950s began the Whit Monday Procession remained strong and vibrant. Vast crowds still lined the processional route, and individual Sunday Schools were attended by numbers of children ranging from 70 in the smallest parish to 525 in the largest. As the Procession moved towards its third century, 1953 saw another year when the Whit Monday Walk celebrated the coronation of a new monarch, that of Queen Elizabeth II.

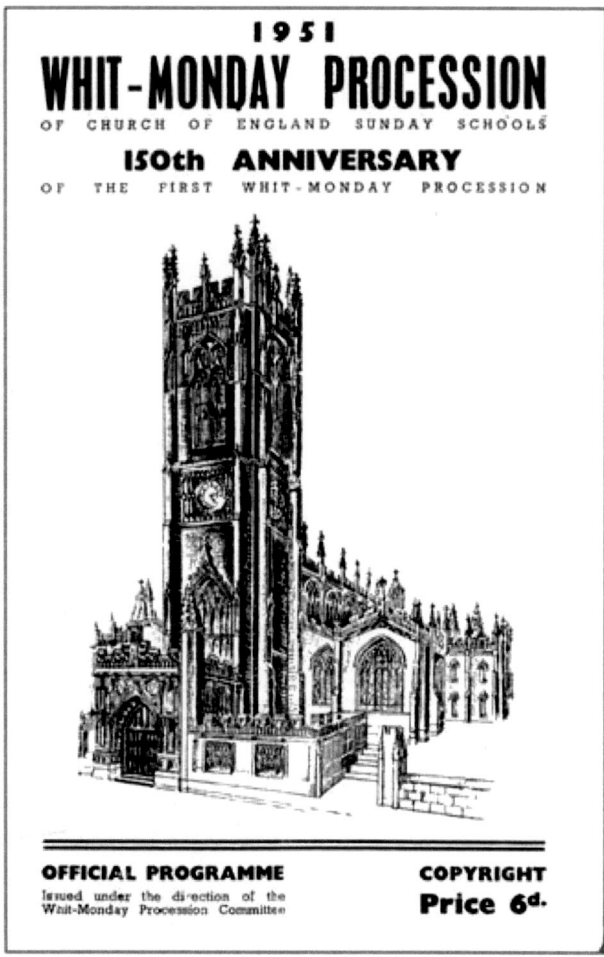

The cover of the 150th anniversary Whit Monday Procession programme in 1951.

Chapter 3

The History of the Whit Monday Procession 1951-2013

A New Queen; Changing Times and Decline

Coronation Year 1953 saw a memorable Whit Monday Walk. The Manchester Evening News carried the banner headline: "A Great Day". It reported: 'This Whit Monday, it was different, Manchester was already a blazing backcloth of coronation colours when 20,000 Church of England children marched in their Procession of Witness. The weather was never better. It was sunshine and smiles all the way, for mothers who had spent weeks preparing the finery. Many were up at dawn, and spectators were behind the crush barriers at 6.30 a.m., to see Manchester's 152nd pageant-filled procession. Albert Square with the whole city centre, was decorated with coronation flags and bunting matching the magnificence of the walkers'. The reporter from the Evening News continued: 'The transformation of Albert Square into an arcade of red, gold and purple banners, with giant golden crowns and pink, blue and white flowers, led to a wave of excitement as the thump, thump of a distant band was heard approaching. Then a gold cross glints. It is the first and oldest church in the twin cities – Sacred Trinity, Salford consecrated in 1635. After its altar servers and choir came the red-coated Gravel Lane Silver Prize Band. Salford this year has a tinge of sadness, the familiar figure of Canon Peter Green was missing. Now in Salford Royal Hospital, he has walked every year since 1901.'

Canon Peter Green, Rector of St. Philip's Salford. A well known figure in the Whit Monday processions.

Dr. W D L Greer, Bishop of Manchester with his chaplain in the Whit Walk.

The 'Evening News' described "a gasp of admiration" as St Ann's Manchester entered Albert Square with a tableau of three stages in the life of Christ. St Matthew's Mission in St Ann's Parish carried a large portrait of the new Queen, with the words in red flowers, "Let us pray for our Queen". The newspaper noted that Canon Eric Saxon, Rector of St Ann's, arrived just in time to walk, his car had had a puncture! It went on, 'School on school arrived. It seemed the Square could not hold anymore. As the Town Hall bells chimed, the Bishop of Manchester stood on a platform beneath an enormous golden cipher of E II R. The mighty congregation sang hymns and the National Anthem. The Bishop pronounced his blessing and the marshalls achieved the seeming impossible, straightening the 20,000 walkers out into procession order. The 1953 Walk was on! It was headed by four-mounted policemen and as it turned into Princess Street there was a ripple of excitement and cheers.' The newspaper reported that people were packed eight-deep along the route from Albert Square to the Cathedral, and that the police had stated that they were the biggest post-war Whit Monday crowds. It reported that seventy-year old Councillor Percy Chadwick, the Walks' Committee Treasurer had missed only one Walk since 1888!

St. Matthew's Mission Church, Deansgate, with their decorated image of Christ in 1951. Photograph courtesy of M.E.N.

The choir, choir master and organist of St. Stephen with St. Mark Hulme move into Princess Street from Albert Square in the 1950s. Photograph courtesy of John Bethell.

According to the Evening News report, as the Procession approached the Cathedral it moved through crowds a dozen deep and the children presented "a rippling sea of red, white and blue". It went on, 'There were bursts of applause for the children in their various tableau, who responded with faces wreathed in smiles. Now the Cathedral bells rang out and as the walkers turned into Fennel Street, before going into the Cathedral, the crowd fell silent.' The newspaper account concluded, 'From the heat, and the noise of the streets, the members of four churches filed into the cool and quiet of the Cathedral. The parishes attending the service were: St Ann's, with St Matthew's Mission, and the Hulme churches of St Stephen, and St Michael, a congregation of 1,400. Sunshine lit up the Cathedral windows and gave added beauty to the new dresses of the girls.'

*St. Paul's Philips Park, Bradford, Manchester, group pose in Albert Square.
Photograph courtesy M.E.N.*

A Golden Whit Monday

The 1953 Coronation Whit Walk was described as "the Golden Whit Monday." This was because the ribbons of the banners and the dresses of the girls were the colour of gold. Whit Monday 1953 was a beautiful and hot day, but as the general procession in the City Centre ended, and the various churches walked back to their parishes, there was a storm and a sudden burst of torrential rain, which caught the last contingents before they reached their destinations. Here was a fore-taste of Whit Monday 1954, for if 1953 was the "Golden Whit Monday," 1954 was to be the "Wet Whit Monday" with laden skies and unrelenting rain, but the Procession went on!

Whit Monday 1953, St. Ann's Manchester carry their coronation tableau along Market Street. Photograph courtesy M.E.N.

The Wet Whit Monday

On Whit Monday 1954 the 'Manchester Evening Chronicle' carried the headline, "Rain lashes but the miracle of the Few happens". It reported, 'It was incredible, fantastic. It was Manchester's Whit Monday Church of England Walk that might have turned out to be a "washout". But the tradition of 153 years that has painted the city streets annually with the quality of a stained glass window, carried it through. Long intervals elapsed after the first of what was thought to be "The Few" marched bravely out into the sparsely lined streets, officials commenting to each other, "There will be no more". Then after an hour with Albert Square almost deserted, and the rain beating on the glistening pavements, the miracle happened. Faintly, came the sound of distant music. It grew louder. It swelled into a triumphant chorus, the strident note of courage born of a tradition that knows no defeat. Into the Square came more swaying banners held proudly, leading columns of little children drenched, but still smiling cheerfully. The Procession which even the most optimistic thought had come to a full stop, was on the march again". The 'Evening Chronicle' story continued, 'The Walks Organising Secretary, Horace W Sumner, declared, "Except for the war years, we have never abandoned the Walk entirely. And however bad the weather we did not intend to start today. This is a tradition which we feel must be maintained". The report went on, 'The first parish to arrive was St Matthias with St Simon, Salford. They came up Brazennose Street slowly, with banners and umbrellas. The rector, the Reverend I. Corbett said, "We would have turned up in a thunderstorm".

St Michael's and St Stephen's, Hulme walked only around their own parishes. St John's and St Luke's, Miles Platting started out, but turned back for their home parishes. St Andrew's Ancoats turned out with a full compliment. The rector, the Reverend J.J. Ambrose said, 'I tried to stop them, but they took no notice of me.' From Ancoats too, came All Souls' with happy rain-coated children. St Mark's Holland Street joined the main procession in Piccadilly. The Church Lads Brigade of St Mary's Beswick carried the colours of their First Battalion with the full turn-out of their church.

The 'wet' Whit Monday 1954. Mildred Nightingale holds a ribbon from the banner of St. Andrew's Ancoats as they start for Albert Square; their Rector having tried to stop them walking in the rain.

St Paul's Philips Park Church Lads and Church Girls' Brigade represented their parish. Shields of all the Bishoprics in the Province of York were carried by the boys of Christ Church, Bradford, who had one of the longest processions. Behind them came St Aidan's, Bradford with choir girls in black mortar boards, choir and altar boys in red cassocks and their parish scout band. The longest journey was made by St Clement's, Longsight who covered four miles in two hours. St Silas, Ardwick made their first appearance in the Procession for eighteen years".

The 'Manchester Evening News' story on the 1954 Whit Walk included the report that St Philip's Salford had especially detoured from their usual route to walk past the home of their old rector, Canon Peter Green who was ill. It noted that Sacred Trinity, Salford had walked without its two large banners to save them from rain damage, and that a two-and-half-year-old had walked in a sailor suit with St Matthew's, Campfield. The 'Evening News' stated that the procession from German Street Sunday School, New Cross was one of the less spectacular. They had few flowers and decorations, stating that they "liked a simple procession". The paper went on: 'St Augustine's, Monsall were led by the Manchester Fire Brigade Silver Band in splendid uniform, whilst St Philip's, Bradford Road had the top-hatted members of Culcheth Military Prize Band adding distinction to their procession. St Stephen's Salford carried a scale model of their church made by their scoutmaster.' The 1954 Whit Monday Procession was watched by American Evangelist, Billy Graham, who was visiting Britain at the time. St Silas, Ardwick had rejoined the Procession after eighteen years, but that church was to close within the year making 1954 its last Whit Walk. The wet weather of this year meant that many of the children's clothes were stained by the driving rain, and by the traditional red roses. 1954 was the last year that as many as 36 churches were numbered to walk in the procession, from then on the number of parishes taking part began to decrease.

St. Andrew's Ancoat walk into Princess Street from Albert Square on the 1954 "wet" Whit Monday. Photographs courtesy of the Nightingale family.

The altar servers of Sacred Trinity Salford lead their parish procession along Blackfriars Road to Albert Square in the 1950s.

1955 – A Beautiful Whit Monday

The *'Evening Chronicle'* headline for Whit Monday 1955 ran: "It was such a Beautiful Day".

St. Augustine's Monsall, led by the Manchester Fire Brigade Band, pass Manchester Cathedral in the 1950s. Photograph courtesy of M.E.N.

It led with a message to its readers, from the Bishop of Manchester, Dr. W.L. Greer, "The way we Act". The Bishop wrote: 'Processions of witness have long been a feature of Lancashire church life, and I hope that they will continue to be so. Our witness to the Christian Faith is perhaps better shown in the way in which Christians speak and act in their daily lives. Membership of the Church of England is growing and I hope that many more people may be drawn into the Church through the witness borne by the Whit Walks.' The 'Evening Chronicle' then gave a guide to the churches taking part. The article began: 'Everyone is talking about the Church of England Whit Walks. What crowds, what glorious weather. Not for five years have the churches taking part enjoyed such ideal conditions. Quietly, dignified, and one of the smallest contingents, came the leaders the Manchester Cathedral of St Mary, St Deny's and St George. Celebrating its centenary, St Oswald, Collyhurst walked immediately behind the Cathedral.

*St. Stephen's Salford with a model of their church in the 1954 Whit Walk.
Photograph courtesy of M.E.N.*

Boys in white shirts and red ties with girls in white, carrying pink carnations made a colourful picture with Sacred Trinity, Salford, St Matthias with St Simon was next with 350 children taking part. St Clement's, Broughton had a fourteen year old girl wearing a crown of pearls and diamante. St Philip's, Bradford Road and St Jude's, Ancoats joined forces for the first time and made a magnificent debut as a combined parish. Eight maidens in white satin formed the focal point for St Catherine's, Collyhurst. St James the Great, Collyhurst has lost many parishioners through housing clearance, but the church took its place as usual. Crimson clad Prestwich Borough Band headed the 180 walkers from St Paul's, New Cross. St Peter's, Oldham Road had a six year old Queen of the May, dressed in white satin and lace, from George Leigh Street School. St John's, Miles Platting walked with two queens. One in a sweeping gown of white lace with a headdress of Lilies of the Valley, the other a retiring queen, wore a white brocade dress with a blue velvet train.'

The Evening Chronicle Guide to the churches went on: 'St Luke's, Miles Platting's contingent of 400 was headed by their choir girls in picturesque mortar boards and blue gowns. What work, what hours of patience went into the floral banner carried proudly by walkers from St Augustine's, Monsall. More than 4,000 flowers, Arum lilies and Lilies of the Valley went into the banner made by a member of the church.' The Guide concluded: 'St Clement's, Longsight carried a tableau of Jesus the Lamb of God, using a once live lamb stuffed by a London taxidermist for the Whit Walk. St George's, Oldham Road included in their number two members taking part in their forty-seventh Walk. A Superintendent from German Street Sunday School missed his first Walk at the age of eighty. Staunch support from former parishioners who had moved miles from their church by re-housing, enabled St Andrew's, Ancoats to put up a good showing. St Barnabas, Ancoats were without a rector, but 240 children and adults joined their procession.'

Re-organisation of the Procession Order

In 1955 the time-honoured practice of churches walking in the Procession in the order of the date of the consecration of their churches was changed. This was a response to the increase in road traffic. The old order meant that churches from the same districts, left and re-entered their areas at different times disrupting traffic repeatedly. The new order of the Procession grouped churches from the same districts in the Walk, to leave and re-enter their areas together. The 34 churches taking part in 1955 were formed into groups.

Salford: St Philip's; St Stephen's; Sacred Trinity; St Matthias with St Simon and St Clement's Broughton.

Collyhurst: St Catherine; St James the Great; St Oswald and Albert Memorial Church.
New Cross: St Paul; St Peter with St James the Less; German Street Sunday School; St George and St Barnabas.

Miles Platting: St John; St Luke; St Philip; St Mark and St Augustine, Monsall.

Ancoats: St Andrew; All Souls' and St Jude.

Beswick and Bradford: St Mary; Christ Church and St Paul Philips Park.

Ardwick: St Thomas; St Jerome with St Silas; St Luke Chorlton on Medlock; St Clement, Longsight and St Aidan, Bradford.

City Centre and Hulme: St Ann's; Cathedral; St Matthew's Mission, St Michael Hulme and St Stephen with St Mark Hulme.

*A 1920s floral banner carried by St. Matthias Salford children
Photograph courtesy of Renee Carr.*

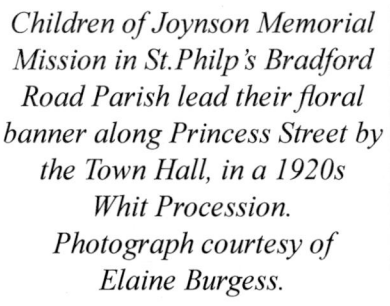

*Children of Joynson Memorial Mission in St. Philp's Bradford Road Parish lead their floral banner along Princess Street by the Town Hall, in a 1920s Whit Procession.
Photograph courtesy of Elaine Burgess.*

An Era of Change Begins

As the mid 1950s were entered the Whit Monday Procession remained a strong and impressive annual event. The number of churches taking part had fallen from the 1901 high point of 45 to 34 Parishes, and the number of children from some 40,000 to 20,000. The Walk, nonetheless, was still rooted in the community of inner Manchester and Salford, and the traditions around it continued. An era of change though was beginning. The increase in road traffic had necessitated the re-organisation of the Processional Order, and City Council re-housing schemes were de-populating the heartlands of the Whit Walk in the inner-city areas. Churches like St Andrew, Ancoats and St Paul, New Cross had lost their Parish populations in pre-war re-housing schemes; the districts around the churches being given over to industry. Though former parishioners returned to their roots on occasions, church and community life declined, and increasingly this led to the closure and demolition of parish churches. There had been de-populating of parishes and closure of churches in times past, but these were the exception rather than the rule. St Clement's, Lever Street, Stevenson Square, closed as early as 1873 and St Mary's, Deansgate in 1890.

The Whit Monday procession moves along Princess Street in a 1950s procession. The contingent in view is from All Souls' Ancoats. Photograph courtesy of M.E.N.

The City Centre churches of St Peter, St James, S.S. Simon and S. Jude, St John and St Matthew, together with St Martin's German Street, St Michael's, Angel Meadow, St Simon, Salford, St Thomas, Red Bank and St James the Less, Ancoats all closed before the Second World War. When these churches ceased to take part in the Whit Monday Procession they were sometimes replaced by others, but the number of parishes in the Walk had gradually decreased. By the mid 1950s re-housing schemes in inner Manchester were becoming the rule rather than the exception. This coupled with the onset of social change, which was to transform society in the 1960s and a growing affluence leading to the present consumer society, impacted increasingly on church and community involvement. The Whit Walks in this climate of change were to enter a time of decline in numbers and popularity between 1955 and 1970 - but in 1956 they remained a major event. With the arrival of Independent Television, Granada televised the 1956 Whit Monday Procession live, and covered the Church of England and the Roman Catholic Whit Walk on other occasions in later years.

In and around Manchester

The Televised Whit Walk

In previous years cinema newsreels had covered the Manchester Whit Processions, but the live televising of them brought a new dimension to the Walks. Those taking part in the 1956 Whit Monday Procession were aware of the cameras at various points on the route, and as they returned to their parishes spectators would call out to the walkers that they had been seen on the television! 33 parishes were represented in 1956, St Jude's, Ancoats having had their last Walk in 1955 before their church closed. The 'Evening Chronicle' devoted its front page to the Procession of 1956 and highlighted features of the Walk. Its headline was "Flowers, dresses, banners and bands – the signs of Faith". The reporter wrote: 'The Bishop of Hulme, the Rt. Rev. K.V. Ramsey gave his blessing to the 155th Whit Monday Walk. The Procession was blessed with sunshine and was as colourful as any in recent years, 20,000 walkers marched through the streets to Manchester Cathedral, and fifty bands went with them and there to catch the spectacle already steeped in history and tradition, was commercial television taking a look in for the first time. The Bishop of Manchester missed the occasion through illness. For many of the schools taking part it was a chilly 6.00 a.m. start, but pink-faced children greeted the early morning cold with a smile. When the bands struck up the nip in the air was forgotten.'

Girls and boys, one with a smiling salute, from St. Matthias with St. Simon, Salford, escort their message in flowers along Market Street in the 1950s. Photograph courtesy of M.E.N.

The article ran on: 'Banners with their religious messages picked out in flowers bordered by leafy greenery were works of art which took days to prepare. A national note was struck by two youngsters dressed as John Bull and Britannia, with German Street Church of England Sunday School, New Cross. Several people travelled great distances to return to Manchester for the Procession, and others conquered infirmities to be present. Among dozens of pretty girls in charming dresses the rose queen, and retiring queen of St Augustine's, Monsall stood out. The two queens had Swiss brocade dresses with trains four yards long carried by six attendants. The youngest person in the Procession was a three-and-a-half year old child with St Philip's, Bradford Road. St John the Evangelist, Miles Platting, celebrating its centenary, headed the Procession behind the Cathedral.' The newspaper reports of the Whit Monday Procession present vivid accounts of the commitment and enthusiasm of a bygone age, for a festival of Faith and Community.

A tradition begun in 1919, "John Bull and Britannia" walk with German Street Church of England Sunday School in a 1950s Whit Walk. Photograph courtesy of M.E.N.

As the second-half of the 1950s enfolded, the Whit Monday Procession retained its strength and popularity but with re-housing plans clearing whole communities the number of churches in the Procession began to decrease year by year. The old traditions of new "Whit Week Clothes" and "Whit Excursions" continued up to the early 1960s, but with an increasingly prosperous society those became outdated. The Sunday Schools which the Whit Monday Procession celebrated ceased to be attended by the majority of children, being replaced by much smaller "Junior Church" groups. By the 1960s churches, which had been a part of the processions for a century had been closed. St Jude Ancoats, St Stephen Salford, St Silas Ardwick, St Andrew Ancoats, St Barnabas Ancoats, St Luke Chorlton on Medlock and German Street Sunday School ceased to be a part of the Whit Walk. The chairman of the Whit Monday Walk Committee, Tom Long of Salford, invited three 'new' Salford Parishes to join the procession and St Clement's Ordsall, St Cyprian's Ordsall and the Church of the Ascension Broughton joined the Whit Monday Walk for the first time in 1961.

As the 1960s progressed re-housing schemes took further toll on inner-Manchester and Salford's churches. St Mark's, Holland Street, St Mary's Beswick, St Catherine Collyhurst and St Matthias Salford ceased to be separate parishes and the number of churches walking in the Procession fell to twenty. 1966 brought a significant change in the history of the Procession. The Government abolished the traditional Whit Monday Bank Holiday, replacing it with a fixed Spring Bank Holiday Monday at the end of May each year.

St Philip's Bradford Road Flower Girls on a Whit Monday, early 1950s. Photograph courtesy of Elaine Burgess.

In and around Manchester

St Andrew's Ancoats prepare to leave Albert Square on Whit Monday 1958. Photograph courtesy of J.Horn.

The Future of the Procession?

In the 1966 Official Programme the Organising Secretary of the Procession, Horace W. Sumner, wrote about "The Future of the Procession". He observed: 'The Whit Monday holiday is to be discontinued by Government decree. It is to be replaced in 1967 and succeeding years, by a new Bank Holiday on the last Monday in May. This will be a "fixed date" and will not always coincide with the Church's Whitsuntide Festival which has had a "moveable date". Whit Monday will therefore no longer be available for holding our annual Procession. We desire the continuation of the traditional annual Procession. Having considered the few alternatives we have concluded that we should seek to hold the 1967 Procession on the new Bank Holiday Monday. The view may be expressed that Whit Sunday is the day on which religious processions should take place and that we should arrange our annual Procession for Whit Sunday. To do so would mean the abandonment of church services and the usual parish processions on Whit Sunday, both of which celebrate the Birthday of the Christian Church. The Whit Monday Procession has for 165 years celebrated the founding of the Sunday School Movement, and their integration into the Church. We remember on that day the efforts of our fore-bearers, not only in the religious education of the children, but also their teaching of the three "R's" in the days before the provision of "day schools" and the coming of compulsory education. The work of the Church and its Sunday Schools is worthy of remembrance, and our Procession is a reminder that this work amongst children still goes on. We feel very deeply that it is worthwhile to maintain our religious traditions in days when the material things of life are so much sort-after, and particularly we desire to give

All Souls' Ancoats children with their floral banner. Late 1950s Whit Procession. Photograph courtesy of The Nightingale Family.

everyone an opportunity to witness to their faith by taking part in our processions. To that end, we would mention that, although Whit Monday has long been regarded as "the children's day" the Sunday Schools did, as long ago as 1830, invite the congregations of the churches to take part. This long-standing invitation is still open. On behalf of the children, we repeat it and say: "Everyone join the Procession with the children".' The Parish of St Cross, Clayton took up the invitation and joined the Procession for the first time.

The 1966 Official Programme carried an article from the Archdeacon of Manchester, the Venerable Hetley Price. He commented: 'The longer a thing goes on the greater the need for seeing the reason lying behind it. The Whit Monday Procession is a great, and by now an ancient institution. What lies behind it? First it's our chance to enjoy ourselves and none the worse for that. Pleasure is part of our human nature, and the Christian faith is concerned with all of that. Secondly, when Christians do anything together - and especially when they do it in large numbers as on Whit Monday - they are engaged in Witness. This does not mean that they have to be solemn, but it does mean that they need to ask what kind of impression their combined activity is creating. Thirdly, at a time when it becomes clearer that the unity and mission of the Church cannot be separated, and when Christians in their separated churches are encouraged to do on their own only what in conscience they must, it is a good question whether or not the Whit Walk might not become much more of a combined operation than has been thought possible or desirable in the past?' Archdeacon Price's question was not answered in the affirmative, and the Whit Walks in Manchester City Centre remained denominational - with the Roman Catholic Whit Friday Procession, on the change of the Whit Week Bank Holiday, moving to Whit Sunday and later being abandoned.

"Whit" Monday no more!

1966 was the last year that the "Whit Monday" Procession bore that title. The Walk in 1967 being held on the new Spring Bank Holiday, the event became "The Church of England Annual Procession". It would, though, for many forever remain the "Whit Monday" Procession.

The next changes in the Procession's tradition was to be to the time honoured route of Princess Street, Mosley Street, Market Street and Deansgate to the Cathedral. Market Street became pedestrianised for shoppers, and with the arrival of the Metrolink, Mosley Street was closed to the Procession. The revised route became Cooper Street, Fountain Street, High Street, Cannon Street and Deansgate. As the 1960s neared their end the growing changes in society, with increasing materialism and secularisation reduced people's enthusiasm for, and commitment to, religious and community events like the Whit Walks.

1969 – The Procession is abandoned

In 1969 the Procession was abandoned entirely for the first time outside the war years, continuous rain being the cause. Some parishes started for Albert Square but turned back on the advice of the Procession organisers relayed to them by the police. In 1970 the last official programme for the Walk was produced and sold. It was a much thinner version than in previous years, and carried an appeal from the Walks' organisers for advertising for 1971. 7,000 children, from 20 parishes took part in 1970, the number of parishes and children

In and around Manchester

The last "Whit Monday" Walks Programme – bearing the title: "Church of England Annual Procession, Spring Bank Holiday Monday".

was to continue to drop, year by year in the 1970s and 1980s. There was no Cathedral service in 1970 and a 1971 official programme never appeared. There were to be none in future years. In the last official programme the Bishop of Manchester, Dr. W. Greer wrote: 'There are many powerful forces in society working against what we stand for. Christian Witness was never more needed than it is today.' The Dean of Manchester, the Very Reverend A. Jowett wrote: 'The Whit Procession has played a great part in the social and religious life of our city. Good wishes for its future success.'

In the 1970s and 1980s, with the decline in numbers taking part in the Procession, and against social change, and population movement from inner-Manchester and Salford, the increasing closure of churches and Sunday Schools, caused questions to be asked about the future of the Church of England Procession.

The Rector of St Cuthbert's Miles Platting (a new church and parish formed from the union of four old parishes, St George, St Barnabas, St Luke and St John the Evangelist) ***Canon Stanley Meadows wrote an article in his parish magazine entitled 'Whither the Whit Walk?'*** He commented: 'We had a very good turn out this year for the Whit Walk. The children were as always a credit to the hard work of teachers and parents, and it was nice to welcome a number of old friends who came back to join in and swell the ranks. What of the future? Should the Walk continue indefinitely regardless of changed circumstances or has the time come to think again? Whit Walks brought a blaze of colour, much needed, music and fun to the drab city streets and a welcome day out for the great mass of "down town" dwellers. I remember the first time I watched the Walk in 1951 when I stood for hours as church after church went by. I remember my first Walk as Rector of St George with St Barnabas. On that occasion we had more than two hundred walking, three banners and the crowds stood six deep in Market Street. Now houses have been pulled down and communities split up, re-development has made drastic cuts in the "down town" population, parishes have had to be united and consequently there are fewer churches to take part. In 1961, 23 parishes took part, this year there will be fourteen and there will be at least one less next year. It is for these reasons that I think we should take a good practical look at the future of the Walks. This does not mean that I am against

Canon Stan Meadows "Whither the Whit Walks?"

them; on the contrary I have always approved of and thoroughly enjoyed them, and so long as this parish walks, I will walk with it. But I should hate to see such a great tradition fizzle out like a damp squib, and that is why I should like us all to do some honest, unsentimental and practical thinking.'

A Shadow over the Future

At this time, Horace Sumner, an East Manchester Funeral Director, and a member of St Philip's Bradford Road, who had been the post-war organising secretary of the Procession died. He had been known as "Mr Whit Monday" and his death cast a shadow over the Walk's future. Canon Gwilym Morgan of St Philips Salford, and the Very Rev. Robert Waddington, Dean of Manchester, took oversight of the Walk and after Canon Meadow's article, in his parish magazine, some positive thinking about the annual Procession was done. Canon Ian McVeety succeeded Horace Sumner as Organising Secretary of the Walk and there was a revival of the Procession. With many of the parishes which traditionally joined the Walk from the inner-city no longer existing, parishes from further afield were invited to join in. They travelled into New Cross by coach and car, and walked to Albert Square from there. Salford churches gathered at St Philip's Church. These new contingents were:-

St Paul, Blackley;
St Mark, White Moss;
St Thomas, Crumpsall;
St Mary, Moston;
St John, Droylsden;
St Martin, Castleton;

All Saints and Martyrs, Langley;
St Margaret, Heywood;
St James Hope, Salford;
St Ignatius, Salford;
St George, Charlestown, Salford.

The *Manchester Evening News* headlined the Walk's revival with the caption, "One Small Step Back". Canon Ian McVeety was succeeded as organising secretary, by Canon Roy Chow, who attended, with the Author, St Mary's Church, Beswick before their ordinations. Canon Chow's leadership ensured the continuation of the Procession, in difficult circumstances, on the Spring Bank Holiday in May each year. The 200th Anniversary of the "Whit Monday" Procession passed without celebration in 2001. Banners and Bands continue to feature in the Procession, the Manchester Diocesan Mothers' Union members and the Church Lads and Church Girls' Brigade are well represented. Traditional red roses are still worn by the walkers and by the spectators, but both are far less numerous than in the heyday of the Whit Monday Procession.

Whit Monday 1959. The Author, Canon Jim Burns, carries the processional cross as St. Mary's Beswick leave their Cambrian Street School for Albert Square.

Immediately behind him is Canon Roy Chow, the present organising secretary of the Whit Monday Procession.

On Spring Bank Holiday Monday 2010 fourteen contingents took part in the Walk. They were:-

The Cathedral;
St Ann, Manchester;
St Philip with St Stephen, Salford;
All Saints Team Parish, Salford;
St Clement, Ordsall, Salford;
St Cuthbert, Miles Platting;
Church of the Apostles, Ancoats;
Church of the Saviour, Collyhurst;
All Saints and Martyrs, Langley;
The Church of the Good Shepherd and St Barnabas, Eastlands;
St Agnes Birch in Rusholme;
St Philip, Gorton;
St Margaret, Heywood;

Church Lads and Church Girls Brigade Bands were prominent in the Whit Monday Procession – a tradition continuing today. Above, St. Luke's, Miles Platting Brigade return along Oldham Road to their church in the 1950s.

In 2011 and 2012, the contingents taking part in the 210th Anniversary Procession of the first 1801 Whit Monday Procession were:-

Manchester Cathedral;
Manchester Diocese Mothers' Union;
St Agnes, Birch-in-Fallowfield;
Church of the Saviour, Collyhurst;
St Cuthbert & The Apostles, Miles Platting;
St Margaret, Heywood;
St Philip, Gorton;
All Saints & Martyrs, Langley;
Good Shepherd & St Barnabas, Eastlands;
St Philip w. St Stephen, Salford;
All Saints Team Ministry, Salford;
St Clement, Ordsall;
St Ann, Manchester.
St. Clement, Chorlton-cum-Hardy

Some 1,800 people joined in the 2011 Whit Walks and a similar number took part in 2012. Again a similar number took part in 2013 when the Walk was held on Whit Sunday afternoon, along a changed route.

On Whit Monday 1801, 1,800 people took part in the first Whit Monday Procession – the wheel had turned full circle!

Having explored the history of the Whit Monday Procession, the memories of some of the people who took part in it are recorded in the next chapter of this book.

Floral banner and the three young ladies with flowers. 1950s Whit Walk.

Chapter 4

Memories of the Whit Monday Procession

Times change; people change; society changes. Many now look back with fond memories of the Whit Monday Procession in their childhood and youths. The memories are of the Whit Walks in the period 1920 – 1960, which saw their heyday. Knowledge of earlier years of the Procession can only be gained through the study of history and documentation. The Author has talked with a number of people who have shared their more recent Whitsun memories with him. All of them have spoken with great affection of their Whit Week experiences of former years.

A tear can sometimes be seen in the eyes of people relating their memories of past Whitsuns. Along the route of the present Procession an observer might note a spectator wiping away the odd tear at memories of past Whit Mondays, and of people who were a part of them. It's called 'nostalgia' and it's part of human emotion. Such feelings should not be lightly dismissed. For many Manchester and Salford people, Whit Walks have been a part of their formative years, and of their lives, and they hold strong church, community and family memories of them. Hearing these memories expressed can remind us of much that the present generation has lost, in its preference for material things to the exclusion of commitment to faith, community and upholding tradition.

A Beswick recollection

The Author's memories of Whitsun in Beswick, East Manchester

The Author of this book was raised in Beswick, two miles from Manchester City Centre. He shares with many in similar parts of Manchester and Salford thankful memories of past Whitsuns. The churches of Beswick, and of neighbouring Bradford, (Manchester) Ancoats, Ardwick and Miles Platting remained significant presences in their communities into the early 1960s. A Church of England bishop once remarked: "In the first part of the 20th century, a good number of people went to church and sent their children to Sunday School, and even those who didn't go to church, knew very well which church they didn't go to!" Whit processions in Beswick and neighbouring areas were events involving the whole community as walkers or as spectators.

The Author, left front, as a choirboy in the Whit Sunday afternoon Walk in Beswick in 1957. Harold Hawksworth carries the cross. The St. Mary's procession is walking through the area now covered by East Manchester Etihad Sport City and Stadium.

St Mary's Church on Hillkirk Street, was the Church of England parish church of Beswick. As a choirboy and altar server, the Author attended St Mary's Church and Sunday School, and remembers with gratitude members of its congregation who served the church and the community. In the early 1950s St Mary's had its own Silver Band; a Church Lads' Brigade bugle band; a church Girls' Brigade trumpet band; a church choir which included 25 boys and numerous parish organisations. The 1951 Whit Monday Procession programme listed the numbers attending St Mary's Sunday School at 510, with 40 Sunday School teachers. The Sunday School building in Cambrian Street was a hive of spiritual and social activity. The Whitsun processions in Beswick included St Mary's; St Anne's Roman Catholic Church; Beswick Methodist Church and Ancoats Congregational Church. The Walks took place locally on Whit Sunday and on Trinity Sunday and into the City Centre on Whit Monday and Whit Friday.

The Author, the first of the two boys in white suits, walks with his parents and cousin, George Moreland, in his first Whit Monday Walk at the age of three and a half in 1947.

The Whitsun Festival

Beswick families began preparations for Whit Week long before the festival dawned. For the children, Whitsun meant new clothes; often two different sets of clothes; one set for Whit Sunday and the other set for Whit Monday. These would be bought each year from the same supplier. On Whit Sunday morning, after church, children wearing their Whitsun finery would tour their family and friends to 'show' their new clothes – the girls in their dresses; the boys in their suits. They would be rewarded with three pence, six pence or from 'better off' relatives in Droylsden, half a crown! A former Beswick boy reflecting on the Whit Sundays of his childhood said: "We wore our new clothes at Whitsun and sometimes we didn't see them again for months." Were they kept carefully in wardrobes, or did they go elsewhere? Whit Sunday at St Mary's Beswick and at other Church of England and Free Churches, saw local afternoon processions. St Mary's walked along streets since cleared in re-development schemes, and partly covered now by Sport City and the City of Manchester Etihad Stadium.

After Whit Sunday's Walk there could be a family gathering for tea and recollections from senior family members of bygone Whitsuns. On Whit Sunday evenings, after evensong, the Sunday School teachers, the Author's mother amongst their number, would go to Cambrian Street Sunday School hall to prepare the floral banners, with fresh flowers being wired into them, for Whit Monday's procession. Then it was home to prepare the children and their clothes for the next day's Walk. Before putting the children to bed for their sleep, disturbed by excitement about and anticipation of the Whit Monday Walk, anxious parents would discuss the weather forecast for the coming morning. The fear of wet weather at Whitsun was the cause of annual anxiety, but a wet Whit Monday seemed to be the exception rather than the rule.

St. Mary's Beswick walk through the old streets of Ancoats, with their terraced houses, long demolished, after singing hymns outside Ancoats Hospital.

Whit Monday

Whit Monday saw an early beginning to the day. Children to be dressed, flowers to be collected from Smithfield Market, or from the local florist – in Beswick this was Frances Dove's Florist on Ashton New Road. It stood with other businesses, where Manchester's Sport City now stands. Mothers would return with bouquets of flowers for the girls and with the traditional Whit Monday red roses for the boys, and for the adults. The scent of a rose never fails to remind the Author of Whit Monday morning. Then the children would be taken to the procession's starting point, along Ashton New Road to Cambrian Street Sunday School. The road would already be lined with spectators. As late as 1961 the St Mary's Beswick procession left for Albert Square at 7.00 a.m.

Ashton New Road was the start of the Walk into the City Centre taken by St Mary's and by the two other local churches – Christ Church Bradford and St Paul's Philips Park. (St Cross Clayton joined the Whit Walk only in the late 1960s). St Mary's Procession would form-up outside the Sunday School building and often move off to the strains of the hymn 'Crown Him with Many Crowns' led by the St Mary's Silver Band. The choir, clergy, church wardens, band and the 'big' banner – 'The Three Wise Men' headed the procession. St Mary's route into the city took the walkers along Every Street, Great Ancoats Street, Adair Street, Travis Street, Whitworth Street, Oxford Street and Peter Street to Albert Square. The route along Travis Street by London Road Rail Station involved going through railway arches, which in days of horse-drawn vehicles, left an unpleasant road surface for the procession to pass over. Complaints about walking under the 'dirty arches' eventually led to re-routing St Mary's along Port Street and Portland Street into Oxford Street. The marshalls would count the number in the procession and announce whether they were 'up' or 'down' on the previous year. The band would play rousing marches such as 'Ballerina'; 'Sons of the Brave': 'The Standard of St George'; 'The Voice of the Guns'; and 'The Thin Red Line'. The crowds responded with applause and cheering. Smiles were on every face.

Naval Cousins
The Author, second right, prepares for the 1949 Whit Monday Walk with cousins Eddie Mitchell, George Moreland and Neville Tinsley.

Local Rivalry

The Whit Walks featured floral banners, each with a faith text; these were wired with fresh flowers. The boys and girls were dressed in the same colours, which were chosen by the Sunday School teachers as their Sunday School's colours. There was an element of local rivalry as to the best dressed children; the decorative arranging of the floral banners; the performance of the bands and the brigade bands and the numbers walking with each church procession. In the Author's childhood in Beswick, the rivalry seemed to be between St Mary's Beswick and Christ Church Bradford. The Church Lads' Brigade of the two parishes vied with each other to win the annual Brigade "Colours" – these were flags which the winners then proudly carried on Whit Monday. Even the youngest children could be seen walking in the Whit Monday Procession – although officially, children were expected to be aged seven at the youngest to take part. The Author walked with St Mary's Beswick at the age of three and a half in 1947.

Long Day

The walk from the inner-city parishes into Albert Square and around Manchester from the Town Hall to the Cathedral, before walking back to their parishes, was a long one. The pattern of the day would be a start for most churches between 7.00 a.m. and 8.00 a.m., arriving in Albert Square about an hour and half later. A short service in the Square (apart from the three parishes attending a Cathedral service) followed. The general Procession to the Cathedral saw dense crowds lining the streets. A veteran of the Whit Walks told the Author that "crowds in Market Street in the 1950s were 12 deep" and that "if you didn't take your place by 7 a.m. you had no chance of having a good view." After passing the Cathedral the churches would wend their various ways back to their home parishes. For Ancoats, Beswick and Bradford churches this involved walking along Cannon Street, Church Street, Dale Street, Port Street, Great Ancoats Street and Mill Street (now Old Mill Street). A stop for a hymn would be made by each church outside the Ancoats Hospital – and then it would be on, along Carruthers Street, Mitchell Street and Ashton New Road where the spectators would be waiting in numbers for the churches to return home.

A St. Mary's Beswick group pose for the cameras in Albert Square in 1961. Photograph courtesy of M.E.N.

A Celebration!

Along the route of the St Mary's procession the public houses would be open, and many people gathered outside them to watch the Walks. They were generally respectful and they sometimes joined in the singing of a well-known hymn. An altar server at St Mary's Beswick, Harold Hawksworth, remembers a very hot Whit Monday when the procession passed a public house on Great Ancoats Street. His father, who was standing outside, offered him a drink. Harold, pointed at the rector, the Reverend Lister, and replied: "I can't, he's here!" There are times in any celebration, for those who wish, to 'have a drink' and the Whit Walks were no exception. They were a celebration of faith, tradition and community.

On return to their various parishes the children would enjoy buns and milk. Some churches organised a field afternoon with games and children's races. Other parishes held these as part of excursions to the seaside, or into the countryside, later in Whit Week. At St Mary's Beswick the latter was the rule.

A Remarkable Event!

The numbers involved in the Whit Monday Procession; the distance walked by the children and the length of time spent en-route made the Whit Walk a remarkable event. After a 7.00 a.m. start the individual churches would be returning to their parishes between noon and 3.00 p.m. depending on their distance from the city centre, and their place in the Order of Procession. The Author remembers a Whit Monday in the early 1950s, when the St Mary Beswick procession had long been finished, but that from St Paul's Philips Park returned to its parish along the Ashton New Road at 3.40 p.m!

Shirley Cumbes, nee Bond, Rose Queen at All Souls' Ancoats in a 1950s Procession. Photograph courtesy of Cyril Cumbes.

In and around Manchester

Whit Social Activities

In the evening of Whit Monday, in some parishes, there would be a Dance and Social Evening – where did the parishioners find the energy! In Whitsun week there would be the Whit excursions, described in the Whit Monday Procession programmes as "festivities". Tickets for the various excursions for children and adults would be collected from the Sunday School building on Whit Tuesday and on the other days of Whit Week the various trips by coach, or train, would take place. At St Mary's Beswick, there was always a Whit Monday Dance in the Cambrian Street Sunday School building, and the parish Whit excursions were to such places as Frodsham, Hoylake, Helsby and Disley in Cheshire. Whit excursions in earlier years were not always to places as far away as Cheshire.

In the 1893 Whit Monday Procession programme, the festivities for Christ Church Bradford, listed the following: "A trip into the fields of Clayton for sports and games." Any familiar with Clayton, in East Manchester, today, long a residential and partly industrial district will smile at the thought of it once being a venue for a Whitsun countryside excursion!

Memories of Whitsun in Manchester and Salford

As with the Author's recollections of Whitsun in Beswick, people in similar parts of the city have Whit Walk memories of Ancoats, Bradford, Ardwick, Salford, Hulme, Collyhurst, Miles Platting, Chorlton on Medlock and Monsall. They involve memories of churches now closed for worship, and of communities dispersed in housing clearance schemes. These areas now have new communities. The old churches; schools; cinemas; public houses and terraced streets have gone, and the old traditions are no longer kept in a changed society. For those who remember the old traditions of faith, church and community, as part of their lives – the memories live on! We recall some of them in the remainder of this chapter.

Along Every Street in Ancoats

Cyril Cumbes, of Heaton Chapel, was a member of All Souls, Every Street, Ancoats. He writes of Whitsun at All Souls: 'As with many churches in the Manchester Diocese, Whitsun at All Souls was a very important time in the Church Calendar. People contributed to Church Saving Clubs at Sunday School, to provide material for the dresses which the girls wore in the procession. The build-up to Whitsun began with the Crowning of the Girls' Friendly Society Rose Queen. There would be a full audience in All Souls' School on the evening before Whit Sunday. Whit Sunday began with Holy Communion in the morning and people returned for the procession around the parish in the early afternoon. The marshalls had to ensure that a full compliment of able-bodied men was available to carry the big banners, and the many tableau and floral banners. The procession around the Every Street, Russell Street, Palmerston Street, Tutbury Street, Pollard Street and Mitchell Street neighbourhoods finished with a service in church. In the early evening people attended evensong in Church. Afterwards the ladies would go into the school room to prepare the refreshments for the return of the walkers in the Whit Monday Procession. On Whit Monday morning the excitement and the tension became evident. The procession would begin at 7.30 a.m. with many churches taking part in the Walk into the City Centre.'

'St Luke's Church Lads' Brigade Band from Benchill Wythenshawe, would join the ranks of the All Souls' Brigade Company and they would receive a cooked breakfast in readiness for the long day ahead. The long day ahead often meant a 2.30 p.m. return to the parish from the City Centre by way of Great Ancoats Street, Pollard Street, Mitchell Street, Ashton New Road and Every Street – the churches further from Albert Square returned to their parishes even later. The return to Ancoats meant a full supply of refreshments and a 'cuppa'! For All Souls' Church Lads' Brigade there was a few hours rest before leaving to take part in the Whit Monday evening Cheetham Hill Whit Procession.'

The All Souls' Ancoats Church Lads' Brigade Band leaves Albert Square in a 1950s Whit Walk. Photograph courtesy of C Cumbes.

'The members of the Brigade returned to the All Souls' Whit Monday Evening Parish Dance in the school room. The ticket cost 1/- (5 pence today) and this included a five-piece band. The end of Whit Week brought about the event which everybody looked forward to – especially the children. This was the Whit Friday outing to country or seaside venues. All Souls' went to places such as Romiley, Charlesworth, Bollington, Bamford, Norden, Aughton, Cleveleys and St Anne's on Sea. These visits seem extraordinary today when young people travel afar. By 1964 much was changing for church life in inner-Manchester. All Souls' Parish was to be affected with first it's union with St Andrew's Ancoats, and then with St Mary's Beswick – those churches being closed and demolished. Finally, All Souls' Church itself was closed and the parish merged in that of the Good Shepherd Eastlands. The building still stands, and those who worshipped in it are left with memories, and gratitude for the efforts and endeavours of many people in guiding us to walk the right pathway in life. There is gratitude also in that we had the opportunity to be part of a huge Manchester tradition, which once saw 45 churches taking part, and continues today, though much reduced in numbers and significance. May those who had the foresight to begin the Whit Monday Procession in 1801 be rewarded by all who strive to continue the Witness of Whit Week in Manchester.'

All Souls' Ancoats – Sunday School children with their floral banner in an early 1950s Whit Walk in Manchester City Centre. Photograph courtesy of C Cumbes.

All Souls', Ancoats 1950s Walk

Walking with the Albert Memorial Church on Rochdale Road

Joyce Mountfield, who was a member of the Albert Memorial Church, Collyhurst, writes from Failsworth. 'My Whitsun memories started as a four-year old walking for the first time to town (i.e. the City Centre). The concern of my mum was whether I would be able to walk so far, but I made it, with the excitement, the bands, the people cheering and my new white dress and bouquet of flowers. I continued to walk every year; still excited, always having a white dress. At the Albert Memorial Church we were not allowed to wear any other colour. The exception was when King George V died and the girls wore mauve dresses.

The Albert Memorial Church Collyhurst on Whit Monday 1958 in Market Street. Joyce Mountfield holds a ribbon from the "big" banner. Photograph courtesy of J Mountfield.

Girls and boys with the Bible on a litter. Early 1950s Whit Walk. Photograph courtesy of J.Mountfield.

We began our journey from an early age being told that the Whit Walks were not a pageant, and that you took part as an Act of Faith, in the Lord Jesus Christ. As children perhaps we didn't think so much about that, as about what flowers we would carry. All our mothers paid a few pence each week of the year to the Sunday School teachers for us to have a Whitsun bouquet of flowers. As children, on Whit Sunday evenings our thoughts would be – will there be all those people in Market Street cheering and dancing? Would the bands be playing good tunes? What position would we be, in the general procession? Would it be our year to go into the Cathedral for a service? The progress a child made in the procession was from holding a ribbon on a basket of flowers, to having a ribbon from the Bible carried in the Walk, and after confirmation to carrying a ribbon on the 'big' banner. What a privilege that was! The anticipation was always that it would be fine, weather-wise, but I remember having a few "soakings" over the years. It never marred the occasion!

I still walk, even though all the Collyhurst churches have been closed and they have been merged into the new parish of The Saviour. It's not the same excitement but I still walk to show my faith in the Lord Jesus Christ.'

The Albert Memorial Church Collyhurst on Whit Monday in the 1930s walking along Rochdale Road. The aunt of Joyce Mountfield holds a banner ribbon. Photograph courtesy of J Mountfield.

Lost in Albert Square

Anne Forster writes from Bromsgrove in Worcestershire, with her Whitsun memories of Manchester

My memories of the Manchester Whit Walks by Anne Forster (Goddard) formerly of Collyhurst: 'I must have been about four when I started to walk in the annual event that was 'The Manchester Whit Walks.' My memories are faint as I was so young but when I look at the earliest photograph that I have, faint whispers of a memory creep back into my mind. An early photo' was, I'm sure, taken by a professional photographer as on the reverse it states 'Kemsley Newspapers Ltd'. I am standing at the front and my hand clutches one of the ribbons that in itself was attached to a large basket that held flowers. Whether these flowers were real or dried, I don't know but the handle of the basket was held on one side by my sister Irene. We always looked smartly dressed. I'm possibly wearing a hand-me-down outfit from said sister and we are both wearing cardigans and matching headdresses. One or two of the other girls are wearing the same headdress so it must have been something that was provided by our St Oswald's Sunday

The choir of St. Oswald's Collyhurst lead their procession along Rochdale Road to Albert Square on a 1950s Whit Monday. Photograph courtesy of Dorothy Park.

School, Collyhurst. My sister and I went to Collyhurst County Primary School but this school was often known as 'The Tin School'. It must have been constructed at one time by corrugated iron or something but by the early 1950s when we went there I think it was made of sturdier wood and brick. Our walk in the procession though was organised by St Oswald's Church, Rochdale Road. My sister and I attended the Sunday School there in the 1950s.

The procession started from St Oswald's Street and there would have been other flower baskets with other children holding onto the ribbons and also banners were held aloft with wooden poles that were carried by young men. Some of these banners also had ribbons attached to them and children would also hold onto these in front and behind. We would have turned right at the end of the street onto Rochdale Road and walked along this road all the way to Albert Square passing closed shops along the way and lots of people standing on the pavements watching all of us in our Whitsun finery. We would have walked down Shude Hill and onto Cross Street and Corporation Street and then to Albert Square. I can't remember exactly what we did when we got to Albert Square, but there was a service and we all milled about in the Square for a while. I suppose we must have also walked back to Collyhurst. One year I remember that after we had reached Albert Square I must have somehow become detached from the group that I was with. I know my dad always used to accompany us as he always liked taking photographs. I must have been taken to the nearest policeman or policewoman. I remember being taken up the steps to the Town Hall and having to wait inside until my dad had been found. How this was accomplished I don't know as there must have been thousands of people in the Square. I do remember though how frightened I was because I was lost.'

Dorothy Thomas writes with Whitsun recollections, from the centre of Manchester: 'These are fond memories of a girl from Morecambe. Our family friends used to invite me to stay with them for the famous Manchester Whit Walks. My family was Church of England, but I was taken by our friends to watch both the Church of England Whit Monday Procession, and the Roman Catholic Whit Friday Walk. Often neighbours were of a different faith, but generally they used to watch each others' processions, cheering when they spotted a neighbour's child. At the age of four, I walked with my church in a "posh" white frock and headdress.'

St. Augustine's Monsall return along Oldham Road from the city centre on the first Whit Walk after the Second World War in 1945. Note the red, white and blue draped from the banner. Photograph courtesy of St. Augustine's Ladies.

The Longest Walk – From Monsall to Manchester City Centre

One of the churches most awaited on the Whit Monday Procession route was St Augustine's Monsall. Its members had probably the longest walk from far-flung Monsall to the centre of Manchester and back. *Now living in Heywood and Miles Platting, Vera Potts and Leone Harrat – who were members of St Augustine's remember the Whit Monday Walks from Monsall. St Augustine's Church was closed in the 1970s but their memories remain fresh. They recall:* 'There was a lot of preparation in St Augustine's Parish for the Whit Monday Walk, and for the other events of Whit Week. The children's clothes – dresses for the girls; attire for the rose queen; uniforms for the boys – had to be planned and made. The floral banners, with chosen texts of faith had to be fitted with fresh flowers. Various tableau would be made. After the Allied Victory in the First World War a tableau of the representatives of the victorious allies took part in the 1919 Whit Monday Procession. Such memories were handed down through St Augustine's families and cherished. Whit Monday morning was exciting. The procession formed-up, headed by St Augustine's "big" banner 'The Good Shepherd' which was draped in red, white and blue ribbons. The clergy, floral banners, bands and the children in their Whitsun finery – often dressed patriotically as sailor boys and as John Bull and Britannia – took their places. Then with the thump of the band's big drum the procession set off along Sanderson Street which would be lined with spectators.'

St Augustine's Monsall, Whit Monday 1945

Vera and Leone continue: 'We walked onto Queen's Road and then along Oldham Road, Great Ancoats Street, Newton Street, Portland Street and Oxford Street to St Peter's Square. At the Cenotaph the 'big' banner would be lowered; a hymn sung and a wreath laid by St Augustine's sailor boys. After the wreath laying, the procession moved on to Albert Square for the service.

The singing was led from a raised dais by a Mr Craddock. The bands led the 30,000 children in singing 'Onward Christian Soldiers', 'All People that on earth do dwell' and the National Anthem. According to its place in the order of the procession each church moved off along Princess Street. St Augustine's was traditionally number thirty-one of the forty churches taking part. So we had a long wait in Albert Square as well as a long walk. We walked along Princess Street, Mosley Street, Market Street and Victoria Street to the Cathedral. Great crowds

Whit Monday 1951 St Augustine's prepare to leave Sanderson Street for the city centre. The Monsall area has now been completely redeveloped. The terraced streets and St Augustine's Church have been long demolished.

clapped and cheered, the Town Hall bells pealed as we left Albert Square, and the Cathedral bells rang as we walked past the Cathedral. The Cathedral Church had led the Walk, headed by mounted policemen and these occasionally escorted individual churches. In some years we attended the Cathedral service and this was thought to be quite an honour.

After passing the Cathedral, we walked along Corporation Street, Cannon Street, Church Street, Oldham Street and Oldham Road. There were crowds everywhere and lots of happy faces. We eventually turned off Oldham Road and arrived back at St Augustine's along Queens Road and Sanderson Street, which was again lined with spectators. A long day! In the evening of Whit Monday there would be a Parish Social in the schoolroom. On Whit Friday the long-awaited children's excursion to Greenfield from Miles Platting Station took place. Most of the boys had eaten their packed lunches before we left Miles Platting Station!'

"Sons of the Sea" Sailor boys leave their church for Albert Square in a 1950s Whit Walk.

The sailor boys approach Manchester Cathedral with St Ann's Church in the background.

St Augustine's "sailors" lay a wreath at the Cenotaph as they walk by St. Peter's Square. Whit Monday 1960.

Whit Memories of Manchester's Fourth Church, and it's Sunday School

St Paul's Church was originally built in 1765 and stood in Turner Street, off Oldham Street. The church was one of the original ten parishes represented in the first 1801 Whit Monday Procession. It had Sunday Schools in Spear Street, Turner Street, German Street and Bennett Street linked with it, but when a second St Paul's Church at New Cross, replaced the first building in 1878, Bennett Street Sunday School, close to the new site of St Paul's, became the only school attached to the church. Bennett Street Sunday School was opened in 1801, and at one time in its history numbered 2000 children, on its registers.

__Enid Cox of Knaresborough, and Ann Crouch were members of St Paul's Church and of Bennett Street Sunday School. They are descendants of the 19th century Hollingworth family who lived in the centre of Manchester – now known as the Northern Quarter. Enid Cox writes:__ 'They were fascinating years in Manchester centre. The town still had the traces of an "overgrown village" about it and was still coming to terms with its City status. The family had addresses in Turner Street and Back Turner Street. That section of the town close to where the Arndale Centre now stands, housed the original St Paul's Church and its parish. The family were 'reedmakers', that is the double-sided comb that separates the warp threads in cotton looms. In that community in those times, Whit Monday with its procession would have been a great day.

*St. Paul's leave the Bennett Street Sunday School on Whit Monday in the 1950s. Note the old terraced houses of New Cross
Photograph courtesy of Enid Cox.*

My own memories are post-war ones. It was once said to me that the Whit Walks were of interest to local businessmen and employers, who would scan the appearance and demeanour of young school-leavers in the Walks for likely recruitment into the employment market. The Whit Walks were also the source of much business for Manchester clothing and shoe traders. I recall that the exit of each Sunday School from Albert Square was in strict order of the date of the consecration of their respective churches. Each year a different group of churches had the privilege of attending the service in Manchester Cathedral. In Albert Square I remember the long wait after the service for each church to move out in the general procession. Refreshments and other needs involved long queues in the Square, with the risk of missing your church's departure. The Whit Walks were very popular and provided a holiday week from day school for the children. The City Fathers arranged wooden barriers and seats for the thousands of spectators who lined the route of the Procession.'

'I remember that when the east-end of Manchester Cathedral was re-built after war damage, a statue of the Blessed Virgin Mary was placed into an external niche in the Lady Chapel wall. Thereafter a stalwart, and very Protestant lady member of St Paul's refused to walk past the Cathedral in the Procession! It is said that another lady refused to be driven past Manchester Cathedral because of the statue of Oliver Cromwell outside the building – that lady was Queen Victoria! My sisters and I wore our best dresses for the Whit Walk, but we were never given the prestige of carrying a ribbon from St Paul's leading "big" banner – much to our mother's disappointment. St Paul's Bennett Street Sunday School had two big banners. One was that of David Stott, founder and the other the 1801-1901 centenary banner. It was quite difficult, especially on windy days, for two men to carry the large banners with their two poles. At St Paul's we had two bands – one hired for the occasion and the other, St Paul's Scout Band. My father was temporarily Assistant Scout Master and one Whit Monday found him behind the big drum. He was a little man and he couldn't be seen behind the drum, but his energy was such that he put one of the drumsticks through one side of the drum, and had to bang only the other side for the rest of the Walk! The Whit Monday Procession was one of the highlights of our Sunday School year. St Paul's had one of the shorter walks to Albert Square, along Oldham Road, Tib Street, Fountain Street, Spring Gardens, King Street and Cross Street. As the Sunday School contingent passed St Paul's Church at New Cross corner, the rector and church members joined the procession. One Whit Monday our whole family hitched a lift on an open lorry, from our home in Longsight to Bennett Street Sunday School.'

St. Paul's Bennett Street Sunday School was led by the Prestwich Borough Band with father and son drum majors.
Photograph courtesy of M.E.N.

Ann Crouch's Reminiscences of Whit Week in Manchester: 'I feel sad when I think back to my Whit Week Walks, that many children no longer take part in these exciting events. Changed circumstances – a transferred Bank Holiday to a fixed date away from Whitsun, and increased traffic – have brought the Whit Walks into decline. Why did I find them so exciting? The Walks began in 1801 as an expression of faith by the Church's Sunday Schools. Later the churches taking part grew in number and were restricted to those churches within walking distance of the City Centre. Churches processed to Albert Square which became crowded with thousands of children; after a service in the Square, the procession to the Cathedral was a colourful sight. The girls in pretty dresses with posies of flowers and the boys in smart suits. Each church had it's banners with ribbons attached. Spectators would clap and cheer their own church. It could be a noisy occasion! Churches had more than one band and there could be a cacophony of sound for the walkers in the middle of the procession. Some considered tunes such as 'Sons of the Sea' unsuitable but the bands played on with music that lifted the spirits. St Paul's was often led by Bess's O th Barn Band. As the bands entered Albert Square they ceased playing and led us in with a drum beat.'

'In 1958 when Bennett Street Sunday School celebrated it's 150th anniversary we led the General Procession after the Cathedral contingent. I felt proud of our Sunday School that day, as did my sisters, parents and children – three generations of Whit walkers! Mine wasn't the only family to boast of that. My Grandpa Thorp – we called him that – President of the Procession Committee, walked with his son, and his wife; his daughter and her husband and their children. I'm proud that members of my family had been taking part in the Walks since around 1870, my grandmother Cox, her mother Elizabeth Hollingsworth and possibly her father William Pennington were walkers too. Bennett St Sunday School was an institution that people came back to long after they had left the parish. When my great aunt Mary Ann walked, she lived in the parish. When my father walked he lived in Moston. When my children walked we lived even further away. My father, Arthur, acted as a marshall on more than one occasion. I still have his lapel ribbon. When he wasn't a marshall he walked with the scout troop, the 2nd 9th Manchester.'

'It wasn't just the Walk that was exciting, Whit Monday morning was the first day of a week of activities for the "Bennett Streeters". The St Paul's Parish Magazine for May 1953 told me that the Whit Week arrangements were: *Monday afternoon: Coach trip around Cheshire, leaving school at 2 pm. Tea at Bulkeley, near Beeston Castle. Cost of coach and tea is 12s6d each for adults and 6s6d each for children. Wednesday afternoon, it is proposed to go to Longford Park.* This trip did not include a coach and meal, but instructions were given that refreshments were available in the café. As I remember it, a number of people would turn up, some refreshments were provided by the Sunday School and we all played games and had races. Another favourite location was Queen's Park, Heywood. Friday was another coach trip, a full day. *Trip to Furness Abbey. The coach will leave school at 8 a.m. This is a beautiful ride through lovely country. Lunch and tea will be at the King's Arms in Ulverston. Cost 26s for adults, children half price.* The week ended on Saturday with a Whist Drive and Social Evening – *To commence at 7 p.m. A dance band will be in attendance. Admission 2s each for adults and 1s for children.* And of course the week had begun by special Whit Sunday services. My parents made sure they were free that week and had put money aside to take us to all three events. I can remember incidents from a number of them, such as having tea in a café in Skipton and a lovely plate of cakes. Or the time we went to Ashworth Valley and a boy missed his footing and rolled down a steep hill – he wasn't hurt fortunately. Whit Week was a highlight of my childhood and teenage years. It was a time for fun, to be with friends, to share the excitement second only to Christmas. Like most children I gave little thought to the Christian message of Whitsuntide or the reason behind the Walks. But now, looking back as an adult who knows more about both, I feel that although I might have been ignorant of the thinking, the activity of taking part in the Whit Week Walks gave me the Christian messages of community, of co-operating with others, of joy and of friendship, profoundly Christian values.'

The St. George's in the Fields sailor boys parade on a 1950s Whit Monday. Photograph courtesy of M.E.N.

St George's in the Fields – a Church without a field in it's Parish!

St George's, Oldham Road, was known as 'St George's in the Fields'. This was because the original St George's Church, built in 1815 stood in the then fields which are now part of the railway line between the Oldham and Rochdale Roads. The second St George's Church on Oldham Road was built in 1877 and was surrounded by terraced houses, and by the railway lines – it remained known as 'St George's in the Fields!'

Norma Rothwell, of Middleton, recollects memories of Whitsun at St George's and of Whit Monday Walks: 'St George's in the Fields was known in the Whit Walk for its Forty Sailor Boys dressed in white naval uniform; they led that church's procession. They carried Union flags over their shoulders, and they received great applause, and many cheers from the spectators. I wonder if my great-great grand father cast a benevolent eye on them in his day when he was the local police 'bobby' for St George's Parish? On Whit Mondays as a small child there was the excitement when I woke up on the big day and new clothes were on a hanger on the wardrobe door. Then there was the anxious peep to see what the weather looked like – would it please be a fine day? One year I remember mum warning me not to walk on pitch bubbles between the setts and cobbles on the roads because it was so hot and the bitumen would be liquefied. I had white patent leather sandals and if the melted tar got on to them it would be very difficult to remove and would leave a dirty, yellowish stain on them. Arriving at our church there was the glorious scent of all the flowers as we assembled in the hall – such a contrast to the usual rather dusty smell. Lilies, pinks and carnations still remind me of this. Once the procession had assembled there was the thrill and excitement as the bass drum of the brass or silver band sounded – the signal to move off. Then the stalwart men hoisted the heavy poles of the big banner into the leather holders and the clergy led off following the gleaming cross held on high and to the notes of a stirring march and we were on our way."

Norma continues: On the route crowds lined the pavements, two or three deep on many roads, but often ten deep in the city centre or on main roads in the suburbs. Ripples of applause followed the procession as it passed by and occasional calls were heard of "give us a smile, luv" or "hold your lily up" until at last was heard "nearly home now, keep going." Other memories come to mind of the peculiarly moving sound of hymns sung in the open air, the stirring music of marches and the bugles and beating drums of scout or brigade bands with the uniformed organisations. There was the tug of the ribbons and cords on the banners, especially on breezy days. Keeping an eye on little five-year-old trainbearers in the year when I was the Sunday School queen and making sure that I did not walk too fast for them. Such solemn little faces they had with the great responsibility they showed towards "their" queen. There were the white tulle picture hats of the banner girls of the Albert Memorial Church, Queens Road, a familiar sight, as were the crinoline dresses and sumptuous floral banners of St Augustine's, Monsall. From the late 1940s and 1950s I had moved further out from the city centre of Manchester to Blackley so "walking" was more local, usually on the church anniversary Sunday, but still at Whitsun we would pack flasks and sandwiches and journey to Market Street to join the crowds and cheer on our old parishes. All the bus services near the city were cancelled or terminated short of the processional route so it was a weary trudge back to Queens Road before we could catch a bus home – but well worth it!'

In and around Manchester

Albert Memorial Church Collyhurst – Whit Monday 1938, on Rochdale Road. The little girl in the photograph is Norma Rothwell. She was dressed in pink with pink carnations.

The banner girls of Albert Memorial in 1938 wearing their distinctive headdresses. Photograph courtesy of Norma Rothwell.

The Band with Tall Hats!

Sheila Shaw walks behind her brother with the "Tall Hat Band" leading St. Philip's Bradford Road in the late 1940s. Photograph courtesy of Sheila Shaw

A feature of the Whit Monday Procession with St Philip's, Bradford Road, Ancoats, was Culcheth Military Band from Newton Heath. A Junior Section led St Philip's Mission Church, Branson Street. The band was known as the 'Tall Hat Band' because it paraded in top hats and tail coats.

From Miles Platting, Sheila Shaw writes: 'My brother walked on Whit Mondays (and on Whit Fridays) with Culcheth Military Band – the 'Tall Hat Band'. I walked behind him with St Philip's Bradford Road, carrying his music, along Oldham Road and Butler Street, as that church returned from Albert Square. The Whit Walks bring back the most wonderful memories. I would go to the city centre early in the morning to get a front-line view of the Procession. I would take a stool and packed sandwiches, prepared for a long, but worthwhile wait. My brother's band at rehearsals sat with their music on a stand, but on the march my brother's music was strapped to his arm. On one march one of the band was so intent on his music that he didn't see a division in the road. The band went one way and he went solo the other! The band always got its act right for Whit Monday in Market Street. What a delight it was to see the 'Tall Hat Band', the many other bands, the banners, children, clergy and all who took part. One Whit Friday, the rain teemed down for the R.C. Walk, but the Procession carried on. The Walks had many fine days. The excitement of Market Street at Whitsun was something not to be missed.'

Sheila Shaw's brother walks with the "Tall Hat Band" at a Whitsun Walk in the 1950s.

Down City Road from Hulme to Albert Square

The ten Church of England Parishes of Hulme which existed until the 1950s, reducing eventually to just the new Parish of The Ascension, were never fully represented in the Whit Monday Procession in the city centre. Only three of the ten Churches of Hulme took part. These were St Mark's, St Stephen's and post-Second World War, St Michael's. Two of Hulme's Churches, St Philip's and St George's were closer to the city centre than most of the parishes which joined the Whit Monday Walk, but they never took part in the Procession. The likeliest explanation for this would be that Hulme, pre-Second World War, had it's own Whit Walks.

John Bethell, now resident in the Isle of Man, has sent the memories of his time as organist and Choir Master of St Stephen with St Mark Hulme, when the church walked on Whit Mondays in the city centre: 'I recall the years 1956-1966 when as organist and Choir Master of St Stephen's Hulme, I walked with my choir in the Whit Monday Procession. We left our church on City Road, Hulme, at 9 a.m. and processed to the Town Hall in Albert Square, along lower Mosley Street, Peter Street and South Street. After the Albert Square service we joined the general processional route to the Cathedral. We then turned back for Hulme along Chapel Street, Salford, and into Deansgate and City Road. Gosh they were weeks indeed. Wonderful and uplifting it was, every year, to take part and to lead the choir, at the head of the church congregation in the Procession. My time in Hulme was indeed a great part of my spiritual and musical life.'

St. Stephen with St. Mark Hulme leave their church for Albert Square, Whit Monday 1958, with choirmaster and choir leading their banner. Photograph courtesy of John Bethell.

Walking with Salford's First Church

Sacred Trinity, Chapel Street, Salford was consecrated as a Chapel of Ease to the Collegiate Church (now Manchester Cathedral) in 1635. It was Salford's first church and it remains open for worship in the 21st Century. The church took part in the first Whit Walk in 1801. ***Anna Yates, of Old Trafford, a former member of Sacred Trinity writes:*** 'I settled into the congregation of Sacred Trinity and found everyone to be very kind. As a young widow with two daughters, I eventually married Jack Hobson, the church warden. Canon Hussey was then the rector and living in the rectory on Blackfriars Road. The church was always second in the order of procession for Whit Monday. We left the schools in Blackfriars and walked along Chapel Street, Quay Street, Deansgate and Brazennose Street into Albert Square. In the Square Canon Hussey was once photographed with members of the church, on the steps of the Albert Memorial.' The contingent from Sacred Trinity once took part in the Whit Monday Procession with the whole congregation, including the children, dressed in 17th century period costumes to mark the church's Anniversary.

John Bethell, organist and choirmaster at St. Stephen with St. Mark Hulme, leads his choir in a Whit Monday Walk in the 1950s.

Canon Richard Lionel Hussey, rector of Sacred Trinity walks in procession with his church wardens – one of whom is Jack Hobson (next to Canon Hussey) Photograph courtesy of Anna Yates.

Canon Richard Hussey with members of Sacred Trinity, pose in Albert Square on a Whit Monday in the 1950s. Photograph courtesy of Anna Yates.

His Last Walk, and Her First

Joan Monckton (nee Ashworth) recalls a moment in her life which she has cherished. She writes from Colwyn Bay, where she now lives: 'For fourteen years I lived in Ancoats, Manchester, and attended the Church of St James the Less.' (Then known affectionately in Ancoats as 'Little Jimmy's'). St James the Less was one of the first churches in Ancoats to close, in 1937. At the age of seven, I took part in my first Whit Monday Walk, with St James the Less, in 1930. As we passed Manchester Cathedral there was a pause in the Procession. The then Dean of Manchester, Dr Hewlett Johnson, was reviewing the Whit Walk outside the Cathedral. He stepped into the road and greeted me. The newspapers carried the caption: 'His Last Walk and Her First Walk'. The Dean was moving to become Dean of Canterbury. The photograph is on the wall of my room, a very much prized possession.' (See photograph page 5).

Keep Playing or you'll get pelted with Fruit

*Drum majors were popular figures in the Whit Walk.
This one, the youngest in the Procession led Newton Heath Loco Band with St. John's Oldham Road.
Photograph courtesy of M.E.N.*

Brian Mooney of Failsworth has his memory of Whitsun: 'I have wonderful memories of the Whit Walks through Manchester City Centre. The first is of being taken by my mother each year as a very young lad, to watch the "scholars", as they were called, walking in the city centre. It was always my ambition as a young lad to walk in the town centre Procession, but as I lived in Failsworth it was obviously too far for our church to walk. In my early teens I joined my school brass band, which led me, through one of my teachers, to join the Moston Silver Prize Band. This band played for St George's, Oldham Road, on Whit Monday (and for St Malachy's, Collyhurst, on Whit Friday). My earlier childhood wish was fulfilled with the Moston band. As we walked into the City Centre from the north side, we had to pass through the old Smithfield Market, and down Shudehill. I remember as a young second-cornet player, being taunted by older members of the band that we should always be playing through Smithfield Market because if we didn't we would have rotten fruit thrown at our feet as we passed on the way out. I never found out if this was a joke or not, as we always 'struck up' in the Market just before Swan Street! While the churches were taking part in the Albert Square service, the bandsmen visited the old Kardomah Café on Cross Street to "wet their whistles" before returning to Albert Square to lead the various churches out. Lyon's tea shop was another venue. We used to go along Princess Street, Mosley Street and Market Street, all of which were packed solid with thousands of people watching. One year our drum major was an ex RAF drum major and I can still remember today the cheers of the crowd as he threw the baton as high as he could before catching it, while the crowds chanted "again, again, again!" Of course he obliged, as the band played stirring marches!'

Americans Watch the Walk – and think it better than the Trooping of the Colour!

James Nutter of Cheadle Hulme recalls Whitsun memories at Christ Church, Bradford-cum-Beswick, as a member of the Church Lads' Brigade: He begins with this: 'I read in the 'Manchester Evening News' after one Whit Monday, that an American and his wife had been in London watching the 'Trooping of the Colour' on Horseguard's Parade. They were told to visit Manchester to see the Whit Procession. They came North, and felt so exhilarated by Whit Monday's experience that they wrote to the newspaper saying that our Whit Walks were an even more joyous celebration of English life than anything they had witnessed in London!'

Jim Nutter, first on the left, without his satchel in 1954. Photograph courtesy of Jim Nutter.

'Oh how the memories flood back. The Whit Walks were a fundamental part of my life, and the memories of them are cherished. They have even been immortalised in a painting by L.S. Lowry. I was born in Euclid Street, Beswick, in 1936 and, until the day of my marriage, spent the next twenty-three years of my life there, embracing every facet of the life and culture of those mainly happy, bygone days. Christened at Christ Church, Bradford, and subsequently a choirboy, it was as inevitable as 'night and day' that I would, with all my pals from the street, graduate into the Church Lads' Brigade, about the age of nine. Each Tuesday, we were drilled in the church school playground, and if it was wet, in the school hall. Nobody ever missed. Discipline was engrained from that age. Respect for authority, recognition of the need to support the other members of the brigade, and a feeling of belonging and identity, and not least, a profound pride in our community and country, were instilled. These elements, without question, helped form the basic social characteristics of the adults we all subsequently became. Our church brigade had a long history of success in the annual marching drill competition held with brigades from all the other rival C of E Churches in East Manchester. St Mary's, All Souls, St Cross in Clayton, to name but a few. The most prestigious award being the 'Fletcher Cup'. We frequently marched on Sunday mornings, through the streets of the parish, celebrating any one of the many commemorations of Christian events and anniversaries, proudly flourishing the flag of the 'colours' denoting our latest 'Fletcher Cup' success. Every time, we marched to our own brigade bugle band, playing the ever recognisable British marches. Christ Church was a thriving, essential and central part of the local community.'

'It was the custom every Whit Sunday for all local children to have new clothes bought for them, which could not be worn before that day. For many children, they were the only clothes they were bought, of right, each year. It was bonanza time for the retailers of Ashton New Road, from Tom Witt's the Tailor, Timpson's Shoes, Gledhill's Menswear and the many other clothes retailers. In my case, I was 'topped and tailed' with everything, which in the early days, were purchased from a credit tailor, such as 'James Stewart's' in Ardwick Green. Paid for at the rate of '2 bob' a week to Stewart's Friday night collector. The same night my dad got his wages. Vest and underpants; shoes and socks; suit, shirt and tie; and even a new hankie. I always felt like the 'dog's dinner' on Whitsunday morning, with my 'brylcreemed' hair, and shiny nose, smelling of carbolic and 'Knight's Castile'. Every kid in the street was similarly kitted-out. The girls resplendent in their new frocks, hair all 'set' and teeth doubly brushed. Absolute Magic! We all pranced around, posing, comparing colours, styles, choices, calling into our aunts and uncles for a 'tanner' for "looking so nice", and for those few in 'the street' having a 'brownie' camera, (but not in my case), a photo or two. The lads in our gang always went to Barmouth Street Baths at 8.30 a.m. on that, and most other Sundays, after the paper round.

The Church Lads' Brigade of Christ Church Bradford, Manchester, line up outside the church ready to bring up the rear of the procession on Whit Monday 1951.

On Whit Sunday we always had a hot bath as well. We wanted to look at our best on that special day. The sense of belonging was palpable. Our street itself always looked a picture, with every house having been given a communal 'spring clean' by the younger married men of the street. Painted window frames, red lacquered walls, and newly varnished front doors. Front steps naturally having 'donkey stoned' that morning. The 'rehearsal' for the Monday Walks took place after lunch on Whit Sunday, when the whole church, led by the rector and choir, followed by the brigade band, brass band, cadets, guides and brownies, 'walked' the parish, accompanied by every child and teacher of the Sunday School, the Mothers Union, indeed, every representative of the church. The men, principally carrying the many banners and flags, relating to the parish, our membership of the Church of England family of churches, our national flags, and if in our possession, the 'colours' denoting our latest successes in retaining the Fletcher Cup and other competitions.'

James Nutter continues: 'Topping everything though, was the annual Walk to 'Town' each Whit Monday. This was *'the event'* of the whole year. 'Dove's The Florists' on Ashton New Road, was a prominent family business attached to the church and parish. Frances Waite, the proprietor and her family were in heavy demand for this extraordinary day, and from early on Saturday, had been preparing the corsages, bouquets and other flower arrangements. The dress code of the brigade, comprised a forage cap and badge, white 'dress' satchel, and clasp belt. Simple, easily identifiable and cherished by every cadet. The more senior members, as well as the bugle band, wore a full 'military' style cap. If you had 'stripes' on your sleeve, your uniform included white gloves and you carried a baton. Each N.C.O. led one line of the ranks. Now that was really something extra. I was considered good enough to be a Corporal, and had this massive honour. Whatever your rank, every member of the brigade, bandsman and cadet, wore a red rose in their hat on this special day. It was making a very important statement. Mancunian, Lancastrian, and above all, English! They cost half-a-crown, if I remember correctly. They were brought at Dove's. I delivered their daily 'papers' from the age of eleven until I left grammar school at sixteen, and during my wonderful time as a member of the C.L.B., I had a 'special' rose given to me by Frances (Mrs) Waite each Whitsuntide. Whit Monday's church assembly began immediately after 'papers' about 8.00 a.m. By then we were all gathered, lined up, and ready to walk. Always at the front of the procession, was the brass band, playing stirring marches and popular, traditional tunes. They were followed by the various branches of the church, led by the choir and rector; the Sunday School teachers and scholars, resplendent in their long dresses, corsages, flowered headdresses and bouquets. They would be followed by the members of the Mothers Union, who had been so instrumental in the general organisation of the clothes and floral dressings. Banners, flags and ribbons accompanied every one of these constituent parts of the church's life, colourfully wafting in the breeze. Coming up in the rear, were the 'Boys of the Brigade'. The bugle band, the cadets and the girls. All marching, and swelling with pride. Unforgettable! The route went down Ashton New Road, up Mitchell Street, Pollard Street, Great Ancoats Street, Newton Street, Portland Street and finally into Albert Square, where all the other churches of Manchester and Salford assembled. A service was held, hymns sung and the churches mingled.'

An East Manchester Church Lads and Church Girls' Brigade parade through terraced streets, long demolished, to join the Whit Monday Walk to Albert Square in the 1940s. Photograph courtesy of Stella McDonald.

'It was the families of those taking part, and the neighbours who lined the 'New Road' and the earlier part of the Walk to town, many of them accompanying the procession all the way. By the time the procession reached Great Ancoats Street, the crowds were three deep. From Newton Street onwards, the crowds became really dense, many spectators having chosen their own strategic spots along the route, waiting patiently on the pavements from an early hour. They brought their own picnics, stools, and crates to stand on, fold-up chairs, 'Union Jacks' to wave, as the procession passed them. All the time adding to the splendour, and excitement of the day. They cheered, sang along with the bands, clapped the marching cadets and generally created a tumultuous party atmosphere. One of my own ever abiding memories was outside the Post Office on Newton Street. There I was, marching at the front of my line of cadets, stripes on sleeve, white gloves, and baton swinging, hearing the crowd singing *'Oh you can't beat the boys of the bulldog breed – bobbing up and down like this'*, when suddenly, out from the dense crowd lining both sides of the street, stepped my dad. *"There he is, there's my son, Jimmy. That's him."* He was telling all and sundry, of the presence of his marching son. I was bursting with pride, absolutely bursting. My eyes never wavered from the front, but my dad knew that I had seen him, and he couldn't stop clapping. It was 1950, I was thirteen years old. Two years later, my dad died of cancer. Recalling it even now, over sixty years later, continues to make me melancholic. Each year some of the churches would be selected to attend the Service of Thanksgiving at the Cathedral. Christ Church returned to Bradford along Oldham Street, Great Ancoats Street, Mill Street, Carruthers Street, Mitchell Street and Ashton New Road – these thoroughfares being lined with spectators. On Whit Monday, in late afternoon, many of us went to Belle Vue for entertainment at the fairground. I spent all my earliest childhood in this idealic world of friendship, neighbourliness and warmth. The sense of community overrode every other consideration. No family had much money, but street crime and vandalism was virtually non-existent. People just 'mucked in'. My childhood association with Christ Church, Bradford, only came to an end when my gang discovered the existence of a great youth club, at Wesley Hall Methodist Church, on Great Ancoats Street. I was by now getting on for fifteen. It was here that I continued to enjoy my youth, met my future wife, married her some seven years later in 1959, and remain happily married, fifty-one years afterwards. I have been lucky in life. I came from a strong, loyal family of five children. I progressed in my career, discovered many parts of the country and in later years, have enjoyed the family joy of married life, and seen a great deal of the world.

Nothing, but nothing, however, will take away the happiness of those early years, of Community, and of Whitsun and it's Walks!'

A Photographer's Recollections of the Whit Walks

Iris Burns, (nee Theobald), second right, wife of the Author, with the Banner Girls of St. Mary's Beswick. This photograph was taken at 7:00am on Whit Monday morning 1961 outside the church, by a Manchester Evening News photographer, possibly Bill Batchelor.

Bill Batchelor, a photographer with the 'Manchester Evening News' covering the Whit Walks writes: 'An event that was perhaps unique to the North West was the annual Whitsuntide Walks (Whit Walks). A throwback, perhaps, to the days when workers in the factories of the cotton towns of the later period of the Industrial Revolution were given, first a day's holiday, and later the whole week off to mark the religious event. On Whit Monday every Church of England congregation would take part in a combined walk of witness and process through the city streets before meeting up for a service in Albert Square. Banners were unfurled and both children and adults would be wearing their finest clothes. Whole groups would be dressed in the same style with the girls looking particularly colourful in their dresses made especially for the occasion. Boys would wear their best Sunday suit and their own band would lead each contingent. The service outside the Town Hall in Albert Square usually began at about 10 a.m. That meant those churches situated in the outlying districts had to begin early – perhaps as early at 7.00 a.m. in some cases – in order for them to arrive in the Square on time. This also meant an early start for every photographer at the 'Manchester Evening News'. It was the biggest processional event for the entire city and, we as photographers on the local evening newspaper, were part of it. The day was planned by the Picture Editor like a military operation with each photographer having been allocated two churches to attend on his way to work at 7.00 a.m. Two early pictures were required from each church group before they began their procession. We would then be in the office by 8.00 a.m. with the undeveloped film, caption the four pictures required for first edition and then rejoin the "walkers" en-route to Albert Square for more pictures. This would be repeated time after time throughout the morning and always we would be on the look-out for a page one picture for that same day's paper, as well as for the souvenir edition packed with photographs that would be on sale the following day.

The Roman Catholic churches would stage their own Procession on Whit Friday of the same week with the Italians walking on the Sunday. The M.E.N. photo team would go into action again. It was such a grand occasion that I recall a time towards the end of my apprenticeship as a darkroom printer in the late 1950s or early 1960s when more than 600 pictures were taken by staff and freelance photographers using 5x4 inch or 9x12 cm plate cameras (a dark slide with two glass plate negatives inside as opposed to role film). No mean task when compared with the ease and speed of today's digital cameras! The job didn't finish at the end of the Whit Walks because then it was the turn of the darkroom printers, of whom I was one in 1960. Since early morning, the darkroom men had been printing hard copy prints from each of the photographs and these were then sent to the picture desk from selection and marking up. In 1960, the M.E.N. had twenty-five branch offices scattered around the region and each branch office had to be supplied with pictures for display in their windows. At the end of the Walk it was time to start printing twenty-five 12x10 inch prints from each of a selection of about twenty-five different Whit Walk pictures. More than 600 12x10 inch prints from Monday's Walk and the same again from the Catholic Walk the following Friday. An early start and a very late finish for the darkroom printers on both these days so that the branch office window prints were in the windows the following day. That was only the start of it because soon orders for photographs were flooding into the office from parents and grandparents anxious to get their own photograph of their "little Suzie or their own little Johnny" whose picture had appeared in the 'Evening News' "special".'

Manchester has the reputation of being the "rainy city" and it certainly does have its share of rain. However, I can recall only one occasion when the annual Whit Walk was cancelled because of the weather. That was one year in the 1960s when the heavens were not kind to the religious procession through the city streets. The rain poured down during the early morning when the walkers were due to leave their respective churches. The M.E.N. photographic team had taken what pictures they could on their way into the city centre and a group of us were now drinking coffee as we waited, together with the staff, inside a café on the corner of Albert Square. The tables inside the café were laden with trays of hundreds of prepared sandwiches awaiting the arrival of the walkers and the thousands of their supporters. They never came! The square was almost deserted and sometime after 10.00 a.m. a decision was taken to cancel the Walk. News trickled slowly into the café. It was a sad time for the walkers and an even sadder day for the café owner, whose staff had prepared all those sandwiches. The food would have to be thrown away and in desperation, the owner told us all to take what sandwiches we wanted. We did just that and linked arms on the way back to the office as we danced a little "jig" down the street. The annual Whit Walks gradually went into decline during the late 1970s and early 1980s. Desperate attempts were made to keep them going but they were abandoned altogether for at least that one year that I can remember. They have since been resumed but have nothing like the following they had known in the past. The M.E.N. gives them a very low profile today and carries perhaps just one or two pages of pictures in the normal day's edition.'

The above written by Bill Batchelor and extracted from "Again There's Just One!" *A "snapshot" in the lives of some of the staff photographers employed by the 'Manchester Evening News'. Compiled by Bill Batchelor and Bob Corfield, two former M.E.N. staff photographers.*

The Whitsun Memories of Iris Burns nee Theobald – who writes about her childhood Whit Weeks: 'Whit Week was always a special and exciting time when I was a child growing up in Beswick in East Manchester. I was six years old when I first went to Sunday School, having moved to Beswick from Reddish. Church and Sunday School played an important part in my life. Sunday School conjures up memories of Bible stories, brightly coloured stickers to stick in an attendance book, Christmas parties, attendance prize giving and preparations for the Whit Week Walks. Preparations for the Whit Week would begin in January. There would be a meeting of Sunday School teachers and parents (usually mothers) who would decide on the material, colours and outfits for the Sunday School children to wear. The church's colours were to be kept a closely guarded secret (that is, do not let Christ Church, Bradford, know the chosen colours!) In the following weeks, dresses were made, headdresses, flowers, shoes and socks were chosen. All this done with great secrecy. I especially remember the dresses chosen for Whitsun 1953, the year of the Queen's Coronation. For Whit Sunday the dresses were a delicate cornflower blue colour with a pink rose bud design; for Whit Monday the colour chosen was an embossed brocade gold material with a Dutch style bonnet to match. On Whit Sunday night my sister Edna and myself would be bathed, scrubbed, hair washed and put in "rags" to achieve Shirley Temple style ringlets. I can remember being too excited to sleep (the rags in my hair would not have helped) and waking early on Whit Monday morning full of eager anticipation and excitement at the prospect of walking to Albert Square.'

Whit Monday 1953 – St. Mary's Beswick leave their school for Albert Square. The Author is front left and his wife-to-be is on the far left. Their respective mothers each produced a copy of this photograph on their engagement.

St. Mary's Beswick Church Girls Brigade march in the 1954 Whit Sunday Parish Whit Walk along Philips Park Road. Iris Theobald is the third girl behind Lieutenant Ada Wakefield, who leads the brigade.

'It was a lovely feeling to wear a new long dress, a headdress, new peep-toe shoes, white socks and all new underwear and to carry a bouquet of fresh flowers. Although we were so excited, my mum would not let us leave home until we had eaten a good breakfast. As we left home in all our finery to walk to Sunday School, neighbours would come out to admire our dresses. Whit Monday morning reflected the community spirit and neighbourliness of the time. When we arrived at Sunday School, Cambrian Street was a place of activity. It was lovely to see the big banner (The Three Wise Men) ready for the confirmation girls to take their ribbons. There were floral tableau (which mothers had helped to arrange the night before) displaying texts such as "Jesus Lives" "Purity" and in 1951 the 150th anniversary of the Whit Monday Walks two banners reading "150 Years, Walks of Witness". Boys and girls in smart brigade uniforms would be lining up, Sunday School teachers in their new outfits would be shepherding their charges into classes and clergy, choir and brass band would take their allocated places. All this would be taking place before 7.00 a.m. At that time in the morning there was a coming together of the community, a feeling of pride in this working class area of East Manchester.

Iris Theobald leads a line of the Girls' Brigade in the Whit Walks of 1954.

There was a sense of spirit, a feeling of togetherness and a sense of belonging to your parish church. Any neighbours differences were put to one side as families stood together admiring the procession in front of them. The Walk into the city centre was a joyous occasion, spectators along the route would applaud with shouts of encouragement such as "hold your lily up". One year it was so hot that black-pitch bubbled up in the roadway and stuck to the soles of the many pairs of new shoes. Another year it rained so heavily, the brigade big drum burst, and I can remember taking shelter under a railway arch. The route was approximately two miles long and took about one-and-a-half hours to walk. On occasions some churches attended a service in the Cathedral. Other churches then met in Albert Square; in the Square there would be hymn singing and an Address. St Mary's Church procession would then make its way back to Cambrian Street for refreshments of buns and milk, served to tired, but happy children. Back home we would put our walking day clothes away in the wardrobe, new shoes would be wrapped in tissue paper and put back in their boxes!'

'As an eight-year old I joined the Church Girls' Brigade at St Mary's, Beswick, this was altogether a different walking experience than as a Sunday School member. I still attended Sunday School, what a big decision an eight year old was faced with, whether to walk with the Church Girls' Brigade or with Sunday School. As a member of the brigade we were very much responsible for looking after our uniform. There was a navy wool tunic, with belt, a white leather sash that had to be whitened, a brass trumpet ring holder that had to be polished, badges that had to be polished, a tie that had to be held in place with a brigade badge, not forgetting white knee-length socks, smart polished shoes, white gloves and a hat positioned at just the right angle. At Whitsun we marched in time to the brigade band and we felt very proud when told how smart we looked. I enjoyed my time as a member of the Church Girls' Brigade and have fond memories of Thursday nights spent in Cambrian Street Sunday School learning marching, drill, P.E. and games. The much respected brigade leaders, Ada Wakefield, Muriel Lee and Lily Hepwood gave freely of their time to the many young girls of Beswick. During my confirmation year I was still a member of the Sunday School and brigade. However, it was tradition for confirmation girls to walk with the big banner. For the first year, confirmation girls in white dresses would walk behind the banner holding a banner ribbon. On full Sunday School attendance the next year, the confirmation girls would walk at the front of the banner. What a privilege this was and such an honour. Whit Week was not only about having new "walking" clothes but also a time to buy a new outfit. Like many others in Beswick, as a family we went to a clothing store in Manchester city centre called Washingtons. Here you could buy everything you needed under one roof and pay weekly for the privilege. Nothing was spared, a new set of underwear, socks, shoes, dresses, coats, gloves, hats, handbags and even a pair of corsets for my grandmother!'

'On Whit Sunday you would put on your new clothes and visit family and neighbours. All would be admired and money would be given to the children for looking so smart. After wearing such finery along with your walking outfits, your new clothes would be put away and worn only for Sunday best. The day after Whit Monday, we would look in shop windows on Ashton New Road to view the Whit Monday photographs on display. Each photo had a number and you could order copies. On Whit Friday the Sunday School went on its annual trip to places such as Frodsham, Lyme Park, Helsby and Hoylake. There we would have a picnic and play games; after a lovely day out we would sing heartily all the way home. I have many happy memories of Whit Week in Beswick. I remember family, friends, neighbours and neighbourhood, people who gave of their time to nurture and encourage young people in their membership of Sunday School, church, choir, brigade and bands. To me, Whit Week was on a par with that other wonderful time in a child's life, Christmas. There was a sense of preparation, excitement and something new to look forward to. Looking back, I give thanks that the Manchester Whit Week Walks were a part of my happy childhood spent with my loving family in Beswick.'

Elaine Burgess – nee Woods, now of Crumpsall, writes of the Miles Platting Whitsun of her childhood: 'My Whit Walk memories begin at the age of three, when my mother and father took me to church with my brother and my late sister. We became part of the Sunday School at St Philip's, Bradford Road, Miles Platting. Everything began for children on Whit Sunday, when dressed in new "Whit clothes" you went around your family to show them off. Children would be given three pence, but one family member, who had always wanted to have a daughter to dress, would offer sixpence to be shown your clothes, if they

Whit Monday 1960. Elaine Burgess, nee Woods, as the Rose Queen of St. Philip's Bradford Road, turns into Market Street.

had "frills" on them! Whit Sunday afternoon saw the walk along Bradford Road, Butler Street and Ridgway Street. Then it was home to get ready for the Whit Monday Procession, and early to bed. My mum used to sit up all night to watch the weather. Whit Monday began for the children at 6.00 a.m. We were dressed and taken to church for the procession. St Philip's were led by Culcheth Military Band, known as the 'Tall Hat Band'. The band would form-up at the top of Ridgway Street and march down the street to the church, to the delight of the spectators. To be allowed to walk in the 1950s children had to have sufficient attendance marks for church and Sunday School. I walked on Whit Monday from the age of three, and eventually became the church rose queen with 100% attendance marks. We usually walked in sunshine, occasionally there would be rain, but the walk went on. In my parents' youth it is said that 1,000 people joined in the St Philip's Procession.

Children of St Philip's Bradford Road with their basket of flowers - 1950s Whit Walk. Photograph courtesy of E.Burgess.

When the St Philip's procession reached Albert Square, we would meet family and friends. In my year as rose queen, St Philip's procession turned into Princess Street from Albert Square, as the 'Tall Hat' Band played the march Ballerina and the Town Hall bells pealed. A wonderful and proud moment. We walked through the centre of Manchester, along Market Street and past the Cathedral, into Oldham Street, Oldham Road and Butler Street – watched all the way by crowds of spectators. After the Procession we arrived home with tired feet, which my grandparents would bathe in hot water and mustard! We always had a meal of homemade meat pie and chips, before a rest in bed – to recover, for the Whit Monday Evening Dance and Family Social in the church hall. Those were days which I shall never forget. In the present, I still watch the Whit Walk. I have rarely missed it in sixty years, and I very much hope that it continues in the future.'

The History and Memories of the Whit Walks

The Culcheth (Manchester) Military Band led St. Philip's Bradford Road, Whit Walk for many years.

St. Philip's Bradford Road Scouts and Guides return to their parish along Oldham Road on Whit Monday 1953.

St. Philip's carry their floral banner along Bradford Road in a 1950s Whit Walk.

Now living in Littleborough, Harold Hawksworth, who was a member of St Mary's Church, Beswick, has recollections of Happy Days at Whitsun, as a child in Beswick: 'As long as I can remember, there was always a build up towards the Whit Walks. It was talked about in the Sunday School, and then I was taken into town (Manchester) to get a suit and new shoes, this was done in time for any needed alterations. All this had all been paid for via the 'clubman' who always came knocking on Friday night (Payday). We were never allowed to wear the new clothes and shoes until the Whit Sunday, when our church, St Mary's, walked round the parish. As a consequence, the shoes weren't broken in, so would wreak agony on the old plates of meat! I also remember, as I got older, joining the Church Lads' Brigade. In the first year, I did not get my uniform in time and, to offset my disappointment, I was asked to walk behind the rector, the Reverend. Lister, in the Whitsun Procession. The following year, I proudly joined my pals in the Church Lads' Brigade. My dad brought me down to earth later that day, when he said "Everyone was out of step apart from you." Most of the Whit Monday Walks I remember being blessed by good or reasonable weather. One year, we had been blessed by a very hot day, but on our way back, storm clouds began to gather and the wind picked up. As St Mary's marched along Pollard Street, near the Salvation Army Citadel, the heavens opened and we had the best part of a mile to go and though we got thoroughly soaked, no-one broke rank. The only concession we made was to roll up the banners to prevent any involuntary hang gliding in the gusty wind.'

Harold Hawksworth leads St. Mary's Beswick from Albert Square on Whit Monday 1957. Photograph courtesy of Harold Hawksworth.

'Never more was the sanctity and dryness of the schoolrooms, on Cambrian Street, more welcome, not to mention the refreshments that were always prepared for our return. I will always remember the Church Lads' Brigade drum major who liked to go the "full Monty" by tossing his mace high into the air and making a perfect catch on its descent thus receiving loud applause from the onlookers. The thing that made this a feat to achieve was the fact that trolleybus wires criss crossed overhead and the trick was to get the mace through, in ascent and descent, without touching them. One year, the drum major of the Church Girls' Brigade decided that, if the lads could do it, so could she. Up the mace went in what initially appeared to be a perfect throw. Unfortunately, a gust of wind caused a slight change in course and the mace touched one of the wires, causing it to spin in the opposite direction. This caused her to miss the catch. Her only saving grace was that she caught it on the rebound. She still got a loud round of applause from the crowds, for her daring. One of the highlights of the Whit Walks was when St Mary's acquired a processional cross and I, as one of the first servers, was given the honour of carrying it in the Whit Monday Procession. The carrying of the cross was shared between me and two of my pals who were also servers.'

Whit Monday 1951 – a spectator's description of the day

John Rowe, now in his eighties and living in the North East, walked in the Whit Monday Procession as a child with All Saints' Sunday School in Chorlton on Medlock. In his teens he watched the Whit Walk as a spectator for the first time. Joining in the Procession each year had meant that he had not been able to watch the other churches which were taking part. He has wondered if this had been the experience of many people who walked every year, and who never saw the Procession in its entirety?

He remembers: 'I decided to see all of the Whit Walk, and 1951 was a good year to do this, because it was the 150th Anniversary of the first 1801 Whit Monday Procession.'

John had a keen interest in the various bands involved in the Walk, and he enjoyed the marches, and the hymns that the bands played en-route. On that day in 1951, he was up and about at 6.00 a.m., and he set off to watch some of the churches beginning their walk to Albert Square. He describes the day, and the scenes he witnessed on a memorable Whit Monday morning sixty years ago. 'The weather was good, and as a young chap I was able to move about at a fair pace. Starting from Chorlton on Medlock, I was in time to see the processions of St Thomas Church, Ardwick, on Grosvenor Street and of St Luke's, Chorlton on Medlock, on Oxford Road. Then I was off to the corner of Whitworth Street and London Road, where St Andrew's, Ancoats, came into view. Their banner bore the text 'Follow Me', but I didn't do so, instead I moved on towards Piccadilly!

Sailor boys of St. Luke's Chorlton-on-Medlock carry their ship in a 1950s Whit Walk. Photograph courtesy of M.E.N.

John's account continues with a description of the activity in Piccadilly, and of the people gathering there. 'As I approached the bottom of Newton Street, I could hear the bugles and drums of the church lads' brigade bands echoing from the high walls of the various offices and warehouses. Crowds were forming in Market Street, and in Mosley Street, even though the start of the Walk was more than an hour and half away. The street vendors were doing a brisk trade selling red roses, red, white and blue, wavers, and Whit Monday programmes. I bought one for sixpence, and I still have it. Looking through the programme has enabled me to recall that Whit Monday as though it was yesterday. A number of churches began to emerge from Newton Street and to cross Piccadilly into Portland Street. I followed with them on the way to Albert Square, as did many others. The Square was a great sight, with rows of banners propped-up against the walls of its buildings, and with the scent of thousands of flowers on the early morning air. The service included hymns led by the bands, which were sung by the vast congregation. Afterwards, there was a sense of anticipation and excitement, as the loudspeakers gave out the names of the first churches to get ready to enter Princess Street from the Square, and begin the Whit Walk. It was, for all taking part, "bliss in that dawn to be alive!"

In and around Manchester

St. Thomas Ardwick walk towards Manchester Cathedral on Whit Monday 1964.

The Writer's account goes on to give a picture of the 1951 Whit Monday Procession as it left Albert Square: 'At the corner of Princess Street the atmosphere of anticipation was palpable as the Walk was about to begin. At just past 9.30 a.m. the bells of the Town Hall began to peal, and four policemen mounted on horses, led Manchester Cathedral, and the Bishop of Manchester, into Princess Street. The Cathedral choir preceded its banner, with their processional cross. There was no band with the Cathedral, but immediately behind it, Prestwich Borough Band struck-up a rousing march as it walked in front of the blue banner of St Paul's, New Cross. The drum major threw his mace high into the air, and caught it again to applause and cheers from the spectators. The Walk's programme informed us that St Paul's Sunday School was celebrating its 150th Anniversary. The thirty-five churches left Albert Square one by one, each of them with their banners, bands, tableau, floral displays, and children in Whitsun finery. St Mary's, Beswick, had a strong turn-out, with the Victoria Hall Band in chocolate-brown uniforms, and a floral banner proclaiming '150 Years Walks of Witness'. Next was St Clement's, Broughton, St Mark's, Holland Street, Sacred Trinity, Salford, St Ann's, Manchester and St Matthew's, Deansgate. St Ann's banner was decorated with lilies.' *The description goes on:* 'St Thomas, Ardwick Green, had their Church Lads' Brigade Band, with the boys each having a red rose in their caps. Then came St Stephen's, Salford, St Luke's, Chorlton on Medlock and St George's, Oldham Road with rows of white uniformed sailor boys. Then it was St Philip's, Salford, whose rector was the greatly respected, Canon Peter Green; St Andrew's, Ancoats, St Saviour's, Chorlton on Medlock, St Jude's, Ancoats and All Souls', Ancoats, with its own brass band formed by the men of the parish. St Matthias, Salford, had a lively military band, and walked in good numbers.'

St. Thomas return to Ardwick Green on Whit Monday 1964.

'The Procession had now been passing on for more than an hour, but the spectators retained their positions, and enthusiastically greeted each church as it moved by. St John's, Miles Platting, St Barnabas, Ancoats, St Philip's, Bradford Road, and St Oswald's, Collyhurst, came along. St Philip's banner was carried on the highest poles in the Procession, and its 'Tall Hat Band' received much applause. St Oswald's had the Blackley Old Comrades Band with them. The next group of schools approached as the Walk reached the two hour point. St Peter's with St James the Less, were followed by German Street Sunday

St. Andrew's Ancoats walk along Ducie Street to London Road in a 1950s Whit Walk, with their banner "St. Andrew and Follow Me". Photograph courtesy of the Nightingale family.

School, who were applauded for their tableau of children dressed as John Bull and Britannia. It seemed odd that a school with the name 'German Street' should display this patriotism. Christ Church, Bradford, had its own Old Boys' Band, and a long line of scholars in its procession. The Albert Memorial Church, Collyhurst, was followed by St Michael's, Hulme, St Stephen's Hulme, St James the Great, Collyhurst and St Luke's, Miles Platting. St Luke's had, what looked like a new (blue and gold) banner and they walked with two silver bands. The Procession had been moving by for almost three hours as the last churches prepared to leave Albert Square. St Augustine's, Monsall, main banner was draped in red, white and blue. Its contingent featured several floral displays, and two finely dressed rose queens. The last three schools were from St Aidan's, Bradford, St Paul's, Philips Park and St Jerome's, Ardwick. Albert Square was now deserted, and along came the street cleaners! The thirty-five churches were wending their way back to their home parishes, with some of the younger children in their ranks surely being a little weary after an eventful morning. The Cathedral had turned into Princess Street at 9.30 a.m.; St Jerome's, Ardwick, followed them at 12.40 p.m! The time had passed quickly, and every minute of it had made for a wonderful experience. The Whit Walk had been a great and colourful act of Christian Witness, through which the churches had reached out to people, and given happiness to the walkers, and to the spectators alike.'

St. Philip's Bradford Road with their banner carried on the "tallest poles" in the Whit Walk. Bradford Gas Works is in the background.

John Rowe concludes his memories of Whit Monday 1951, reflecting: 'The Whit Walks were a unique demonstration of the Christian Faith, and an opportunity for the churches to present a lively witness to the people of a great city in its town centre. Across the years there were those who criticised the Walks for being 'too worldly'. In my view this was a narrow understanding of the Christian Faith. The Whitsun processions were a big part of my childhood, and they have been an abiding memory ever since. The Whit Walk in 1951 was a special occasion for me, and for many in Manchester and Salford who will still remember that day. The years have gone by, and though the Walk has declined in numbers, and in popularity with spectators, it is good that this great tradition is maintained. Long may it march on!'

Memories of Whitsuntide at St John's, Miles Platting

Hilda Fitton (nee Meehan); Barbara Mackenzie (nee Meehan); May Kay (nee Greathead); Dorothy Preston (nee Flitcroft) and Roy Flitcroft, have memories of their childhood Whitsuns at St John's, Oldham Road, Miles Platting. Dorothy Flitcroft and Hilda Fitton expressed them to the Author.

Dorothy recalls: 'The Reverend Malan was our Rector when I was a child at St John's Church. Miss Lambert, was a respected Sunday School teacher. Whitsuntide was the highlight of our year, and for the children it was better than Christmas. We had new clothes, paid for weekly in the months leading to Whit Week, by our parents. The church gave the girls their Whit dress length, and I was fortunate in that my aunt, who was a machinist, made my dress. St John's Church had a green "big" banner depicting a figure of St John the Evangelist. This was proudly carried at the head of our Whit procession. This same banner is now carried in the Church of England Procession in Manchester, by All Saints and Martyrs church, Langley – with the church's name adjusted.' *Hilda Fitton adds:* 'On Whit Sundays St John's walked around our parish, which was made up of the terraced streets leading off Oldham Road. Children wore different new clothes and shoes for this occasion, than those special ones chosen to be worn on Whit Monday. Whit Sunday evening was spent getting ready for the next great day. For the girls this meant having their hair put into "rags" to curl it, which didn't make for a good nights sleep! Not that this mattered for we kept one eye all night, on the weather. Whit Monday saw parents making an early start, collecting the flowers for the procession from the local florist on Oldham Road. The St John's Whit Walk was organised by Miss Lambert, the Sunday School Superintendent. She decided who would carry baskets of flowers, and who would hold the banner ribbons. Miss Lambert presided at the choosing of the parish rose queen, at Christmas each year. In my years at St John's Church, the clergy included, the Reverend Malan; the Reverend Knowles and the Reverend Basil Higginson.'

St. John's Miles Platting walk along Mosley Street in an early 1950s Whit Monday. Photograph courtesy of H. Fitton.

'St John's held a third procession of Witness each year on the anniversary of the consecration of the church. Whit Monday, though, was The Great Day. We left the church at 8.00 a.m. in the morning, and led by Newton Heath Silver Prize Band, Miles Platting Mission Silver Band and St John's Church Lads' Brigade Band, we walked along Oldham Road, and into the city centre. As we passed the Cenotaph in St Peter's Square, our banners and flags were lowered in respect to the Fallen.'

May Kay, nee Greatbanks, walks as Rose Queen with St. John's Miles Platting in the early 1950s.

Nurses from Ancoats Hospital walked in the Whit Monday Procession from St. John's Miles Platting in the 1960s. Photograph courtesy of M.E.N.

'As our procession moved through the centre of Manchester, after leaving Albert Square, the crowds of spectators would be densely packed on the pavements. The bands played hymns, such as 'The Church's One Foundation' but also patriotic tunes, like 'Sons of the Sea', the lively sounds of which, cheered the walkers and spectators alike. The spectators would wave Union Jacks and red, white and blue 'wavers'. After leaving the general procession at Manchester Cathedral, St John's and the other Oldham Road parishes, would walk home along Oldham Street, New Cross, and Oldham Road, all of which would be lined with spectators. If the weather was very hot, the children were afraid of getting the melting tar from the cobblestones in the roadway onto their new white shoes. I remember one Whit Monday in the mid 1950s when St John's started off for Albert Square in torrential rain. We had to seek refuge from the weather in St George's Church, Oldham Road, as we reached that point, and our Whit Monday was over! Representatives were sent to Albert Square to report to the Walks' organisers. In Miles Platting we had Roman Catholic neighbours, but any rivalry was friendly. Church of England people watched the Roman Catholic Walks, and Roman Catholics saw our processions. We have only good memories of those happy days.'

Whit Monday at German Street Church of England Sunday School

German Street Sunday School, as recorded in chapter five, had an unusual history. It was built in German Street, off Oldham Road, in 1826, after a previous building had been erected in 1785 as 'St Paul's Turner Street Fourth School'. It later became a part of the St George's district in Manchester; it was later the centre of the beginning of the parish of St Peter, Oldham Road, and it was then given its own parish church of St Martin in German Street. On the closure of St Martin's Church in 1906, German Street Sunday School retained its independence, in the parish of St Peter, Oldham Road. The school hymn was: 'We won't give up our Sunday School'.

Whit Monday 1959. German Street Church of England Sunday School's last Whit Monday Walk. Their banner had to have a police escort during the First World War because it bore the word "German". Photograph courtesy of V. Kingham.

St Martins, German Street

WE WON'T GIVE UP OUR SUNDAY SCHOOL

Composed for German Street Sunday School by Rev. W.B. Atkinson

We won't give up the Sunday School,
Where first we learnt of God;
Where first our little feet were taught
The path our Saviour trod;
Where, drawn by one endearing tie,
Dear friends have often met,
Some gone to glory long ago,
While some are with us yet.
We love, we love the old place
We love its Christian rule;
Whatever others think or say,
We love the Sunday School.

We won't give up the Sunday School,
As onward still we go,
And, with the flowing tide of time,
In years and stature grow,
Long may it shed a hallowed charm
Around the Sabbath days,
And cheer us on our heavenward road,
By precept, prayer, and praise. – We love, &c

We won't give up the Sunday School,
Which godly men of old
For their Redeemer's sake upreared,
And in His name controlled:
While year by year, the hand Divine,
Their loving mission blest,
Until with many of their flock,
They entered into rest. – We love, &c

We won't give up the Sunday School,
It yet has work to do,
As great as in the days gone by,
As noble and as true.
We'll help it on with heart and hand,
To guide the children home,
Until to crown the good old cause,
Our blessed Master come. – We love, &c

During the First World War, German Street was re-named 'Radium Street', but the school kept its original name.

Whit Monday 1959 – German Street Church of England Sunday School carry their floral banner along Princess Street in the school's last Whit Walk. Photograph courtesy of V. Kingham.

Val Kingham, nee Rawlinson, has her memories of Whitsun at German Street, which she has sent from Middleton Junction, where she now lives: 'I first walked on Whit Monday, with German Street Church of England Sunday School, at the age of three. I held a ribbon attached to a basket of flowers. On Whit Monday morning the children would meet at the school, and after a prayer, the banner 'The Sower' would be raised; the brass band would strike-up and we would walk from German Street, into Jersey Street, and across Great Ancoats Street into the city centre. The closer we got to Albert Square, the greater the crowds of spectators would become. When I was twelve, I was privileged to have a ribbon from the main Sunday School banner in the procession. When the school had walked through the centre of Manchester, we returned along Oldham Street and Oldham Road. The crowds watching would be dense, and the excitement of the children would be great. My father was a Roman Catholic, but his family would come from Hulme to watch the Church of England Walk, and they would give me gifts of money, as our procession passed by them. After the Walk ended, the children would be given a party in the school hall. This was all part of the wonderful Whit Mondays of former times in Ancoats. Horace Sumner, who was the Organising Secretary of the Whit Monday Procession, was a member of German Street School, as were his assistants, Harold Bromley and Alan Gleaves. My grandparents were members of the nearby St Barnabas Church in Rodney Street, Ancoats, which had some connections with German Street School.'

'German Street Sunday School, like St Paul's Bennett Street Sunday School, off Oldham Road, was an imposing building. Our Sunday School Superintendent, was a Mr Burton, and he conducted Sunday afternoon services in the school. The services were held in a large room which had a big coal fire. The school organ was in this part of the building. It had been brought, from the old Church of St Paul, Turner Street, when that building was demolished, and replaced by St Paul's, New Cross. Many Ancoats children were taught the Christian faith at German Street Church of England Sunday School. Violet Carson, Coronation Street's 'Ena Sharples', had connections with the school, and with the adjacent St Peter's Church. The school gave a great deal to the local Ancoats community, and especially to the children. With re-housing leaving the district without a resident population, the life of German Street School came to an end in 1959. In that year I walked in the school's last appearance in the Whit Monday Procession, at the age of thirteen. Appropriately the school attended the Whit Monday Procession service in Manchester Cathedral, and we led the Walk, after the Cathedral, through the city centre.'

Whitsun at St Mark's, Holland Street

Renee Emery, nee Edwards, has recollections of Whit Mondays as a member of the Church Girls' Brigade at St Mark's Church, Holland Street, Miles Platting. She writes from Congleton in Cheshire: 'I attended St Mark's Church, Holland Street, when I was twelve years old. I joined the Church Girls' Brigade as St Mark's did not have a Brownie and guide pack. Our Captain was Elsie Lee. The uniform was a thick dark-blue serge dress, a forage cap, white sling with a brass ring and red belt. On the Whit Monday Walk if the weather was warm and sunny you would be very hot, particularly after playing a trumpet or carrying and playing a drum. If it was raining the uniform absorbed the water and became heavy if you did not have a raincoat. Unlike Brownies and Guides, I don't remember any of us working for any badges, which I would have like to do. Most of our time was taken up with band practice and games for the corps. For a few months, before the Walks we attended St Catherine's Church, Collyhurst, one night a week for band practise. The bandmaster was a blind person, but he knew which person played a wrong note on the trumpet and would go immediately to that girl, although we were marching round the hall. He had a young assistant called Harvey, who taught drum players.

The week prior to the Whit Walk we sometimes had a parade round part of the parish boundary as a dress rehearsal. On Whit Sunday it would be the church Walk round the parish, with stops, when the rector would give a short sermon. For Whit Monday there was always a lot of speculation as to which band the church would hire to lead the Walks, and there was great competition between the parishes as to who had managed to get the best band. St Mark's, on several occasions had the Manchester Tramways Band to lead the way, whereas nearby St Philip's always had the "Tall Hat Band." The Whit Monday Walk began at about 8.00 a.m or earlier if your church was to go into the Cathedral for a service. St Mark's took the route down Holland Street, across Butler Street, Woodward Street and along Ancoats Lane to Newton Street, then along Portland Street, Princess Street and into Albert Square, where each church had an allotted space, and time for the return walk. The first churches in would watch the later ones arriving and compare bands and rose queens, but we all thought our own church to be the best!

Enid Meredith in her crinoline dress, Renee Emery's cousin, walks in 1953 with St. Mark's Holland Street. Photograph courtesy of M.E.N.

The first church arrivals into Albert Square were those going into the Cathedral for the short service. St Mark's return walk progressed from Albert Square, into Mosley Street, Market Street, Deansgate, past the Cathedral, into Cannon Street, Oldham Road, Butler Street and back to the church in Holland Street. The Walk would end between 2.00 pm and 3.00 p.m. It was lovely, as the crowds would line the streets, clap, cheer, wave flags and streamers. However, this was not the end for St Mark's Girls' Brigade. As most units were small, on Whit Monday evening, we marched with St Luke's, Cheetham Hill, Girls Brigade round their parish. I remember being very tired but proud by the end of the day. We also swelled the numbers of another church at Moston on their church anniversary walk. The only other large Girls' Brigade contingent was St Aidan's, Bradford, who did not require extra numbers. My brother John was the drum major in an Ancoats Church Boys' Brigade.'

'At Whitsuntide in Manchester and in most of the North West it was the time that children had a full set of new clothes ready for the Whit Walks, and for girls in the late 1940s, early 1950s, if you were lucky you may have also had a long dress – even if you were not the rose queen or one of her attendants. I counted myself one of the lucky ones as my mother was a dressmaker, and so for a few years I also had a long dress, the first of which was white with pink flowers and pink trimming, however, I was upset as Miss Pimblott, the Sunday School teacher had only asked me if I was going to have a long dress, but did not stipulate she wanted all the dresses in white; my upset was for my mother who after making my other Whitsun clothes, including a coat, had stayed up all night to finish my dress. Therefore I was put at the back of the group, whereas my cousin Enid, was at the front of the group; my disappointment being that Enid (a very pretty child) was wearing a pink crinoline dress with matching bonnet and was leading our class! When I was thirteen I left the Girls' Brigade as we moved house to Newton Heath, where I attended St Cuthbert's Church, Clayton Bridge, the mother church being All Saints, which we all attended when St Cuthbert's closed. All Saints and St Cuthbert's only walked on Whit Sunday round the parish and I remember being on the Banner at St Cuthbert's (this honour was always for long standing attendees and older girls), however as the number of Sunday School girl attendees was very low being a small community, I was very surprised and quite thrilled to have a banner ribbon.'

Walking with St Stephen's, Salford, and other Whit Memories

Canon. Ian Anthony, of Little Lever, has three Whitsun memories which he recalls: 'I have three main memories of the Manchester Whit Walks. One was when I was a small child and the other two were much later. The first memory as a child was when my family had attended St Stephen's Church in Salford in around 1953. The Walks were still a big thing in those days; the Church of England Walks on Whit Monday and the Roman Catholic Walks on Whit Friday. You knew the time for the Walks was drawing near because large wooden stands were erected along the route in Manchester. To a small child they seemed peculiar structures because I could never work out whether they were for sitting on, leaning on or standing on. Whichever they were for, they looked very large and uncomfortable. People went to great effort to make these days both on the Monday and the Friday particularly special. There was a good deal of rivalry between what went on the two days. I can remember watching the Roman Catholic Walks and being impressed and surprised by the outfits worn by the priests. Each one wore a frock coat and top hat and carried a walking cane. They looked very smart and were greeted with huge cheers by their people as they passed in the procession. I think they turned out looking like that as a result of some ancient law which prevented Roman Catholic priests from walking through Manchester wearing their robes. However, having said that, one parish, St Sebastian's, I think, was looked after by some monks and they walked with their parish in their white habits. Another cheer went up on Whit Friday when the nurses who were Roman Catholic and walked with St John's Cathedral walked past. Clearly these two sets of cheers showed great appreciation of the spiritual and temporal care that folk enjoyed at the hands of these two groups of people.'

Canon Ian Anthony was impressed by the outfits worn by the Roman Catholic clergy in their Whit Walks.
The priests of Corpus Christi, Miles Platting in their top hats and frock coats on Whit Friday in the 1950s.
Photograph courtesy of Stella McDonald.

'In the St Stephen's procession I was a train bearer to the rose queen and I must have been about four or five years old. We wore long blue trousers and light blue shirts. The appearance on Whit Monday was the culmination of many events. We had had the crowning and we had also been taken to a photographic studio to have the official photograph taken. In my case, the appearance on Whit Monday had been fraught with problems. By the time the day came round, we, like many other families had moved out of Salford and were now living in Little Hulton about seven miles away. This was in the days before everyone had cars and bus services were not always reliable. The walks started very early in the morning because we had to walk from our own church (near Salford Station) to Albert Square in the centre of Manchester and arrive by a certain time. My mother's problem was how to get me to Salford in time with as little fuss as possible. The idea she came up with was to leave me to stay the night at the home of an auntie in Salford. The advantage of this was that she could come from Little Hulton on the first bus possible on the day without being encumbered with a small child. When she arrived I would be up, fed, dressed and ready for off. I was taken to the house of my auntie the night before. She had gone to a lot of trouble to make up a bed for me and was kind and welcoming. Unfortunately, this was the first time I had spent a night away from home and I was only four years old. Clearly, I was coming round to the idea that I was not keen on this arrangement and let my opinion be known by crying my eyes out as my mother tried to leave. In desperation, she abandoned the plan, took me home and we had to get back to Salford the next day by public transport by about 7.00 a.m.'

'The second occasion when I was involved with the Whit Walks was when I was much older in my teenage years. I was thinking about ordination and had come into contact with Jim Burns (the Author of this book) who was also an ordination candidate. He was involved in the Whit Walks and invited me and a couple of other chaps to walk with his church with the servers. We turned up ready to walk in our servers robes. It is embarrassing to remember that we carried rosaries to demonstrate how high church we were!'

'The third occasion was when I went to watch the Whit Walks with some friends from my church in the 1960s. I can remember standing near the Cathedral watching as the processions filed past. An ancient clergyman, stood in a sort of outdoor pulpit. He stood there "taking the salute" as these many groups of walkers filed along. It was deemed something of a privilege to be allowed to take part in this bit of the Procession. I seem to remember some sort of communal hymn singing taking place at this point. They sang "Lord of the Dance" which was deemed very trendy and cutting edge at that time. We felt very pleased with ourselves because most people did not know it but we had been singing it at our church for ages.'

Some Whit Monday Anecdotes!

The Whit Monday Procession was an act of Christian witness, but it was also a community event which has left many memories of the human side of people who participated in it, displaying life's rich pattern!

Here we recall some of those memories.

A Defiant Bandsman

There is the story of a man who was the bass drummer in a band which played every Whit Monday for the same church. Enthusiastic bandsman though he was, the man didn't look forward to the final stage of the procession each year as it returned from the city centre. This was because it involved the climb up a steep incline in the Ancoats area. At this point each year the band master would call a difficult march for the tired bass drummer to play. The drummer would play his part whilst muttering under his breath uncomplimentary remarks about the band master, much to the great amusement of the rest of the band! The same man, who was approaching retirement, had cause to see his doctor, before one Whit Walk, with a health concern. The doctor strongly advised him to give up playing the bass drum, as it could further damage his health. The man replied that he couldn't do that, as the band was "his life" and the Whit Monday Procession was special to him. The doctor, to emphasise his point, said: 'If you continue to play the bass drum on Whit Monday you could die.' The drummer retorted: 'Well doctor, I'll have to die then because I'm playing on Whit Monday!'

The Cartwheeling Lady!

Another memory is that of a very patriotic lady who embraced the Whit Walk with the greatest of enthusiasm. Each year on Whit Monday, she would decorate her house with pictures of the King and Queen, bunting and flowers. The band leading the local procession would assemble a distance away from the church, and then march along the street to meet the procession. The lady would be at the band's starting point applauding with great energy. It is said that, on occasions, her excitement would overcome her inhibitions, and she would cartwheel in front of the band, to the disapproval of the rector of the church!

By Their Fruit ye Shall Know Them

It is recalled that on one Whit Monday, a family watching the Walk in Mosley Street, had a young boy amongst its number who had become bored with the long procession. His parents, to occupy the boy, asked him to look for the name of each church on its banner, and announce it, as the church approached. St Ann's and St Paul's, presented no difficulty for him, but when St Barnabas, Oldham Road, came close to where he was standing the youngster shouted: 'The next church is St Bananas!' The spectators around him as St Barnabas passed-by cheered, 'Come on St Bananas!'

The Missing Crooks

It remains a legend to his descendants, that in the 1920s a Miles Platting father, proud to have his three daughters walking in the Procession on Whit Monday, rose at dawn to go to the Smithfield Market to buy three crooks of flowers to be carried in the Walk, as was then the custom, by his daughters. In those days the public houses could be open in the early morning, and returning from the Smithfield Market with the crooks of flowers, the man met friends outside an Inn. They urged him to imbibe with them, to celebrate the day and the presence of his three daughters in the coming Whit Walk. His acceptance of their offer was a mistake. He arrived home with the three crooks of flowers, long after the Procession had ended – much to his wife's displeasure, which she displayed by wielding the crooks of flowers, about his shoulders!

Girls of St Barnabas, Oldham Road, with their banner on the wet Whit Monday of 1954. Photograph courtesy of M.E.N.

Hold your Lilies Up; and other words of advice!

In the Manchester City Centre Procession, the spectators would often offer words of encouragement to the children in the Walks. This would especially be the case if the weather was wet. When the children knew that they still had a distance to walk in the rain, comments such as: 'There's not far to go now' and 'you're almost home' sometimes didn't help! The command to the children, from spectators to: 'Hold your lilies up' wasn't always well received either. The origin of this last expression, lay in the earlier days of the Whit Walks, when all the children carried lilies. It came to be understood in later times, as an exhortation to the children to hold their heads up. The least appreciated advice for the children on a wet day was: 'It's only God watering His little flowers'. The soaking-wet "little flowers" often wished that God had chosen to do otherwise than water them!

We have recalled here some tales and memories of Whit Monday Processions. No doubt there are many other tales and memories of it, and of other processions, which have been told, and re-told across the years, and which will continue to be told.

We look next at the churches which took part in the Whit Monday Walk across the years.

Chapter 5

The Churches, Communities, Personalities, Banners and Bands of the Whit Monday Procession

J H Barratt, Chief Marshall and Procession Committee member leads St. Augustine's, Monsall procession in a 1950s Whit Walk.

In the heyday of the Whit Monday Walk it was never the case that all of the Church of England Churches within walking distance of the city centre took part. Some parishes did not join the Procession because they were involved in their own local Walks. Added to this, at one stage, the number of churches taking part was restricted. Generally the same parishes walked year by year. Occasionally a new church joined in, but it was not until the 1970s that a number of new contingents from the more distant suburbs replaced the many churches, closer to the city centre, which had closed because of re-housing schemes and population movement. In this chapter we look at the organising of the Whit Walk, and at the churches which took part – their banners, bands, personalities and the communities from which they came. Readers may well remember personalities from their church and community who were their parish representatives on the Procession's organising committee. They did not change greatly over the years and the 1951 Whit programme lists them as follows:-

The Committee for the Whit Monday Walk.

N Cumbes	All Souls', Ancoats.
W Atherton	St Matthew, Deansgate.
J Backhouse	St Luke, Miles Platting.
J H Barratt	St Augustine, Monsall.
A Bateman	Albert Memorial, Collyhurst.
N Blackett	St Mark, Holland Street.
J W Bloor	St Stephen, Hulme.
Mrs E M Blow	St Luke, Chorlton on Medlock.
J Church	St Catherine, Collyhurst.

J Ellis	St Paul, Philips Park.
A Gleaves	German Street Sunday School.
J Heywood	Christ Church, Bradford.
W Howell	St Stephen, Salford.
S J Hulme	Sacred Trinity, Salford.
Miss M Hunt	St Matthias, Salford.
Miss E J Johnston	St Ann, Manchester.
Miss E Jones	St Thomas, Ardwick.
Miss E Lambert	St John, Miles Platting.
T W Long	St Philip, Salford.
W McCauley	St Philip, Bradford Road,
J Morley	St Jerome, Ardwick.
G Morris	St Peter, Oldham Road.
A Nutter	St Oswald, Collyhurst.
J Pennington	St Aidan, Bradford.
Miss D I Savage	St Saviour, Chorlton on Medlock
M J Shaw	St Michael, Hulme
J Stanton	St Barnabas, Rodney Street
Miss E Thomas	St Clement, Broughton
Miss C Turner	St Mary, Beswick
A Wardley	St Jude, Ancoats
A White	St Paul, Bennett Street
J Whitehead	St James, Collyhurst
L Wilkinson	St George, Oldham Road

The Executive Committee of the Procession in 1951 was:

President:	The Rt Reverend J L Wilson, Dean of Manchester
Chairman:	Councillor W H Cox
Organising Secretary:	H W Sumner
Assistant:	H Bromley
Treasurer:	Councillor Percy Chadwick
Auditor:	G F Thorp

The Executive and the Committee issued the Annual Programme and set the General Arrangements for the Procession in Albert Square on Whit Mondays.

The Whit Monday Programmes

The best source of information about the Whit Monday Walk, apart from the newspaper reports of it, are found in the annual Whit Monday programmes. They list past figures of the executive committee, and they name its current officers and members of the committee. The programmes detail the Arrangements for Procession days, and give each parish its own section for details of its church, Sunday School, banners, bands and what it calls "festivities". These are the Whit Excursions and Socials.

The Past Chairmen of the Procession Committee:

1801-1823 The Reverend T Blackburn
1823-1840 The Reverend Thomas Jackson Calvert
1840-1883 Alderman William Booth
1884-1915 George Milner (Freeman of Manchester)
1915-1919 Alderman N Meadowcroft
1919-1930 Benjamin A Redfern
1930-1939 Walter S Nesbitt
1939-1940 Councillor T W Richardson
1940-1947 C F Howarth
1947-1962 Councillor Walter H Cox
1962-1971 Tom W Long

After 1971 the successive organising secretaries of the Procession, Horace W Sumner, Canon Ian McVeety and Canon Roy Chow had the responsibility for organising the Walks and for their general arrangements.

For the General Arrangements and Instructions for Whit Monday see Appendix 1 page 189.

There were between 30,000 to 40,000 walkers, in the Procession's heyday, from forty-five different starting points in Manchester and Salford. They processed along every main road into the city centre – around the centre, and then they returned to the various starting points. This was a major task for the police, and they performed it twice in one week in the city centre, with the Roman Catholic Whit Friday Procession requiring the same level of supervision. Adding to the responsibility of the police were all the other district processions during Whit Week in Manchester. A policeman who was a friend of the Author's grandfather, once described the Whit Monday Procession as: 'The police's nightmare!' He said: 'We had forty-five processions converging at the same time, and from all directions, on Albert Square.' The walkers came from the city centre; from the north, east, south and west of the city bringing Manchester to a standstill. We look now at each of these churches, and at the districts of inner-Manchester and Salford from which they walked.

The Procession, as we have seen, began in 1801 with the then ten churches in, or close to, the city centre.

The Cathedral and Collegiate Church

The Collegiate Church, later the Cathedral, led the Whit Walk from the beginning. Until 1939 the Cathedral was joined in the Walk by Chetham's Hospital, Blue Coat School, with the boys in their traditional uniforms. The school was housed in ancient buildings opposite the Cathedral. It was founded in 1653 by Humphrey Chetham. Its banners were: "Quod Tuum Tene"; "Our Lady and Child" and "St George and the Dragon". In the 1930s its band was Longford Hall. Its "festivities" allowed the boys to "go to their homes for a holiday week" at Whitsun!. The school numbers in 1937 were given as 89. The Girls' Jubilee School, Bury Old Road, also joined the Cathedral in the Procession. Founded in 1810, by 1937 its school numbers were 30. These two schools preceded the main Cathedral contingent.

Chethams Hospital Blue Coat School enter Manchester Cathedral in the 1930s. Photograph courtesy of Chethams' Music College.

The Cathedral itself did not include a Sunday School in its procession from the 1930s onwards. Its banner depicted John Huntingdon, the first warden of the 'College of Christ at Manchester' – the Collegiate Church. In the 1951 Walks programme, the Cathedral clergy and Fellows of the College were: Canon Peter Green, Archdeacon Arthur Selwyn Bean, Canon Howard Woolnough, The Rt Reverend Edward Worsfold Mowl and the Dean – The Very Reverend John Leonard Wilson. In the 1900s the Cathedral had a mission church in the populated part of its residual parish in the Strangeways area. St Saviour's stood in Park Street off Cheetham Hill Road. It briefly became the centre of a separate parish before closing in the late 1940s. In the early years of the 20th century St Saviour's Mission joined the Cathedral in the Whit Walk.

Chethams School Band - the boys would be involved in the Whit Monday procession with the Cathedral. Photograph courtesy of Chethams' Music College.

Sacred Trinity, Salford

Sacred Trinity Church was consecrated in 1635, and its school founded in 1892. It became the parish church of the Greengate district of inner-Salford. Its banner was 'The Emblem of the Trinity'. Its bands included LMS Manchester Silver Band and Gravel Lane Silver Band. Its school in 1937 numbered 246, and in 1951, 150. Its clergy included Canon Peter Green, the Reverend J W Rideout and Canon Richard Hussey.

'Festivities' included trips to Lightoaks Recreation Ground, Middlewood and Southport Sacred Trinity remains a parish church still standing, in Chapel Street, Salford.

The choirboys and altar servers of Sacred Trinity Salford pose before a 1930s Whit Monday Procession. Photograph Courtesy of R. Carr.

St Ann, Manchester

St Ann's was consecrated as the second church in Manchester in 1712 – and it was then known as "the new church" – the Collegiate Church being "the old church". Its banner was 'the Good Shepherd'. Its bands included Pendleton Public Prize Band, and Cheetham Hill Public Prize Band. Its clergy included Canon Tonge, Canon Dorrity, Canon Paton Williams and Canon Eric Saxon. Founded in 1841, in 1937 its school numbered 100, and in 1951, 40. 'Festivities' in 1937 included trips to Wythenshawe and to Southport. In 1951 the excursion was to Worsley.

St. Ann's Manchester celebrated 250 years in 1962. Children carried a model of their church in the Whit Monday Procession. Photograph courtesy of M.E.N.

In and around Manchester

St Mary's, Parsonage, Manchester

St Mary's was the third church in Manchester, consecrated in 1757. With St Ann's, it served a then resident population around Deansgate in the 19th century. Its parish population was removed by housing clearance in the late 19th century, and St Mary's, which stood in what is now Parsonage Gardens, was closed and demolished in 1890. St Mary's Parish was united with that of St Ann's to serve a small remaining population around the Deansgate area.

St Thomas, Ardwick Green

Consecrated as a Chapel of Ease on Ardwick Green, in the then village of Ardwick, in 1740, St Thomas became the parish church of a densely populated part of Ardwick as it developed into a suburb of Manchester. Its school was founded in 1870, and it had links with Ardwick Industrial Sunday School which took part in its 19th century Whit Walks. St Thomas' banner was 'The Figure of St Thomas'. Its bands included, Onward Hall Mission Band and, Gorton and Openshaw Silver Prize Band. In 1937 its school numbered 300, and in 1951, 250. 'Festivities' included trips to Cringle Fields, Southport and Ainsdale. St Thomas closed for worship in the 1970s and the building is now used to house offices for voluntary organisations. Despite its 'early' consecration date, St Thomas' was not one of the original ten churches of 1801.

Pat Heald with the banner of St. Thomas' Ardwick on an early 1950s Whit Monday. Photograph courtesy of Pat Heald.

Three little girls with their teacher, Mrs Glegg of St. Thomas Ardwick Green. A Whit Walk 1950s. Photograph courtesy of P. Heald.

St Paul's, Manchester

St Paul's was consecrated in 1765 and originally stood in Turner Street. It had Sunday Schools in Turner Street, Spear Street, Bennett Street and German Street. Bennett Street and German Street were linked at one stage with St George's in the Fields. St Paul's was re-built at New Cross in 1878, and with the resulting parish boundary change, Bennett Street reverted to its original links with St. Paul's. St Paul's banners were: "School Founder – David Stott" and "Centenary". Its bands included Pleasely Colliery and Prestwich Borough bands.

At a point in its history St. Paul's Bennett Street Sunday School numbered over 2000 children on its registers. In 1937 its numbers were 395, and in 1951 – 180. Festivities were numerous, including excursions to Queens Park; New Brighton; Heywood; Glossop; Moston; Matlock; Bath; Buxton and London!

St. Clements's Church, which stood in Lever Street, Stevenson Square, was a Chapel of Ease in St. Paul's parish with links to Spear Street Sunday School. St. Clement's was closed and demolished in 1873. St. Paul's Church at New Cross was itself closed and demolished in the late 1970s.

St John's, Deansgate

St John's, which stood in Byrom Street at the bottom of St John's Street, off Deansgate, was consecrated in 1769. Its school was founded in 1827. Its banner was 'the Lamb of God' and 'St John'. Its band was the Manchester Postal Band. In 1937 its school numbered 200. 'Festivities' included excursions to Southport each Summer. St John's had served a 19th century residential population around the Quay Street area of the city centre. With house clearance schemes, the parish was deprived of people. The church was closed and demolished in 1931 and its parish united with St Matthew's, Campfield. St John's Sunday School remained a part of the Whit Walk, linked to nearby St Matthew's, until 1940.

St Peter's, Mosley Street

St Peter's was consecrated in 1788. It stood in St Peter's Square, on what is now the site of the Cenotaph. The parish served the Knott Mill district, off Oxford Street. Its school was founded in 1794. Its banner was 'St Peter'. As with the other city centre churches, St Peter's lost its resident population in the late 19th century with commercial development. It was closed and demolished in 1906, its parish being joined to St James, George Street. Its Sunday School in Hewitt Street, Knott Mill, continued to walk in the Whit Procession, linked to St Matthew's, Campfield, until 1940. In 1939 its school numbered 63 children. Its 'Festivities' included excursions to Pot Shrigley and to London.

St James', George Street, Piccadilly

St James' which stood on the site now occupied by office buildings in George Street, was consecrated in 1788. Because of the loss of its resident population it closed, and was demolished in 1928. Its school stood in Major Street off Princess Street. Its banner was 'St James'. St Peter's, Mosley Street Parish, and that of SS Simon and Jude, Granby Row, were added to that of St James in 1906. St James Parish was later divided between St Ann, Manchester, and St Andrew's, Ancoats. All of the city centre churches, including in the 1950s, that of St Matthew, Campfield, were finally joined to St Ann's. In 1928 St James George Street School, numbered 80 children.

St Matthew's, Campfield, Deansgate

St Matthew's was consecrated in 1825, and its school founded in 1827. The noble church, designed by the architect Barry, was closed and demolished after war damage in 1951. St Matthew's stood on a site, now occupied by office buildings, next to the Museum of Science and Industry on Liverpool Road – and "around the corner" from St John's, Byrom Street. Its banner was 'The Church'. Its bands included Central Hall Band and Besses' o'th Barn Boys Prize Band. On the closure of St Matthew's Church, its Sunday School building became a Mission Church in St Ann's Parish. The school continued to join the Whit Monday Procession until the 1960s. Its numbers in 1937 were 139 and in 1951, 90. Its 'festivities' included trips to Longford Park; Chesterfield; Holcombe Brook and Southport. St Matthew's, though a city centre parish, was not formed until 1825, and therefore it was not one of the original ten city centre churches represented in the first Whit Procession of 1801. The last two of the original ten, were parishes just outside the centre of the city.

St Michael and All Angels, Angel Meadow

On a site at the bottom of Angel Street, off Rochdale Road, St Michael's was consecrated in 1789. Its school was founded in 1800, and later re-built in Gould Street in 1910. Its banner was 'St Michael'. Its school in 1937 numbered 70 children. Its band in that year, was St Paul's Blackley CLB Bugle Band. Its 'festivities' included a Field Day. St Michael's Parish became the worst slum district in 19th century Manchester, beset with every kind of social problems. It contained 'St Michael's Flags' a vast burial ground for Cholera victims. It is remarkable that St Michael's Parish, set in such a district continued to take a prominent, disciplined and colourful part in the Whit Monday Procession for 139 years. During the late 19th and the early 20th century St Michael's was served by a number of devoted 'slum' priests. It is said, that in stark contrast, in the first years of the Whit Monday Walk, many of St Michael's parishioners arrived at the church to take part in the procession in 'fine carriages'! In 1929 St Michael's was joined in a united parish, with St Thomas' Red Bank, and St Paul's, New Cross. St Paul's became the Parish Church of New Cross with Angel Meadow, and Red Bank. It now had a sizeable parish population. St Michael's was closed in 1930, and the church demolished. The Sunday School continued to take part in the Whit Walk, linked to St Paul's, until 1939. The site of St Michael's Church is now laid out as 'Angel Meadow Gardens'.

Ladies of St. Michael's Angel Meadow leave their church on Whit Monday 1902.
Photograph courtesy of Manchester Libraries.

St Stephen's, Salford

The last of 1801's ten churches was St Stephen, Salford. It was consecrated in 1794, and its school founded in 1794. St Stephen's stood on a site off Chapel Street, Salford; now a children's play area. Its banner was 'St Stephen'. Its bands included Swinton and Pendlebury Borough Prize Band, and Hugh Stevenson's Silver Prize Band. Its school numbered 306 children in 1937, and 300 in 1951. 'Festivities' included trips to Ainsdale and 'country excursion'! With housing clearance in lower Salford, St Stephen's lost its parish population. The church was closed, and demolished in 1956, and the parish joined to nearby St Philip's.

As the Whit Monday Procession developed, additional parishes joined in the Walk from the growing suburbs on the fringes of Manchester and Salford. East Manchester began a strong and constant participation in the Whit Walk, from an area which had been the cradle of the Industrial Revolution in Ancoats.

St George's in the Fields, Oldham Road

St. George's Oldham Road flower girls in a 1950s Whit Monday Procession. Photograph courtesy of M.E.N.

St George's was consecrated in 1818, and re-built on a new site in Oldham Road in 1878. Its school was founded in 1816. Its banners were: 'Feed my Lambs' and 'Fear God, Honour the King'. Its bands included Manchester Transport Band and Wythenshawe Prize Band. 'Festivities' were excursions to Lyme Park, and Stratford Upon Avon. In 1951 its school numbered 203 children. St George's was closed in the late 1960s, and then demolished. The parish was joined with others in a new Parish of St Cuthbert, Miles Platting, serving a much smaller population in the re-developed area.

St Andrew, Ancoats

St Andrew's was consecrated in 1831 and stood, then, amongst 'pleasant fields' in Travis Street. Its school was founded in 1837. Its banner was 'St Andrew' and 'Follow Me'. Its band was Wesley Hall Prize Band. In 1937 its school numbers were 104, and in 1951, 90. 'Festivities' included, in 1937, 'a Coronation Social Tea' and excursions then and in other years, to Stratford on Avon; Southport and Carr Mill. Canon Scott, a residentiary Canon of Manchester was also rector of St Andrew's until 1925, and was a well-known figure in the Whit Walks. Early re-housing schemes in St Andrew's Parish in the 1930s took away the entire parish population, and left the church standing amongst wasteland. It became known as 'the church without a parish.' St Andrew's continued walking on Whit Monday until 1958, when the church closed, and was demolished. The parish was joined to adjacent All Souls', and the site of the church is now occupied by industrial premises.

In and around Manchester

St. Andrews' Ancoats pass into Piccadilly, on their church's last Whit Monday Walk in 1958, with their floral cross. Photograph courtesy of the Nightingale family.

The b anner of St. Andrew's Ancoats is carried along Great Ancoats Street on Whit Monday in the 1950s. Photograph courtesy of the Nightingale family.

St Jude, Ancoats

St Jude's was consecrated in 1837, and re-built in Mill Street in 1866. Its school was founded in 1837. Its banner was 'St Jude's Church' Its bands were, St Jude's Brass Band and Star Hall Salvation Army Band. In 1939 school numbers were 270, and in 1951, 60. 'Festivities' were excursions to Tatton Park; Longford Park; Styal Woods; a picnic at Lyme Park and a rally at Wythenshawe Park. St Jude's closed, with housing re-development, in 1955. The parish was merged into that of St Philip, Bradford Road. The site of the church, opposite the former Ancoats Hospital, has been re-developed.

All Souls', Ancoats

All Souls' was consecrated in 1840, and the church still stands on Every Street, though once used by another denomination. The school was founded in 1840. Its banners were 'The Good Shepherd' and 'Suffer Little Children to Come unto Me'. In 1937 school children numbered 510, and in 1951, 140. Canon Shinwell was a notable rector of All Souls'. 'Festivities' included excursion to Styal; Infants' Procession; Tea Party; trip to Charlesworth and a church dance! All Souls' was closed in the 1980s, and its parish taken into the new parish of the Resurrection and the Good Shepherd, Eastlands; serving a reduced population in the re-developed district.

St Philip, Bradford Road, Ancoats

St. Philips' Bradford Road, floral banner and rose queen. Whit Monday in the 1960s, walking along Oldham Road to their parish. Photograph courtesy of Elaine Burgess.

St Philip's was consecrated in 1850, and its school founded in 1850. It stood in Ridgeway Street, off Bradford Road. Its banners were 'The Light of the World', 'The Good Samaritan' and 'The Good Shepherd'. Its bands included Culcheth Manchester Military Band (the 'Tall Hat Band'), Culcheth Manchester Junior Military Band and Star Hall Salvation Army Band. St Philip's Parish included Branson Street Mission Church and Joynson Memorial Mission Church, off Hulme Hall Lane. The number of children in 1937 was 640, and in 1951, 150. 'Festivities' listed; excursion to Pointon; Southport; and a church dance. St Philip's was a strong contingent in the Whit Walk. A relative of the Author was often heard to boast that the church had 'three "big" banners; three bands; and in the 1920s, 1,600 children in its Sunday Schools'. St Philip's was closed in the 1970s and a new Church of the Apostles built on its site to replace it.

St Barnabas, Ancoats

St Barnabas was consecrated in 1844, and its school founded in that year. The church stood in Rodney Street, off Butler Street, Oldham Road. Its banners were 'St Barnabas' and 'The Good Shepherd'. Its band was Miles Platting Mission Band. Its school numbers in 1937 were 300, and in 1951, 110. 'Festivities' were trips to Greenfield, and to New Brighton via the Mersey Tunnel! St Barnabas was closed in 1958 and demolished. Its remaining parish, after re-development, was joined to St George's, Oldham Road.

St James the Less, Ancoats

St James the Less was consecrated in 1870 and it stood in Little Newton Street, off Great Ancoats Street. Its school was founded in 1869. Its banner was 'St James the Less' and 'St George and the Dragon'. Its band was Russell Memorial Band. In 1936 its school attendees numbered 150. Its 'festivities' included various excursions into the countryside and to the seaside. St James the Less was closed and demolished in 1937. Its parish, with a reduced population, was joined to St Peter's, Oldham Road, and partly to St Andrew's, Ancoats.

St Peter's, Oldham Road

St Peter's was consecrated in 1860. Its school was founded in 1865. Its banner was 'St Peter with Keys'. Its bands included Salford Military Prize Band and Openshaw Original Prize Band. In 1937 its school numbered 148 children, and in 1951, 70. St Peter's was known as the 'Cotton Church' because its parish contained a number of cotton mills in which many of the parishioners laboured. 'Festivities' included excursions to Hazel Grove, Norbury and the Wizards Field Alderley Edge. St Peter's closed for worship in the 1970s and its remaining Parish population was joined to the new parish of the Church of the Apostles, Ancoats. The building has been restored to become a centre for the Halle Orchestra, and it still stands in Blossom Street.

The Culcheth (Manchester) Military Band - 'The Tall Hat Band' played for St. Philip's Bradford Road on Whit Mondays and for other churches in the Whit Walks. Photograph courtesy of Eric Humphreys

St. Peter's, Oldham Road, turn into Fennel Street – 1960s Whit Monday Walk. Photograph courtesy of M.E.N.

German Street Church of England Sunday School Ancoats, and St Martin's Church, German Street

This school and church present an unusual story. German Street Sunday School was founded in 1785, and at that time it was linked with St Paul's, Turner Street, as was Bennett Street Sunday School. Later both schools were attached to the Parish of St George's in the Fields. Bennett Street School reverted to its links with St Paul's at New Cross in 1876. German Street School became the centre of the new Parish of St Peter, Oldham Road, in 1854. When St Peter's Church opened in Blossom Street in 1860 the link between the church and the school in German Street seemed final. It was not to be, as a dispute arose between the church

St. Luke's, Miles Platting, walk along Oldham Road in the early 1950s returning to their church. Margaret Simpkin is the girl in the middle. Photograph courtesy of M. Simpkin & S. McDonald.

and the school. This may have been about the school's insistence on a measure of independence from St Peter's Church, but there might have been other differences. The surprising solution to the dispute, was that St Peter's built its own school in Bengal Street, and the then Bishop of Manchester, Dr Fraser, created a second new parish centred on German Street Sunday School, and dedicated to St Martin. St Martin's Church, German Street, was consecrated in 1873. The story did not end happily. St Martin's Church had a tiny parish population, and the building bordered by Primrose Street, and Silk Street, was only 'around the corner' from St Peter's. St Martin's closed for worship after only thirty-three years, in 1906. Its parish was divided between St Peter's, Oldham Road, and St Barnabas, Rodney Street. German Street Church of England Sunday School continued its existence, and independence within St Peter's Parish, until 1957, when it was closed and demolished. German Street School and St Martin's Church both took part in the Whit Monday Procession. The Church of St Martin from 1873 to 1906, and the school independently after 1906. The church banner was 'St Martin dividing his cloak with the Blind Beggar'. The school's banners were 'The Good Shepherd' and 'The Sower'. The bands included the Northern Military Band and the Shaftesbury Institute Band. 'Festivities' listed were excursions to Burnage, Hyde, Windermere, Grange-over-Sands, Wythenshawe, Ingleton, Morecambe and Clitheroe.

St Mark, Holland Street, Miles Platting

St Mark's Church which stood in Holland Street, was consecrated in 1884. Its school was founded in 1875. Its banners were 'St Mark's Church' and 'The Good Shepherd'. Its bands included Victoria Hall Brass Band and the Manchester Corporation Transport Band. The numbers of children in the Sunday School were, in 1937, 248, and in 1951, 123. 'Festivities' included trips to Alderley Edge, Southport and London. St Mark's was closed for worship in the 1970s and demolished. Its parish became part of the new parish of the Church of the Apostles, Ancoats.

St John the Evangelist, Miles Platting

The banner of St. John's Miles Platting - used by the church until its closure. It is now carried by All Saints and Martyrs Langley.

St John's was consecrated in 1855, and its school was founded in 1855. The church stood on Oldham Road, close to Varley Street. Its Banner was 'St John'. Its bands included Miles Platting Mission Band and Droylsden Military Band. In 1939 its school numbered 250 children, and in 1951, 200. 'Festivities' were trips to Heaton Park and Knutsford, and a church Whit Monday dance. St John's had the distinction of having a 19th century rector imprisoned in Lancaster Castle, for contempt of court regarding his 'High Church' ritual practices, which contravened a then public worship law! St John's was closed and demolished in the 1970s and the new Church of St Cuthbert was built on its site.

St Luke's, Miles Platting

St Luke's was consecrated in 1875 and it stood off Hulme Hall Lane. Its school was founded in 1870. Its banner was 'The Good Shepherd'. Its bands were Street Fold Prize Band, and Harpurhey and Moston Silver Prize Band. In 1951 its school numbers were 350. 'Festivities' were an excursion to Lyme Park, Disley. St Luke's was closed and demolished in the 1970s, and its parish became part of the new St Cuthbert's.

Children of St. Luke's, Miles Platting, prepare for the Whit Monday Walk in the 1940s. Photograph courtesy of Stella McDonald

St Augustine, Monsall

St Augustine's was consecrated in 1888. The church stood by Sanderson Street, Monsall. Its school was founded in 1888. Its banner was 'The Good Shepherd'. Its bands were Newton Heath Loco British Rail Brass; Manchester Fire Brigade Band, and Moston and Harpurhey Band. Its school children in 1937 numbered 250, and in 1951, 250. 'Festivities' were excursions to Blackpool, Southport, Broadhurst Playing Fields and Greenfield. St Augustine's closed and was destroyed by fire in the 1970s. Its re-developed parish area was joined to the parish of the new Church of the Saviour, Collyhurst.

St Paul, Philips Park, Bradford

St Paul's was consecrated in 1907. The church stood by the gates of Philips Park, Bradford, and was surrounded by the industry of that area. Its school was founded in 1905. Its banner was 'St Paul's Church'. Its bands included Jackson Street Mission Band; St Paul's C.E.M.S. Silver Band and Central Manchester Silver Band. Its school children numbered 290 in 1939 and 200 in 1951. 'Festivities' included excursion to Knutsford; Southport; a Field Day and a Tea Party. St Paul's Parish population declined with re-housing schemes, and the church was united with St Cross, Clayton – eventually being closed in 1969 and the building demolished. St Paul's union with nearby St Cross, Clayton, brought that parish into the Whit Monday Procession for the first time in the 1960s.

St Augustine's Monsall return to their parish from Albert Square on a 1930s Whit Monday.

St Cross, Clayton

St Cross was consecrated in 1874. Its school was founded in 1830. Its banner was 'The Good Shepherd' Its bands included British Railways Manchester Band; Central Manchester Silver Band and Culcheth Manchester Military Band. Its school numbers in 1968 were 80. St Cross Church on Ashton New Road is of historical and architectural interest. Designed by William Butterfield, it is the only church of its design in Manchester. The building was opened in 1866 but not consecrated until 1874, because of a dispute about its proposed title, and its 'High Church' practices. The title proposed 'The Church of the Holy Cross' was rejected, and the eventual compromise reached was that of 'St Cross'.

Christ Church, Bradford Cum-Beswick

Christ Church was consecrated in 1862 and the building at that time stood amongst fields. This quickly changed and in the 1880s Christ Church had the biggest parish population in Manchester Diocese with 29,000 souls. Its school was founded in 1865. Its banners were 'The Good Shepherd' and later in its history, 'The Lamb of God' a banner which had originally belonged to St John and St Matthew's, Deansgate. Its bands were Hulme Public Prize Band, Hugh Stevenson's Silver Prize Band and Christ Church Old Boys' Brass Band. 'Festivities' included excursions to Llandudno, Menai Bridge, Heaton Park, Wythenshawe Park and in 1893 to the "Fields at Clayton!" school numbers in 1937 were 580, and in 1951, 400. Christ Church had a Mission Church of St Cuthbert, which stood next to the parish's Bradford Memorial school in Score Street. St Cuthbert's joined Christ Church in the Whit Walk until the mission church closed in the early 1950s. Christ Church itself, which stood in Charlesworth Street – late – Church Street, became structurally unsafe; it was closed in 1963 and demolished. An original plan to build a new Christ Church gave way to a scheme to unite Christ Church and neighbouring churches in a new parish of the Resurrection. In 1972 a church and school of the Resurrection were built. The school stands on the site of the former Christ Church. The 1972 the church building developed structural problems. It had to be demolished in the 1980s and it has been replaced by another building opened in 2011.

St Mary, Beswick. The Bishop Lee Memorial Church

St Mary's was consecrated in 1879, but the building was never completed to the original plan. Because of its secondary dedication title, to Bishop Lee, the first Bishop of Manchester, there was speculation as to whether St Mary's would replace Manchester Cathedral. The original design would have produced a church of cathedral-like proportion. The uncompleted building was impressive in itself. The school was founded in 1876. Its banner was 'The Three Wise Men' – a unique choice in the Whit Walks. Its bands included Gorton and Openshaw Silver Band; Burnage Postal Band; Victoria Hall Silver Band and St Mary's Silver Band. In 1939 school numbers were 290, and in 1951, 510. 'Festivities' included excursions to Hoylake, Helsby, Frodsham, Poynton and Southport, and a Whit Monday dance in the school room. St Mary's Church was stricken with dry rot in 1963 and demolished. Its parish was eventually merged in the Parish of the Resurrection. New housing now occupies the site of the Church. St Mary's Church was used for the wedding scenes in the 1960s film 'A Kind of Loving'.

St Silas, Ardwick

St Silas, on Ashton Old Road was Consecrated in 1842. Its School was founded in 1844. Its banner was 'The Good Shepherd'. Its band was Levenshulme Prize Band. Its school numbers in 1939 were 150. 'Festivities' included 'a day at Belle Vue'. St Silas did not join the Procession from 1945 to 1954. It rejoined that latter year, but the church closed and was demolished, stricken by dry rot, in 1955. St Silas Parish is merged in the Parish of the Resurrection. Industrial premises occupy the site of the church.

St Jerome, Ardwick – The Houghton Memorial Church

St Jerome's Church in Baden Street, was consecrated in 1913. Its school was founded in 1914. Its banner was 'The Light of the World'. Its bands included Hyde Road Depot Silver Band and Burnage Silver Prize Band. School numbers in 1939 were 298, and in 1951, 250.

'Festivities' included, annually, an excursion to Heaton Park. Because of the date of the consecration of the church, St Jerome's was, for many years, the last contingent to leave Albert Square in the Whit Walk, until the order of procession was changed in the 1950s. It is recorded that the then Rector of St Silas, Ardwick, objected to the founding of St Jerome's Church in 1913. This was because the new church took away half of his Parish of St Silas. He was far-sighted, because when St Silas' Church developed dry rot in 1954, its parish population was declared to be too small to necessitate the re-building of the church. St Silas was joined to St Jerome, as St Jerome with St Silas' – the daughter church absorbing the mother church! St Jerome's was itself to be closed for worship and become part of the Parish of the Resurrection. The building still stands and is to be re-deployed for community use.

St Aidan, Bradford

St Aidan's was consecrated in 1899. Its school was founded in 1879. Its banners were 'The Good Shepherd' and later 'St Aidan'. Its bands included Crossley Lads' Club Band; Hayfield Public Prize Band; L.N.E.P Openshaw Band; St Andrew's Pipe Band and Culcheth, Manchester, Military Band. School numbers in 1939 were 210, and in 1951, 400. 'Festivities' were excursions to Middlewood and to Summershades Pleasure Grounds, Oldham. St Aidan's was closed for worship in 1972 and the church demolished. The parish is now part of the Church of the Resurrection Parish, which covers seven former East Manchester parishes. St Aidan's is the last of the churches of East Manchester, seventeen of which took part prominently, and over many years, in the Whit Monday Procession. In the suburb which was 'the cradle of the Industrial Revolution' the Whit Walks were an important part of community and family life.

St Aidan's, Bradford, Manchester, leave Albert Square on a 1960s Whit Monday.
Photograph courtesy of M.E.N.

In and around Manchester

Boys of St.Aidan's Bradford, carry symbols of the Eucharist in a 1963 Whit Walk.

We move on now to other similar areas of Manchester and Salford which were represented in the Whit Walk of Church of England parishes. From North Manchester there were five Parishes.

St Thomas, Red Bank

St Thomas in Derby Street, Red Bank, was consecrated in 1842. Its school was founded in 1847. Its banner was 'The Good Shepherd' Its band was Windsor Institute Silver Prize Band. In 1937 its school numbered 110, and in 1939, 120. 'Festivities' included an annual excursion to Southport. St Thomas' Church was closed and demolished in 1929. Together with neighbouring St Michael Angel Meadow, its parish was united with St Paul's, New Cross. An unusual union of parishes, as both St Michael's and St Thomas' had bigger parish populations than the surviving St Paul's. St Thomas' Sunday School continued to take part in the Whit Procession until 1939 as part of St Paul's Parish. The Sunday School building in Derby Street still stands, but the site of the church is occupied now by an industrial development.

St Catherine, Collyhurst

St Catherine's Church was consecrated in 1859. Its school was founded in 1859. Its banner was 'Suffer Little Children' Its bands included Cheetham Hill Prize Band and Beswick Prize Band. Its school numbers in 1937 were 235, and in 1951, 200. 'Festivities' were excursions to Wilmslow, North Wales and Bamford. St Catherine's was one of the small number of churches which had a central pulpit, with the 'Lord's Table' behind it, and whose clergy wore the black Geneva preaching gown, rather than the white surplice. St Catherine's closed and was demolished in 1966. Its site by the River Irk in Collyhurst Road, remains undeveloped. The remaining parish was merged into the new Parish of the Church of the Saviour Collyhurst.

St Oswald's, Collyhurst

St Oswald's, on Rochdale Road, was consecrated in 1855. Its school was founded in 1855. Its banner was 'St Oswald'. Its bands included Blackley Home Guard Band and Heaton Mersey Silver Prize Band. Its school numbers were, in 1937, 294, and in 1951, 170. 'Festivities' were excursions to Blackpool and Disley. St Oswald's Church was closed and demolished and the new Church of the Saviour built on its site in the 1970s.

St James the Great, Collyhurst

St James, off Collyhurst Street, was consecrated in 1874. Its founders appealed to a Manchester business man for funds to build a mission room. His generosity was such that the founders told him, 'We asked for a mission room but you have given us a "Cathedral"!' St James' School was founded in 1875. Its banner was 'Feed my Lambs' and 'The Good Shepherd'. Its bands included Street Fold Methodist Prize Band and British Railways Gorton Band. The number of school children in 1939 was 157. 'Festivities' were 'Field Day at Boggart Hole Clough' and excursions to London and Greenfield. A well respected incumbent of St James' for many years was the Reverend Stephen Henson. It is recorded that his bulldog joined him in the Whit Walk, with the National Flag on its back. St James' was closed and demolished in the 1970s. Its parish is merged in the Church of the Saviour.

The Albert Memorial Church, Collyhurst

'The Albert' as it was known, was due to be consecrated as St Anne's Church in 1864, but upon the death of Prince Albert, Consort to Queen Victoria, it was given his name in memoriam. The church stood on Queens Road. Its school was founded in 1862. Its banner was 'A Little Child shall Lead Them'. Its bands included Queens Road Methodist Brass Band and Gill Street Methodist Silver Band. School numbers in 1937 were 272, and in 1951, 240. Albert Memorial Church closed, and was demolished in the 1970s, and its parish joined to the Church of the Saviour.

The Reverend Barry Blowers was rector of the Church in 1968, and an Executive Member of the Whit Procession Committee. In the 1968 Whit Monday Programme he wrote: *'Sociologists and Psychologists, have attempted explanation for the tradition of the Manchester Whit Walks. They have described them as an opportunity for self-expression by deprived communities, and as a cascade of colour to relieve a drab environment. With improved social conditions they suggest that the Walks are now a fruitless attempt to keep an irrelevant tradition alive. My experience of the Walk, and surely only those who have been involved in it are qualified to comment, has made me realise that the Whit Walks are prompted by influences more profound. The environment, the route, the content and the numbers may have changed, but it is still allegiance to Christ which sustains the Walks.'*

From North Manchester we move to inner-Salford, another area which was always strongly represented in the Whit Procession. We have looked at Sacred Trinity and at St Stephen's Salford earlier. The other representatives have been:

St Philip's, Salford

St Philip's, Salford carry their Good Shepherd banner past Manchester Cathedral on Whit Monday 1953. Photograph courtesy of M.E.N.

St Philip's, by the former Salford Royal Hospital building, was consecrated in 1825. It then stood in fields, and it served as a chapel for the military, and the well-to-do! Its school was founded in 1825. Its banner was 'The Good Shepherd'. Its bands included Irwell Old Prize Band and the Y.M.C.A. Manchester Band. School numbers in 1937 were 440, and in 1951, 185. 'Festivities' were excursions to Ambleside, Blackpool, Southport, North Wales and Boggart Hole Clough. St Stephen's, Salford, was united with St Philip's in 1956, and the parish is now linked with Sacred Trinity, Salford. Canon Peter Green was a much-loved and respected figure as Rector of St Philip's, and Residentiary Canon of Manchester Cathedral from 1911 to 1951. He was known as the 'greatest parish priest in England'. Canon Peter Green did not 'suffer fools gladly' and two stories, amongst many, can be told about him. An altar server arrived late for a service and Canon Green was not pleased. The boy pleaded, 'better late than never, Canon?' Canon Green retorted: 'better never late!' On another occasion, St Philip's Sunday School teachers had a dispute amongst their number in Albert Square, during a Whit Monday Procession. The Canon was furious, and it is recorded that he walked back to Salford in stony silence. Outside the church he exclaimed: 'I accept the resignations of the Sunday School teachers!' They were forgiven, and loved their rector no less. In 1951 when he was unable to join the Procession of St Philip's because of illness, the church detoured, on the way to Albert Square, to pass his house. A fitting tribute to Canon Green, who had walked in every Whit Monday Procession from 1911 to 1951 with St Philip's, and before 1911, for ten years with Sacred Trinity, Salford.

Nurses from Salford Royal Hospital walked on Whit Monday 1955. Here with the rector of St. Philip's, Salford, Canon Gwilym Morgan. Photograph courtesy of M.E.N.

St Simon, Salford

St Simon's Church stood in the Salford street which still bears its name, off Blackfriars Road. The church was consecrated in 1849. Its school was founded in 1854. Its banners were, 'The Light of the World' and 'St Simon'. Its band was Longford Hall Mission Silver Band. School children in 1937 numbered 100, as part of St Matthias Parish. 'Festivities' included an excursion to Mobberley. St Simon's Church was closed in 1927 and demolished. Its parish was joined to nearby St Matthias. The site of the church is covered by re-development, but its memory is preserved in a Lowry portrait.

St Matthias, Salford

St Matthias stood on the Blackfriars Road. The church was consecrated in 1842. Its school was founded in 1842. Its banner was 'St Matthias Church'. Its bands included Hyde Road Methodist Band and Salford Military Band. School children in 1937 numbered 350, and also in 1951, 350. 'Festivities' were excursions to Mellor and to New Brighton. St Matthias closed in the 1960s and the church was demolished. Its parish was united with St Clement, Broughton.

St Clement and St Matthias Salford carry their banner of Hope along Deansgate to Albert Square in a 1960s Whit Walk. Photograph courtesy of M.E.N.

Children of St Matthias, Salford, leave their church in a Whit Monday Walk. Photograph courtesy of Renee Carr.

St Clement, Lower Broughton

St Clement's, in Broughton Lane, was consecrated in 1881. Its school was founded in 1874. Its banner was 'Behold I Stand at the Door and Knock'. Its bands included Gatley Prize Band and Windsor Institute Silver Prize Band. School numbers in 1937 were 210, and in 1951, 266. 'Festivities' were excursions to Prestwich Clough and to Southport. St Clement's Church was demolished in the 1960s, and replaced by a new building on the same site.

The Church of the Ascension, Lower Broughton

The Church of the Ascension was consecrated in 1871, it stands in Ascension Road. Its school was founded in 1871. Its banner was 'The Ascension'. Its band was Wythenshawe Prize Band. Its school children numbered 80 in 1966. The Ascension was one of three Salford parishes which joined the Whit Monday Procession for the first time in the 1960s.

St Cyprian, Ordsall Salford

St Cyprian's stood in Ordsall Lane, by Ordsall Hall. The church was in the process of union with nearby St Clement's Ordsall, when it joined the Whit Monday Walk for the first time in 1961. Its banner was 'St Cyprian's Sunday School'. St Cyprian's walked only twice as a separate contingent, and on the closure and demolition of the church in the mid 1960s, it was united with St Clement's Parish.

St Clement, Ordsall

St Clement's was consecrated in 1878. Its school was founded in 1874. Its banner was 'St Clement'. Its band was Salford Military Band. 'Festivities' included an 'outing to Prestatyn'. School children numbered 80 in 1966. St Clement's joined the Whit Walk, with St Cyprian's in 1961, and from 1963 to 1969, walked as the United Parish of St Clement with St Cyprian.

From inner-Salford to Hulme, an area close to the city centre on the south side of Manchester, but never represented by more than three of its churches in the Whit Monday Procession.

St Mark, Hulme

St Mark's by City Road, was consecrated in 1852. Its school was founded in 1852. Its banner was 'The Lion of St Mark'. Its band: This was not listed in the Procession Programmes. School children numbered in 1937, 65, and in 1939, 290 – a big increase in two years - ? 'Festivities' included an excursion to Southport. St Mark's closed and was demolished in the 1940s. Its parish was united to nearby St Stephen's.

St Stephen's, Hulme

St Stephen's stood in City Road; it was consecrated in 1869. Its school was founded in 1864. Its banner was 'The Good Shepherd' and 'Memorial'. Its bands included Stretford Borough Band and Hulme Temperance Band. School children numbered 255 in 1939, and in 1951, 400. 'Festivities' included excursions to Hayfield and to Southport. St Stephen's closed and was demolished in the 1960s. Its parish was joined with other Hulme Parishes in the new Parish of the Ascension.

St Michael's, Hulme

St Michael's was consecrated in 1864. Its school was founded in 1863. Its banner was 'St Michael's Church'. Its band was South Salford Prize Band. In 1951 the number of children in St Michael's School was 102. 'Festivities' included trips to Southport and Carr Woods, Bamford. St Michael's joined in the Whit Monday Walk in the late 1940s. St Michael's closed and was demolished in 1963. Its parish became part of the new Parish of the Ascension.

Banner girls of St Michael's, Hulme take their place in a 1950s Walk. Photograph courtesy of M.E.N.

All Saints', Chorlton on Medlock

All Saints' Church, Oxford Road, was, prior to the Second World War, the last parish to leave Albert Square in the Whit Monday Procession. In the Whit Monday programme 'All Saints' Parish Sunday School' was listed, without reference to the church. Its banner was 'The Good Shepherd' and 'Tribute to the Fallen'. Its bands were Essex Street Baptist Silver Band and Salford Prize Band. In 1939 its school children numbered 100. 'Festivities' were given as 'A Country Outing'. All Saints' was destroyed in the blitz of 1940, in World War Two. Its parish was merged in the Parishes of Hulme and Chorlton on Medlock. Though the church has long gone, its name lives on, uniquely, in the Manchester suburb known as 'All Saints'. A well known incumbent of All Saints', was the Reverend Etienne Watts, a radical left-wing clergyman. The site of the church is now a public garden

St Luke, Chorlton on Medlock

St Luke's was consecrated in 1804. Its school was founded in 1865. Its banner was 'St Luke' and 'The Good Shepherd'. Its bands included British Railways Manchester Band and Openshaw Original Prize Band. In 1939 its school numbered 160 children, and in 1951, 140. 'Festivities' were trips to Tatton Park and Middlewood. St Luke's closed and was demolished in the early 1960s. Its parish was joined with St Paul, Chorlton on Medlock, and with that parish it later became part of the new Parish of Christ Church, Brunswick. The site of St Luke's Church is now covered by new housing close to the Mancunian Way.

Girls of St. Luke's, Chorlton-on-Medlock walk in a 1950s Whit Monday Procession. Photograph courtesy of M.E.N.

St Saviour, Chorlton on Medlock

St Saviour's was consecrated in 1836, and stood at the junction of Upper Brook Street and Plymouth Grove. Its school was founded in 1836. Its banner, given by All Saints', Chorlton on Medlock, on that church's closure was 'The Good Shepherd'. Its bands included Burnage Prize Band and Ardwick Silver Band. In 1951 its school children numbered 200. 'Festivities' were a trip to Charlesworth. St Saviour's joined the Whit Monday Procession after the Second World War, and is listed in the 1949 Whit Monday Procession Programme. A new St Saviour's Church replaced the original building in the 1960s. Owing to revised road building plans, this new Church was demolished in the 1980s, and St Saviour's Parish became part of the new Parish of Christ Church, Brunswick.

St Saviour's, Chorlton-on-Medlock, walk along Princess Street on a 1950s Whit Monday. The Life Boys march with them. Photograph courtesy of M.E.N.

St Clement, Longsight

St Clement, Longsight, was consecrated in 1876 and stood in Grey Street, off Stockport Road. Its school was founded in 1876. Its banner was 'The Good Shepherd'. Its band was St Mary's, Droylsden CLB Band. 'Festivities' included a 'Trip to Southport'. St Clement's joined the Whit Monday Walk in the late 1950s. The church was closed and demolished in the 1970s, and its parish became part of the new Parish of St Luke, Longsight.

S.S. Simon and Jude, Granby Row

S.S. Simon and Jude was consecrated in 1842, and the church stood in Granby Row on a site now occupied by the Manchester College of Technology. Its banner was 'The Church'. S.S. Simon and Jude was closed and demolished in 1906, and its remaining parish was united with St James', George Street.

St Clement, Longsight, walk along Mosley Street, Whit Monday 1956, with their "big" banner. Photograph courtesy of M.E.N.

Beyond 1970

The last official Whit Monday Procession programme was published in 1970. After that year an increasing number of the churches, which had traditionally taken part in the Procession were closed, and they ceased to be represented in the Whit Monday Walk. In the 1970s and 1980s a revival of the Whit Walk saw churches from Manchester's outer suburbs joining the Procession, together with a group of new churches formed from the union of former parishes in the inner areas.

St Paul	Blackley
St Mark	White Moss
St Mary	Moston
St Thomas	Crumpsall
All Saints' and Martyrs	Langley
St Margaret	Heywood
St Crispin	Withington
St John	Droylsden
St Luke	Cheetham
The Church of the Resurrection	Bradford *and*
The Good Shepherd with St Barnabas	Eastlands
The Church of the Apostles	Ancoats
The Church of the Saviour	Collyhurst
St Cuthbert	Miles Platting
St James Hope	Salford
St Ignatius	Salford
St George	Charlestown
All Saints' Team Parish	Pendleton
St Agnes	Birch in Rusholme
St Martin	Castleton
St Philip	Gorton

These new contingents were generally smaller than had been the strength of the 'old' Whit Monday parishes, and they took a more informal approach to the Procession. A number of these 'new' parishes no longer join in the Walk.

Much Lost

In the inner-areas of Manchester and Salford, where the Whit Monday Procession had its strength, there has been great change, with house clearance and population movement. People whose roots lay in these communities have moved away, and in doing so, they have gained much in material terms. That they look back with such good memories of former times, is an indication that perhaps they feel that much has been lost in terms of community spirit and involvement – of which the faith based Whit Walks were a great example. The rector of St Paul's, New Cross, the Reverend Thomas Owrid, writing in his parish magazine in May 1929 said: 'I look forward with great anticipation to Whitsun, and to the thrill of joy walking in the great Whit Monday Procession'. The Whit Monday Procession in its heyday was a great event; there was church and community commitment to it, and enthusiasm for it. It gave birth to the Whit Walk tradition which took root in inner Manchester and Salford, and spread to processions on other days, and in other places around Manchester. It is to these 'other' Whit Walks that we will turn in part 2 of this book.

A Whit Monday Message

Canon Peter Green of Salford was regarded as the greatest parish priest in England. He took part in the Whit Monday Walk from 1901 until 1951.

In the 1949 Whit Monday programme he wrote about the Processions Sunday Schools.

To All Sunday School Workers

from

The Rev. Canon Peter Green, M.A., D.D.

St. Philip's Clergy House,
6, Emcombe Place,
Salford, 3

May I, as an old Sunday School teacher who has taught almost without break for sixty-two years and who still has his class on Sundays, send greetings to my fellow teachers?

I believe that there is today nothing more important than the work of the Sunday Schools.

A famous Sunday School teacher once said: "Years after we are dead our boys and girls may have forgotten what we **said**; they will not forget what we **were**."

Let your character, with God's help, build the characters of the coming generations of English citizens.

Yours very sincerely,

PETER GREEN.

PART 2

Whit Walks in Manchester's Suburbs

The Manchester and Salford Whit Friday R.C. Procession

Whit Walks and Walking Days in Towns and Villages around Manchester

Chapter 6

The Whit Walks in the Manchester Suburbs

In addition to the city centre Whit Monday C of E, and Whit Friday R.C. Walks there were processions in the city's suburbs during Whit Week. The Whit Monday Procession being the forerunner of these, and of other Whit Walks and Walking Days.

In many districts these processions have been discontinued, but in other areas the tradition lives on. The Church of England and Roman Catholic parishes involved in their respective city centre Walks, also processed around their districts, the former on Whit Sunday, and the latter on Trinity Sunday. Those churches which were not a part of the city centre processions, including the Free Churches, held their own district Whit Walks. In this chapter we look at some of these processions, beginning with a very special Whit Walk.

An Old Tradition in a New Community
'The First Wythenshawe Whit Walk'

An early Whit Walk in Wythenshawe.
Photograph courtesy of Manchester Libraries.

The new housing development of Benchill, Wythenshawe, took up the Whit Walk tradition, brought with its new residents from inner-Manchester, at Whitsun 1934. In his book '50 Years From the Farm', Don Egan includes the Reverend Colin Lamont's description of his arrival as priest in charge of Benchill in 1934. Colin Lamont writes: 'With the church hall premises not yet built, my ministry was initially based at Hollyedge farm. The first service at the farm was led by the Bishop of Middleton and 160 people were present. On my arrival at the farm I had put a notice on the Farm gate advertising a Sunday School on the next Sunday. On the first Sunday 60 children attended; on the second Sunday 160 were present; on the third Sunday 220; on the fourth Sunday 300, and on the fifth, 350. The farm was filled to capacity and beyond. Benchill was then a building site, with no church, church hall, vicarage, shops or pubs, but plenty of mud. The newly arrived residents felt cut-off from Manchester with its great Whitsun Festival. They wanted something of their own in Benchill. It was decided to hold a Whit Walk on Whit Sunday 1934. A lady in the congregation made an improvised banner. The Northenden Band agreed to lead the Walk free of charge. When the day dawned, there was early rain, but this cleared by the afternoon. 1,000 men, women and children, of all denominations joined the first Wythenshawe Whit Walk. As the procession set-off along Woodhouse Lane, to the stirring music of the band, I had a lump in my throat. Mothers cried with excitement at the sight of the children of Benchill taking part in their own Whit Walk. There were cheers and clapping everywhere.

St. Luke's Church, Benchill, Wythenshawe, 1938, the fulfilment of a 1934 mission. Photograph courtesy of Manchester Libraries

After the Walk hundreds of buns, bottles of milk and cups of tea were served. This was the Birth of New Life, and Hope, for a new community, expressed through an inherited and time honoured tradition!' Benchill became the Parish of St Luke the Physician, with its own church, built in 1938.

The Whit Walks – Around the Districts

In May 1967 the 'Manchester Evening News' published a 'Whit Sunday, Whit Walks in the Districts' Souvenir Newspaper. It gave photographs of, and information about, the Whit Walks in the suburbs of Manchester. Its front page was headlined: 'The Smiling March of Youth'. A second-page heading read: 'It's So Wonderful to be Young at Whitsun!'
The district processions listed were: see appendix 2 page 190.

Massive Celebration

The 'Evening News' Whit Sunday District Walks Souvenir gives an indication of the number of Whit processions happening on Whit Sunday in Manchester and Salford's suburbs. There were very many other churches taking part in processions, not covered by the District Walks Souvenir. Considering this, it becomes obvious that Whitsun in Manchester, with two great processions in the city centre, and other Whit Walks in all of the city's suburbs was a massive celebration. In the 1950s Manchester at Whitsun, even with less traffic than today, must have been a motorist's nightmare, with thousands and thousands of children, banners and bands taking over the roads! A tradition, the remembrance of which, deserves to be perpetuated for posterity. The Whit Walks in the suburbs were sometimes united processions of all the local churches, and sometimes, they were individual church processions. Whichever was the case, they involved churches with their banners, bands, Sunday and day schools, youth organisations and adult organisations. They would be watched by many spectators, and embraced by the whole community.

Helen Gilbertson writes from London about her experiences of a district Whit Walk in Levenshulme: 'I was a member of the 2nd Levenshulme Brownie Pack in the 1970s, as an eight-year old. Our Whit Walk was with St Mark's Church in the Levenshulme district. The St John's Ambulance Society joined in our Walk to be on hand if needed. I have the best memories of Whit Week in Manchester, and, of my childhood in the St Mark's Levenshulme Procession. I wish the Author of this book all good luck in reminding people of the part that the Whit Walks played in our lives.'

Helen Gilbertson, centre, walks in the 1970 Whit Sunday Procession with St. Mark's, Levenshulme.

Photograph courtesy of Helen Gilbertson.

Cutting Up a Wedding Dress for the Walk

Carole Elmer, now of Bolton, has good memories of walking with Chain Bar Methodist Church in Moston. She writes:

A Whit Sunday Walk at Bar Methodist Church. Photograph courtesy of Carole Elmer.

'I was the rosebud queen at Chain Bar Methodist Church in 1952; I was then five-and-a-half years old. My abiding memory of that Walk was of having my neck almost broken by the children holding my train as attendants! My family was not over endowed with money, at this time, and my mother had to tell me that a new long frock was beyond its resources. Our next-door neighbour in Moston came to the rescue. Quite willingly, and very generously, she 'cut-up' her wedding gown to make me a long dress for the Whit Walk! On the day of the Walk I remember that I felt like a queen – though one with a sore neck! My sister, Christine, reminded me that our older sister, Amy, as a teenager, didn't want to join the Walk, and having to do so, she decided to carry a mirror with her to catch the sun and dazzle everybody. This she said, would make her Whit Walk more interesting! My parents were Sunday School teachers, and they had their memories of Whit Sunday Walks with Harpurhey Methodist Church. My first procession was at the age of three-and-a-half. My mother made posies for my sisters and I, and very pretty they were. My final memory of the Whit Walk was in my teenage years watching the boys marching with the Scout Band!' Carole Elmer's recollection of her neighbour's generosity in giving her wedding gown for the long white dress of the rosebud queen, reveals the community spirit that the Walks inspired.

In the suburbs the Walks included:-

Cheetham Hill United Procession

In the 1901 Centenary programme of the Whit Monday City Centre Procession, a list of the churches which would be having processions that day, in the suburbs, was given. These district Whit Monday processions eventually gave way to Whit Sunday Walks, with the exception of the Whit Monday evening procession at Cheetham Hill. This continued until the late 1960s. Some of the bands which had taken part in the Whit Monday morning procession in the city centre, were marching again in Cheetham Hill in the evening. The Cheetham Hill procession was centred on Cheetham Hill Road and Waterloo Road. A good number of people walked in the procession, and many spectators lined the route. Amongst the churches which took part were:

St Luke's, Cheetham;
St John the Evangelist, Cheetham;
St Mary, Crumpsall;
St Mark, Cheetham;
Trinity Church, Cheetham;
Crumpsall Methodist Church;
Cheetham Hill Methodist Church;
Queens Road Church.

Newton Heath Free Church Procession

The Newton Heath United Procession took place on Whit Friday afternoon. The Walk was centred on the Oldham Road, Church Street and Droylsden Road area. The Free Churches of this district joined in the procession, and they included in their number:

Newton Heath Evangelical Church;
Culcheth Methodist Church, The Welcome Mission Church;
Newton Heath Methodist Church;
St Paul's Mission;
The Salvation Army;
The Free Church of England Church.
Other processions in Newton Heath included the Church of England Walks of:
St Wilfrid;
St Anne;
All Saints *and*
St Cuthbert, Clayton Bridge;
The Roman Catholic procession of Christ the King.

The Whit Monday evening Cheetham Hill Procession, 1949. Norma Rothwell, with her brother carrying the flag, join Victoria Methodist Church in the Walk. Photograph courtesy of Norma Rothwell.

*The Queens Park Congregational Church, Harpurhey, Whit Sunday Walk in 1948.
Norma Rothwell is the girl who is the second from the right.
Photograph courtesy of Norma Rothwell.*

The First Walk of the Week in Droylsden

The first Walk of the Whit Week Festival took place in Droylsden on Saturday, the eve of Whit Sunday. This was a procession of Church of England and Free Churches. The route lay through the centre of Droylsden's Market Street, but the starting point was varied between Droylsden Football Ground, Droylsden Primary School playground and later, Fairfield Square. A United Service was held at the starting point of the procession, and it then wended its way around Droylsden, taking in Ashton Hill Lane, Market Street, Manchester Road, Scott Road and Greenside Lane. The churches involved were:

St Mary's Parish Church;
St John's Mission Church;
St Martin's Church, Greenside Lane;
Moorside Methodist Church;
Droylsden Methodist Church;
Droylsden Congregational Church;
The Salvation Army;
Bethel Church;
Fairfield Moravian Church.

The numbers in the Droylsden Walk declined by the 1990s, to three churches. St Andrew's Church, Edge Lane, and Edge Lane Methodist Church held their own Walk in their area of Droylsden.

There were district Whit Walks in all of the suburbs, including Denton, Reddish, Gorton, Openshaw, Failsworth, Moston, Stretford, Blackley, Harpurhey, Prestwich, Levenshulme, Newton Heath and Ardwick. No district of Manchester and Salford was without its parish, or its united Whit Walk. To record the details of them all would require a library of books. It is sufficient to say that each of these Walks saw the churches leave their places of worship, and go out into their communities to witness to their faith – and by so doing brought those communities together in an exceptional way.

In and around Manchester

The Newton Heath Whit Friday afternoon procession passes along Oldham Road led by Newton Heath Methodist Church in the 1970s. Photograph courtesy of Eric Humphrey.

Renee Emery, nee Edwards, who recalls her childhood Whit memories with St. Marks Holland Street, in chapter 4, walks with All Saints' Newton Heath in their 1960s Whit Sunday parish procession. Renee is the second girl from the front holding the banner ribbon. Photograph courtesy of R. Emery.

The Bible is carried, decorated with flowers in the Whit Sunday Newton Heath Walk, in the 1960s, along Oldham Road. Photograph courtesy of Eric Humphrey.

St. Wilfrid's, Newton Heath, Whit Sunday Walk, 1960s, along Oldham Road. Photograph courtesy of Eric Humphrey.

The History and Memories of the Whit Walks

St Benedicts Church of England Parish Walk in Ardwick

St. Benedict's, Ardwick, process through the streets of their parish in a 1950s Whit Walk. Photograph courtesy of Richard McEwan.

St. Benedict's, Ardwick included a "boy bishop" in their parish Whit Walk in the 1950s. Note the bricked-up houses in readiness for clearance demolition. Photograph courtesy of Richard McEwan.

St. Benedict's, Ardwick, process into the first post-war housing development in their parish walk. St. Benedict's parish underwent housing clearance schemes in the 1950s and 1960s. The church is now closed for worship. Photograph courtesy of Richard McEwan.

St. Benedict's, Ardwick, the rector preaches from the balcony of the flats in the 1950s.

In the next chapter we look at Manchester City Centre's other great Procession – the Roman Catholic Whit Friday Walk.

Salford RC Cathedral

Chapter 7

The History and Memories of The Whit Friday Roman Catholic Procession in Manchester

There is no definite date recorded for the beginning of the Whit Friday Procession in the form that it became established, with the meeting point in Albert Square and a procession through the city centre. As with the Church of England Whit Monday Procession, the Whit Friday Walk had its origins in the Sunday School movement. In 1784 a Sunday School Committee had been set-up for all the denominations in Manchester. In 1800 the Church of England withdrew from this and formed its own committee. This decision led to the beginning of the Whit Monday Procession in 1801. Had the committee for all the denominations continued, it is interesting to consider the possibility that, though unlikely in those times, the Manchester Whit Walks might have become an ecumenical procession. This was not to be; Whit Monday became the day of the Church of England Procession and eventually, after taking different routes on different days, the Roman Catholic Procession was established on Whit Friday.

The First Four Chapels

In 1834 there were only four Roman Catholic Chapels in Manchester and Salford. These were, St Chad's, which then stood in Rook Street in the city centre; St Mary's, Mulberry Street; St Augustine's, Granby Row and St Patrick's, Rochdale Road. These chapels were described as 'missions'. In each of the missions a Sunday School was established and a Roman Catholic Schools' Society was eventually set-up. It became the practice for the children of these Sunday Schools to meet at their school and to march to their Catholic Chapel for Mass. These processions were the forerunners of the Whit Friday Walk.

A Glimpse into the Past

In the 1914 Whit Friday Programme, P. Prendergast, wrote an article, with the title above, on the origin of the Catholic Procession in Manchester. He states: 'Naturally a great deal of doubt surrounds the origin of the great Catholic Procession that takes place year by year on the Whit Friday in Manchester, for as we look back into the bygone days and realise the circumstances that then prevailed, the necessity there was for Catholics for long years even after the passing of the Emancipation Act in 1829, of fulfilling the duties of

The Bishop of Salford, The Right Reverend Thomas Holland. The 1965 programme of the Manchester Roman Catholic Whit Friday Procession.

their faith in a quiet and unostentatious way, we can well understand why so little in the way of recorded history has come down to us from those times. For the commencement of this now historic event we must go back to the early days of Catholic Manchester's second spring, the days of Fr. Henry Gillow, Fr. Parsons, Fr. Crook and Fr. Daniel Hearne. There were then in the year 1834 only four Catholic chapels in the whole of Manchester and Salford: St Chad's (Rook Street), St Mary's (Mulberry Street), St Augustine's (Granby Row) and the newly-built St Patrick's (Rochdale Road).

In each of these missions there was established a Sunday School for the religious instruction of the young and rising generation. But with the rapid growth of the town in those years, and the influx of thousands of Catholics from Ireland – consequent to 'persecution and famine' in their own land, and to the wondrous industrial progress made in connection with the cotton trade – the outlying districts of the town were soon in a sad way in respect to provision for the fulfilment of religious duties and instruction for the young. To remedy the evil as far as possible a board of management, consisting of the priests of the four missions, along with many prominent and enthusiastic laymen, was formed, called the 'Catholic Schools' Society,' whose object was the provision of religious instruction to the people of the outlying districts of the town. Monthly collections were made, teachers appointed, suitable buildings obtained, and in a wonderfully short space of time Sunday Schools were established and carried on with great spirit and great benefit to a numerous class of poor children on every side of the town. In connection with this Catholic Schools' Society, and the missionary work it entailed, there comes down to us today the names of Mathias Grey, of old St Augustine's; Mr Perry, of St Mary's; Mr Corden and the Brothers McAllister, of St Patrick's.'

He continues: 'In 1836, two years after the formation of this society, a survey was made for the Statistical Society of the various Sunday Schools in Manchester and Salford, and the returns for the Catholic schools and scholars were given as follows: Sycamore Street, Oldham Road, 231; George Leigh Street, Oldham Road, 350; Dyche Street, Angel Meadow, 1,050; Newton 75; Granby Row 900; 'Little Ireland' 335; Lloyd Street 415; Green Street, Hulme, 104; Bury Street, Salford, 500; Charlestown, Union Street, 115. Thus there were establishments, as the results of this society, many centres, which formed the foundations of new Catholic missions.

A 1960s Whit Friday procession moves along Market Street. This section of the Whit Walk features Our Lady's Church, Moss Side. Photograph courtesy of M.E.N.

The Sunday School children marched to their chapel for Holy Mass, a simple, practical and certainly in those days, a courageous manifestation of their faith. At St Patrick's, Livesey Street, there assembled each Sunday morning for the half-past nine Mass scholars from Sycamore Street, George Leigh Street, Dyche Street and Newton. After the Mass and before their dispersal the beautiful custom was observed by them of marching around the cemetery reciting the 'De Profundis' with the usual prayers for the dead.'

'At St Mary's, Mulberry Street, scholars assembled from Lloyd Street, Green Street, Hulme, Bury Street, Salford and Union Street, Charlestown; at St Augustine's scholars from the Granby Row school, from Chancery Lane, Ardwick and from 'Little Ireland'. It is in these various Sunday morning processions of those bygone days that we have the origin of the present great Catholic Whit Friday Procession. From the years 1838-9, now some seventy-five years back, with rapidly increasing strength in numbers, with the formation of guilds and confraternities, the effect and power of a combination of forces, quickly suggested itself to those in authority, and on various occasions, such as the openings of the Presentation Convent in Livesey Street, St Wilfrid's, Hulme (1842), St John's, Salford (1844), such combined processions took place. It is recorded that at the opening of St John's, thirteen Sunday Schools were represented in procession, with a total number of scholars of some 6,000. For some years after this we learn of the Manchester schools assembling for an annual procession like to that of the Church of England churches in Whit Week.'

'The Salford schools held independent processions of their own. When Whit Friday first came to be the recognised day for the Catholic procession we are not able to state, but how is quite obvious; from the Church's law of abstinence the Friday was and is now generally regarded by those outside as the practical test day of Catholicity. The Friday, therefore, naturally became the Catholics' day. On June 28th, 1838, 5,000 Sunday School children from the Catholic Chapels walked in procession to Ardwick Green, as part of the celebrations for the Coronation of Queen Victoria.'

A Cathedral in Salford!

With the influx of Roman Catholic immigrants from Ireland, the Catholic community in Manchester and Salford began to grow in numbers. On Whit Tuesday 1844, the site for the building of St John's Cathedral was inaugurated. Ten Sunday Schools, with 6,000 children, marched to the site in Chapel Street 'with banners waving and bands playing' By 1846 a Catholic Procession was taking place in Manchester. The schools assembled at New Cross, and proceeded along Great Ancoats Street, Pin Mill Brow, Ardwick Green, Rusholme Road and Oxford Street. It is recorded that the procession included ladies wearing 'blue ribboned bonnets and brown-

St. Aloysuis Church, Ardwick Green. The boys walk in a 1960s procession. Photograph courtesy of Maureen Molloy.

serge dresses, with medallions pinned to them'. The Salford schools, at this time still held their own independent Whit Walks. In 1848 St John's Cathedral was solemnly opened, and children from three Salford, and ten Manchester Sunday Schools marched to witness the event. The route of the procession lay over a bridge which levelled a toll of thirty shillings for the children to pass! With the opening of St John's Cathedral and the formation of the Diocese of Salford, the Roman Catholic presence in Manchester and Salford became firmly rooted. On occasions of significance to the Catholic community, churches and schools would join in combined processions to celebrate, and witness to, the event.

Whit Friday becomes the Day!

A general assembly of schools meeting on Whit Friday in Albert Square in 1887 introduced the traditions now associated with the Whit Friday Procession. With the improvements made in the way of colour and dress distinguishing the various guilds and confraternities, as well as the vast increase in numbers, the civil authorities of the town, seeing the importance of this procession, at length recognised it as a town event in holding up all traffic and patrolling the route. This reflected the growth of Roman Catholic parishes, and their day schools, which took over the work of the Catholic Sunday Schools. These churches and schools were built in the expanding suburbs of Manchester and Salford, and they came from the same areas of the two cities, as the Church of England parishes which took part in the Whit Monday Procession.

In his book 'Irish Catholics in England' Steven Fielding writes of the tensions existing in some of these communities with significant populations of people with Irish descent. He observes that in the 1880s and 1890s the two Whit Week processions could put strains on relationships within these areas. He states: 'In the Knott Mill district there could be fights at Whitsun, that might be provoked by comments such as "You can't rule the weather" or "God knows His Own" if the day had been fine for one of the Whit Walks, but wet for the other'! Fielding relates that in the Collyhurst neighbourhood, on Whit Monday 'houses would be decorated in red, white and blue, with photographs of the King and Queen in the windows. On Whit Friday houses would display the Green of the Irish immigrant families, with photographs of the Pope adorning the windows'.

As noted in previous chapters, patriotism was expressed in the Whit Monday Procession, through the use of red, white and blue; the presence of John Bull and Britannia, and of sailor boys. Bands played tunes such as 'Sons of the Sea' and 'We've Got a Navy'. In the Whit Friday Procession the presence of families of Irish descent lent an air of the country of their forefathers to the Whit Walk. This was seen in the use of Green, and in the participation of pipe and fife bands playing tunes like 'The Wearing of the Green' and 'The Minstrel Boy'.

Whit Friday Established

Towards the last decades of the nineteenth century the Whit Friday Procession became, with the Anglican Whit Monday Procession, an established part of Manchester life. If there were tensions in some areas, there was also mutual goodwill, with many Catholics watching the Whit Monday Walk and numerous Anglicans being spectators on Whit Friday. There were families which included both traditions within their number, and for whom both Whit Walks left happy memories. As the end of the nineteenth century approached, the Whit Friday Procession grew in numbers and attracted huge crowds of spectators. The route of the Walk was by way of Mount Street, Peter Street, Deansgate, Market Street and Piccadilly, where the Bishop of Salford watched the Procession pass-by to return to each of the parishes.

The banner of St. Patrick's R.C. Church, Collyhurst is led, in returning from Whit Friday Procession, by the parish's girls pipe band, in the 1950s. Photograph courtesy of S. McDonald.

The 'Manchester Guardian' gave an account of the Procession in 1895: 'Whit Friday Catholic Procession in Manchester. Whit week saw the usual abandonment of Manchester to holiday making. Children and grown-up people forgot for a time, as far as possible, that there were such things as school and business. The streets were thronged with crowds of visitors, and the fields of the neighbouring country were besieged by bands of romping children, out for their annual treat. The long stretches of green grass with the sunlight on them, and the fresh pure air breathing over them, their embroidery of wild flowers, and the soft symphonies of the birds in sky and thicket, must all have been very pleasant after the dull greyness of the city, with its rattling traffic and atmosphere of smoke. Such days are days of real happiness and delight, when man turns from the scenes of his own handiwork and throws himself into the bounteous lap of Nature, where he becomes, for the once at any rate, loyal, loving and contented.

The Guardian report continued:
The Catholic Procession on the Friday, took place under most favourable conditions, and in spite of the regrettable breakdown over the singing of 'Faith of Our Fathers' and a change in the placing of the schools in Albert Square, the spectacle, witnessed by about a quarter of a million of people lining the streets along the route, has never been surpassed. A Catholic procession has always the aid of many and splendid banners, which of themselves make a bright and striking display. But the display made by the banners was well supported by the distinctive sashes or hoods – always of bold colour – worn by most of the children, and also by the older members of the numerous confraternities in connection with the schools. Many of the girls, both large and small, make it a point on these occasions to appear robed in white when the weather permits. Yesterday, the weather not only permitted, but strongly invited white; and upon this pure ground the scarlet and blue sashes at once seized the eye. More delicately pretty were the dresses of several groups of little ladies who had long veils falling over their white frocks, and, for the only colour, chaplets of light green leaves or of flowers. The banners, the dresses – all the kaleidoscopic mixing of colour – were yesterday lighted up with the brilliance of a summer sun. The sky was almost

Italian in its unbroken blue; and as the bright Procession, with its large crucifix and the great statue of the Madonna moved through the streets, it seemed as if some breath from an old Florentine festival of San Giovanni was passing over the usually cold grey city. The spectators gave frequent signs of their appreciation of the effort on the part of parents, scholars and priests necessary to produced such an effective spectacle. The tiniest children naturally had the most applause, and they deserved it. The sun was hot, and they were kept long afoot; but they all bore up well, and marched bravely along under the spell of the fine white frocks and the bright sashes. Another section of the Procession which seemed to strike popular sympathy, was the little band of Italian women following the crucifix and the Madonna. Banners, sashes, hoods – all had to yield in point of brilliance to the gay colouring of their dresses, aprons and head-shawls.'

The Men's Confraternity of Corpus Christi, Miles Platting, walking to Albert Square on Whit Friday 1930. Photograph courtesy of S. McDonald.

In 1900, 18,000 children walked in the Whit Friday Procession. It included 22 parishes with their day schools, confraternities and banners. Some of the Confraternities represented were, the Children of Mary, the Agnesians, the Blessed Sacrament, the Union of Catholic Mothers and the men of each parish.

In 1904 the marshalls sent directions to each parish priest for the ordering of the Procession these became the statuary arrangements for Whit Friday. See appendix 3 page 191.

The 1904 Whit Friday Programme listed the Schools taking part:-

1. St John's Cathedral, Salford.
2. St Sebastian's, Salford.
3. St Boniface, Salford.
4. St Thomas of Canterbury, Broughton.
5. St Peter's, Greengate, Salford.
6. St Joseph's, Salford.
7. Mount Carmel, Salford.
8. St Mary, Mulberry Street.
9. St Brigid, Bradford, Manchester.
10. St Anne's, Ancoats.
11. St Alban's, Ancoats.
12. St Patrick's, Collyhurst.
13. Corpus Christi, Miles Platting.
14. St Edmund's, Monsall.

15. St Chad, Cheetham.
16. The Boys' Industrial School.
17. St Wilfrid, Hulme.
18. The Holy Name, Oxford Road.
19. The Holy Family, Chorlton on Medlock.
20. St Aloysius, Ardwick.
21. St Augustine's, Granby Row.
22. St Michael's, Ancoats,
and the Manchester Italian Society.

In 1905, the Girls' Independent School and St Joseph's Industrial School joined the Procession.

The 1905 Whit Friday programme listed the numbers likely to walk with each parish. These ranged from 350 to 2,000. It included photographs of the churches and their clergy. By 1910 the numbers walking in the Procession were 20,000 and by 1922 they had risen to 25,000. In 1910 the Procession was held on Trinity Sunday rather than on Whit Friday. During the First World War the Whit Friday Procession was abandoned. The 1924 Whit Friday programme contained an appeal from the parish priest of St Malachy's, Collyhurst, Fr. Vincent Marshall, for spectators to donate a shilling towards the building of St Malachy's schools. Fr. Marshall was later to become Bishop of Salford.

Corpus Christi, Miles Platting, in their 1953 parish walk in the shadow of Bradford Gasometer, on Trinity Sunday. Note the Coronation bunting on the since demolished terraced houses. Photograph courtesy of S. McDonald.

The men of St. Patrick's, Collyhurst, walk along Rochdale Road on their way to Albert Square, Whit Friday 1936. Photograph courtesy of S. McDonald.

In 1924 the schools represented were:-
1. St John's Cathedral.
2. St Boniface, Salford.
3. St Peter's, Greengate.
4. St Sebastian, Salford.
5. St James', Pendleton.
6. St Joseph, Salford.
7. Mount Carmel, Salford.
8. St Mary's, Mulberry Street.
9. St Chad's, Cheetham and St William's, Angel Meadow.
10. St Edmund, Monsall.
11. Corpus Christi, Miles Platting.
12. St Casimir, Miles Platting.
13. St Patrick, Miles Platting.
14. The Boys' Industrial School at St Joseph's, Longsight.
15. St Brigid's, Bradford.
16. St Anne's, Ancoats.
17. St Aloysius, Ardwick.
18. Holy Name, Oxford Road.
19. St Wilifrid, Hulme.
20. St Augustine, Manchester.
21. St Alban, Ancoats.
22. St Michael, Ancoats and the Italian Society.

Emblems of the Faith

By the 1920s and 1930s the Whit Friday Walk had increasingly grown in numbers. The Procession included the 'big' banners associated with all Whit Walks, but not the floral emblems, carried by other denominations. The Manchester Italian Catholic Society, founded in Ancoats, joined St Michael's, Ancoats, in the Walk, carrying emblems of the Faith, including the Statue of the Madonna, decorated with lilies. During the Second World War the Whit Friday Procession was again abandoned, but it was re-started in the post-war years. A move was made by the Manchester Chamber of Commerce for the Whit Walks to be changed, or abandoned permanently. This was resisted by all denominations, and it gave the walkers a firmer intention to continue.

*Girls of St. Aloysius Ardwick return to their parish from a 1960s Whit Friday walk.
Photograph courtesy of M. Molloy.*

The Churches of the Whit Friday Procession

Though some of the original parishes involved ceased to be part of the Procession, and others replaced them in later years, the participants, in general, remained the same across the years. These were, as listed in the Whit Friday programmes, with school numbers and bands:- See appendix 4 page 192.

Whit Friday Heyday

By the 1950s and early 1960s the Whit Friday Procession had reached its heyday, numerically with 25,000 walkers. It had become a great, demonstration of the Roman Catholic Faith, and it included Catholics of English, Irish, Italian, Ukrainian and Polish descent, who had been united in community through their common faith. 'The Manchester Evening Chronicle' of Whit Friday 1962 carried the headline: ***'25,000 Walkers conquer the heart of the City'.***

Corpus Christi, Miles Platting, with their "boy" bishop in a 1950s Whit Walk. Note the long vanished terraced houses of the parish. Photograph courtesy of S. McDonald.

'The Evening Chronicle' reporter wrote: 'They came, they walked, and they conquered the heart of the city. This was the famous Roman Catholic Whit Friday Procession which once again transformed Manchester into a breathtaking spectacle of colour'. The reporter noted that the Bishop of Salford had watched the twenty-four parishes go by, in a test of endurance, because he had suffered a slipped disc and had joined the Walk against his doctor's advice. The reporter highlighted the presence of many nationalities in the Procession. It stated: 'There were swirling Irish and Scots Kilts; National European Costumes and brightly dressed children, which made for a blazing ribbon of colour'. The 'Chronicle' article gave mention to the 500 strong Polish contingent, who walked for the first time from their Church of Divine Mercy, Moss Side, led by General Wladislaw Anders, leader of the 'Free Polish Forces in World War Two' and by men who had fought under him in the War. The article continued with reference to the Italian Society contingent: 'The Italians once again won loud applause as they proudly carried their giant crucifix and the statue of the Madonna through the city'. The reporter noted that St Peter's, Greengate, had 'the smartest drum major's assistant in

town, with a six-year-old boy walking alongside him'. He wrote of children in Albert Square: 'wide-eyed with excitement' and of children in 'dazzling national dress'. The feature ended with the story of an altar server at St Sebastian's, Pendleton, who was filming the Procession to send it to relatives in Canada.

'The Evening Chronicle' listed the churches taking part in the 1962 Whit Friday Procession:-

1. St John's Cathedral
2. St Boniface's, Lr. Broughton
3. St Peter's, Greengate
4. St Sebastian's, Pendleton
5. St James', Pendleton
6. St Joseph's, Salford
7. Mount Carmel, Salford
8. St Thomas', Hr. Broughton
9. St Chad's, Cheetham Hill
10. Ukrainian Society
11. St Edmund's, Miles Platting
12. St Patrick's, Collyhurst
13. St Malachy's, Collyhurst
14. Corpus Christi, Miles Platting
15. St Vincent's, Openshaw
16. St Willibrord's, Clayton
17. St Brigid's, Bradford
18. St Anne's, Ancoats
19. St Aloysius, Ardwick
20. Holy Name, Oxford Road
21. Our Lady's, Moss Side
22. St Wilfred's, Hulme
23. St Augustine's, Chorlton on Medlock
24. Polish Society, Moss Side.
25. St Michael's with St Alban's, Ancoats and the Italian Society.

The Italian contingent carry the statue of the Madonna through Piccadilly on a 1950s Whit Friday.

The Whit Friday programme for 1962, as usual, had given the marshall's advice on the weather to the walkers: They stated:

'Hope for a Fine Day, Not Alarmed by a Wet Day, Satisfied with a Manchester Day!'

The Whit Friday programme was printed in similar style to that of the Whit Monday Church of England programme. It generally carried a photograph of the Bishop of Salford on the front cover, and it sold thousands of copies. There are copies of the Whit Friday programmes dating back to the 1900s in the Salford Diocesan Archives at St Augustine's Church, Chorlton on Medlock. In the 1965 Whit Friday programme the Bishop of Salford, the Rt. Reverend Thomas Holland urged his people to be 'Christ bearers' in the Whit Walk, and to see its deeper religious significance.

St. Michael's, Ancoats, procession, in Portland Street – Whit Friday 1960s. Photograph courtesy of M. Molloy.

The Bishop's Letter

The Italian Catholics, with St. Michael's Ancoats, carry their decorated crucifix in a 1950s Whit Friday walk.

'This programme tells us all the usual details: where we assemble, when we start, the order we walk in and the route we follow. The old hands know it all by heart! But does the programme set out to tell us all we need to remember? Is this the lot? The Walk is a tremendous sight. Nobody denies that. But so is an iceberg! And yet they say the bigger part of an iceberg is under the surface. There is twice as much again out of sight! If this Walk is to be the Genuine Article the part you don't see must be very big indeed! The part you don't see is in our minds and hearts. That's the part to be sure about. What is it? It is God's gift of divine Faith: a loving homage to His truth. It is deep trust in His eternal promises. It is love of God and love which, for God's sake, embraces all men. These are the spiritual assembly point, the route and order of the procession. The whole programme must be timed and carried through with these spiritual realities present – out of sight perhaps – but strongly sustaining the whole exercise. We should all begin with Mass and Holy Communion if we can, and be Christophers – Christ bearers – on the march!

God bless you all!
Your loving Bishop
THOMAS '

The changes in society that began in the 1960s affected the Whit Friday Procession as it had other Whit Walks. Re-housing brought about population movement, and caused the closure of some Roman Catholic Churches which had long been a part of the Whit Friday Walk. In 1967 the change from the Whit Holiday to the new Spring Bank Holiday, necessitated the moving of the Whit Friday Walk to Whit Sunday. The traditional route along Mount Street, Peter Street, Deansgate, Market Street and Piccadilly was shortened to Cross Street, Market Street and Piccadilly. In 1965 some 20,000 people walked in the Procession, the number being down from the 25,000 of the 1950s. In the 1970s a change was made from the traditional Whit Walk to a solemn Corpus Christi Procession. The 'big' banners were still carried, but the bands were dispensed with. The Corpus Christi Procession was eventually discontinued, and a great Manchester and Salford tradition came to an end. The memories of the Whit Friday Walk remain with those whose lives it touched. Some of those many memories are included here.

The 1970s Roman Catholic Procession. St. Dunstan's, Moston, walk along Cross Street, in the "new" Corpus Christi Procession on Whit Sunday. Photograph courtesy of E. Humphreys.

WHIT FRIDAY MEMORIES

Tom Farrell, now of Gatley, has fond memories of the Whit Friday Walk in his childhood in Chorlton on Medlock, which he regards as an important chapter in his life: 'The Whit Friday Walk; at last the big day had arrived. I was up early looking through the bedroom window, checking on the weather. It was so important I had a fine day, luckily it was fine and clear, and no doubt the sun would make an appearance later. I hurried down the stairs, and into the kitchen where mam had prepared my breakfast. Porridge, toast, and a nice cup of sweet tea, although I must admit I wasn't feeling very hungry. The excitement of the day was getting to me. Mam insisted that I get something inside, it was important as she put it, to put a lining on my stomach, as it was going to be some time, before I would have a chance to eat again. I managed to finish my breakfast without really enjoying it, but at least mam was happy, or so she seemed. My school uniform, plus shirt, socks and boots were neatly laid out on the couch, ready for me to change into. My elder sister Veronica was busy getting herself ready for the big day and my younger sister Dorothy, and brother Ged, were running around getting in everyone's way. Mam was fussing around, making sure everything was just right. Cap and tie straight, socks pulled up, and shoes shining like patent leather.

Pipe Bands featured in the Whit Friday Walk with St. Augustine's, Chorlton-on-Medlock, and other churches. Here the Mc. Sweeney Pipe Band pass through an area of terraced houses now demolished. Photograph courtesy of S. McDonald.

I can't remember ever looking so smart and clean. I didn't mind after all this was a special day. Then as was the custom, I was ushered outside into the street to show myself off along with all the other children who were dressed for the occasion. Friends, relatives and neighbours, all milling round stuffing pennies into the pockets of our jackets. I soon had enough money to keep me in sweets for a long time. Mam stood in the doorway, pride showing on her face, she had turned out a proper little gentleman, and was now enjoying every minute. At last mam said it was time to go, and with my hand in hers we made our way through the busy streets towards the school. The colourful throng of men, women and children, were all gathered in the school playground. Teachers were busy marshalling the children into their respective groups, this was the assembly prior to the annual Catholic Whit Friday Procession, which would be leaving the school shortly, to walk into the city centre. The procession would make its way into Albert Square, via Oxford Road, Oxford Street, through St Peter's Square, into Mount Street before entering Albert Square itself. There all the different schools taking part would be met by the Bishop, all would receive his blessing, before making the return journey to their respective parishes. Our school would be returning through Piccadilly, Portland Street, Princess Street and on to York St, Chorlton on Medlock.'

The Children of Mary, in their pale blue cloaks, were represented in many parishes in the Whit Friday Procession.

'The Whit Walks were the highlight of the year for the majority of the school children, and no doubt for many of the grown ups, whether taking part or just watching. The boys all looking smart in their new uniforms, the school badge proudly worn on the breast pocket, and the girls in their beautiful frocks. The May Queens, and train bearers, wearing long white dresses. The Children of Mary in their blue capes, all looking radiant as they waited for the Walk to start. Eventually we were all organised into our different groups, the school playground that half an hour before, had been a bedlam of noise, was now fairly quiet. We were all lined up in order as the banners were unfurled, all finely embroidered with religious pictures of the saints etc., pride of place going to the school banner, proclaiming to all who we were 'St Augustine's, Manchester', one of the oldest parishes in the Diocese. The splash of colour, contrasted sharply with the grey buildings that surrounded the school. It was as if a rainbow had reached out, and settled on our ordered ranks, and its effect was electric, you could sense the pride surging throughout the assembled ranks. The parish priest, and his curate were the last to join the line. Dressed in their long black morning coats, and top hats, carrying the traditional umbrellas, that hopefully would not be needed today. The bands were in position, and waiting the signal to start. Suddenly the big drum struck up, and on the fifth beat, the band took up the challenge with a rousing march, we were on our way.

The sounds of the music drifted over the playground, and you could feel the excitement, heads shoulders, and backs straightened, and with teachers keeping a watchful eye on our lines, the procession started its long walk into Manchester. The spectators lining the route, were there in plenty, as we neared the city centre they were packed six and ten deep. There was hardly a vacant space left anywhere. They clapped, cheered, more so when a son or daughter was spotted among the marchers, you could hear the audible disappointment when the band stopped playing, followed by a mighty cheer, when it started up again. We loved it, big beaming smiles were in evidence, we all knew we were the centre of attraction, and we made the most of it. I scanned the faces of the onlookers, hoping to see my mam and dad, or other relatives. You soon knew if you had been spotted, there was an almighty shout, and the cheers would grow louder. Our young hearts beat faster with pride, we had to stifle the urge to wave back, our teachers had impressed on us the need to look dignified, and disciplined, and to give the impression that we hadn't noticed. We did manage a slight smile of recognition as we passed the crowded pavements.

Eventually we arrived in Albert Square, the Bishop in all his splendour was standing on a dias in the middle of the Square. All the schools entering were then lined up, and the Bishop then gave us all his blessing before we started the return journey back to the school. It was about 1.30 p.m. when we finally arrived back, tired but happy. The teachers who had looked after us so well during the walk, were now busy making sure we were all reunited with our parents. The Whit Friday Procession was one of the highlights of my childhood, and its memory will never diminish. As an adult I often returned to Manchester to watch the processions, and without fail my mind went back to the time when I had walked proudly with my school, and the surge of pride within me as St Augustine's passed. These processions were a part of the history of Manchester, but sadly times have changed. The pageantry and spectacle, that we as children on Whit Friday experienced are no more.'

Maureen Molloy (nee Leah) now of Moston, recalls her formative years in Ancoats, and of her exciting Whit Friday: 'My memories of the Whit Friday Walk, and of Trinity Sunday processions around our Ancoats Roman Catholic parish, are those of pride, excitement and nervousness. In the weeks leading up to the big event at Whitsun, my mam would take me to Timpson's shoe shop on Ancoats Lane, where Miss Wade would sort me out with new shoes – Whitsun always meant new shoes! A new school uniform came from Cappallo's Store on Rochdale Road. Every year they measured me, but the uniform never seemed to fit when it arrived, and my mam had to take it back to the shop. When I walked on the church banner with my parish, St Michael's, Ancoats, my Aunt Dolly made a beautiful long white dress for me to wear. On the Thursday before Whit Friday I was bathed in our big sink, and my hair was washed. It was then put into rags to curl it. When Whit Friday dawned I was up early and dressed in my new finery. When I walked in my white dress, a large bouquet of flowers was brought from Smithfield Market the night before Whit Friday. These white lilies were put into a bucket of water to keep them fresh overnight. When the time came to walk from Jersey Street to St Michael's Church in George Leigh Street, my excitement was intense. On arrival at St Michael's school I met up with my friends.

Girls of St. Patrick's, Collyhurst, return from Albert Square on a 1950s Whit Friday passing along Oldham Road.

The procession would form-up with the altar boys, banners, bands, the Agnesians, the Children of Mary and the men's and women's confraternities. The Kerry Pipers' Band always led St Michael's and when it started to play the thrill of the occasion ran through the walkers and the spectators alike. St Michael's was always the last church to leave its parish for Albert Square. I can still remember the crowds along the route. I was only a child but it seemed to me that everyone in Manchester had come to watch, cheer and applaud as we made our way through the streets. The schools met together in Albert Square in front of the Town Hall, before returning to their respective parishes. Each school passed along Deansgate and Market Street to Piccadilly, where the Bishop of Salford gave a blessing. St Michael's was always the last parish to reach Piccadilly, and the Bishop would then join us in walking up Newton Street and across Ancoats Lane. As we entered George Leigh Street the Kerry Pipers lined either side of the road and we walked through their Guard of Honour. The band then played the hymn 'Faith of our Fathers' which everybody joined in singing.'

'A great day, but still to come was Trinity Sunday evening and a second procession of witness around the streets of the parish, and part of the city centre. This was a popular event for Mancunians of all denominations. St Michael's Church was followed in the procession by the then Manchester Italian Catholic Society, and the streets were lined with spectators for the Walk. The route took in George Leigh Street, Lever Street, Stevenson Square, Thomas Street, Shudehill, Rochdale Road, Thompson Street, Oldham Road, German Street, Jersey Street, Ancoats Lane and back to the church. The most important part of this route for me, was along Jersey Street where I lived. We didn't walk as far on Trinity Sunday evening as we did

Maureen Molloy, nee Leah, and her aunt Maureen Grimshaw, walk from their church of St. Michael's, Ancoats, as the 1954 Whit Friday Walk begins. Photograph courtesy of M. Molloy.

on Whit Friday, but the procession was just as exciting. Ancoats, in my childhood, was a good place to live with its community spirit, and it has left me with many memories. My parents and I would watch neighbours walking in Church of England processions from St Peter's and St James the Less, church. Our other local Roman Catholic Churches were St Alban's off Ancoats Lane, and St Patrick's in Livesey Street, where I went to my second school. It would be good if the Whit Walks could be revived, but there are many difficulties in the changing times of today.'

Norah Hawksworth, (nee Fogarty) sends her memories of Whitsun from Littleborough:
'My witness of faith at Whitsun was with St Anne's Church in Ancoats, Manchester, in the city's Whit Friday Procession. As a child at school, like everyone else in the late 1940s and early 50s, I along with my sisters and brothers and school pals looked forward to the 'Whit Walks'. It was a time to show our faith in numbers whether you walked to Albert Square on the Whit Monday or Whit Friday with the schools and churches. Whichever one you walked with, you supported the other on their special day and, together, we supported the Italians who walked on Trinity Sunday, from St Michael's, in Ancoats, around the Oldham Road area. It was not just a time of pretty dresses or suits and seeing, for hundreds of yards, children in a splash of colour, each different for their school or church. It was, for many families, a time to dress their children in new clothes. I know, being the eldest of seven, it was new dresses, coats and shoes for me and my sisters and new suits, shirts and shoes for my brothers, with mother praying that we would not grow out of them too quickly. It took most families almost twelve months to save up for the new clothes so they were always appreciated. There was a special pride and joy of going round to friends and family showing off our new outfits and, if we were well behaved, we would get a three penny bit or sixpence which we saved to use

The clergy of St. Anne's Ancoats, - left to right: Fr. Richardson, Fr. Hunt, and Fr. Scanlon in Whit Friday clerical dress, as St.Anne's begin their Whit Walk through now demolished terraced streets to Albert Square in the 1960s. Photograph courtesy of Norah Hawksworth

as spends. My overall memories though, were of sharing and everyone taking part, showing how we belonged together in a community. Times were hard, but you could rely on each other when in need and the faith of the Walks encompassed what it meant to each one of them and this faith was witnessed by all.'

Pat Breakley, now of Failsworth, looks back to Whit Friday memories with Corpus Christi, Miles Platting: 'When I think of Whit Week in Manchester it brings back so many happy memories. As a child I walked in the Roman Catholic Whit Friday Procession, through the City Centre with my church and school at Corpus Christi, Miles Platting. The church was situated on Varley Street, and the children waited there to get into line on Whit Friday morning, for the Whit Walk. Corpus Christi Flute Band led our procession, which included large banners in many beautiful colours, and other bands. Corpus Christi walked along Oldham Road into the city centre, watched by crowds of people cheering and waving flags. What a wonderful sight this was, set against the drab Manchester streets. When we arrived in Albert Square, we gathered with all the other Roman Catholic Churches and schools. My uncle, Norbert Connell, a member of Corpus Christi Flute Band would take the children for a drink in one of the coffee bars in Albert Square. The schools meeting in Albert Square, came from Collyhurst, Ancoats, Salford, Ardwick, Openshaw, Hulme, Chorlton-on-Medlock and other districts. Memories then of my childhood Whitsuns.'

Corpus Christi, Miles Platting, walk along Bradford Road, Miles Platting in a 1960s Trinity Sunday Parish Walk. Photograph courtesy of S. McDonald

Corpus Christi Miles Platting led by altar boys band and banner in a 1950s Parish Procession. Photograph courtesy of Sheila McDonald.

Pat Breakly continues 'As an adult, I became a spectator at the Whit Friday Walk rather than a participant. With others, I followed the procession along Oldham Road and into the city centre, meeting old friends on every step of the way. As Corpus Christi passed Granelli's ice cream shop on Oldham Road, everyone would buy an ice cream from the shop – it had a wonderful taste. I can almost taste it today! Like so many good things the ice cream shop has now gone. As the Corpus Christi procession reached the bottom of Oldham Road, we walked past the part of Ancoats known as 'Little Italy'. It was called by this name because many Italian immigrants settled in its streets in the nineteenth century. The Italian community became ice cream makers for much of Manchester. I still walk around the old streets of Ancoats and the memories come back to me. St Michael's Roman Catholic Church, now closed, was in George Leigh Street, and the Manchester Italian Society still meet outside the church in June each year, and process from there to Albert Square. As Corpus Christi's procession arrived at Great Ancoats Street, we might meet St Michael's, St Patrick's, Livesey Street and St Malachy's, Collyhurst. As Roman Catholics our Procession was held on Whit Friday, but many of us watched the Church of England Whit Monday Walk in Manchester. The people walking in it, from St Luke's, St John's, St George's and St Mark's, Miles Platting, were all from our same community. We were of different religions, but we were old friends, and we were close. Those great days of Whit Friday, and of Whit Monday, were long ago, but we all still keep in touch. That is how strong the bond was with the people of the old community from which we came in Manchester's Miles Platting and Ancoats.'

Corpus Christi, Miles Platting, return from Albert Square on a rainy 1960s Whit Friday. Photograph courtesy of S. McDonald

The boys of Corpus Christi, Miles Platting, - Whit Friday 1960s – walking along Oldham Road.

The Whit Walk of the Manchester Italian Association

The original name of the Association was the 'Manchester Italian Catholic Society', now changed to the 'Manchester Italian Association'. The Italian Community first took part in Whit Walks in 1890. Its members had begun to settle in the Ancoats area, in the Roman Catholic parishes of St Michael's and of St Alban's. During the period leading up to the 1890 Walks members of the Italian Community visited the homes of their fellow countrymen to collect donations for their first ever procession through Manchester. In that year four men carried

Girls of Corpus Christi, Miles Platting, - Whit Friday 1960s

the statue of the Madonna, which then just consisted of a figure of the Virgin Mary, brought over to England from Italy. There were banners, with women and children in national costume. By 1900 the Italian Society, as it then was, had grown in stature and influence. It still relied on contributions from its members to help to buy banners or statues for the Whit processions. Around the 1900s the Madonna and Child statue became surrounded by lilies and other flowers, and it was a deeply-loved part of the Whit Walks. A statue of Christ at Calvary, also adorned with flowers was eventually added to the processions. In the annual Whit Friday Roman Catholic Procession, the Italian Community joined with St Michael's, Ancoats, in the Walk through the streets of Manchester city centre. In addition the Italians walked with St Michael's on Trinity Sunday evening, around what is now the Northern Quarter of the city, and around part of Ancoats. In recent years the Italian Community has held its own procession, with members of St Michael's former parish, in June or July, on a Sunday afternoon. The Walk moves from George Leigh Street, Ancoats, along Ancoats Lane, Swan Street, Miller Street, Corporation Street and Cross Street to Albert Square. It then returns to Ancoats either by the same route, or along Princess Street, Portland Street and Newton Street. In 2013 the procession included members of St Patrick's Collyhurst, St Malachy's Collyhurst, St Anne's Ancoats and St Peter's Middleton. It was 1,000 strong, and it was watched by a good number of spectators. 'The Manchester Evening News' reported: 'Manchester's Italians Mark 120 Years of History'. The newspaper stated: 'The Italian Community in Manchester will take to the streets to mark 120 years of history. The Madonna Del Rossario Procession will take place from Ancoats, the home of the first Italian immigrants. The procession will feature brass bands and pipe bands'.

Manchester was the place where the Whit Walk tradition began in 1801, with the first Whit Monday Procession. Whit Walks and Walking Days featured later, in towns and villages across Lancashire. We turn to some of these processions in the areas around Manchester in the next chapter.

The Manchester Italian procession with Madonna and child, decorated with lilies, leaves St. Michael RC Church, Ancoats, on a Whit Friday, for Albert Square. Photograph courtesy of M. Molloy.

In and around Manchester

The Italian Catholics lead their banner of St. Peter in a Whit Walk in the 1970s.

The Madonna and Child carried in the Whit Friday Procession by the Italian Catholics.

*Ruth and Matthew Malloy with the banner of St. Michael's, Ancoats, - which is carried to Albert Square each year with the Italian Catholics in their continuing procession.
Photograph courtesy of M. Molloy.*

Chapter 8

The Whit Walks in Towns and Villages around Manchester

Processions of Witness, following a similar pattern to the Manchester Whit Walks, became an established custom in all the towns and villages of Lancashire – and on some occasions they spilled over the border into Yorkshire and Cheshire. In the Lancashire towns and villages the processions did not generally take place at Whitsun, where they did not they were known as 'Walking Days' rather than as Whit Walks. The processions, whatever they were called, included banners and bands, and in the villages Morris Dancers and floats mounted on tractors or wagons, decorated with flowers. Unlike the Manchester Whit Monday Procession, no definite start date can be traced for most of the processions which followed its inception. The mid, to later nineteenth century is the most likely dates at which the Walks in the towns and villages began. In each case their origin lay in the Sunday School movement, but they developed their own local styles and customs. In Manchester, spectators would applaud and cheer the processions. This was rare in the other Walks, but in some of these processions it became, and still remains, the custom for spectators to give the walkers, both children and adults, gifts of money as they passed by. It is sometimes stated that Whit Walks and Walking Days no longer take place. In some towns and villages they have been discontinued, but in other places they remain a part of the annual calendar, though they have generally declined in support, from their heydays. We now look at a number of these traditional processions, some having come to an end – others still walking on!

Oldham and District

Whit Walks in the Oldham area date back to the nineteenth century. They were interrupted by the two World Wars.

A 1900s Whit Walk – the Minister of Heyside Congregational Church, Oldham, the Reverend Samuel Wilson and the children with their banners. Photograph courtesy of the granddaughter of Reverend Wilson – Betty Langton.

The *'Oldham Evening Chronicle'* of 22nd May 1948 carried the headline: 'Ten Thousand People in Enthusiastic Revival of Whitsun Walks in Oldham'. The report recorded that united hymn singing for Whitsun took place by Alexandra Park, attracting large crowds of spectators. The *'Evening Chronicle'* article ended with reference to Corpus Christi Parish, which it described as the first Roman Catholic Church to revive the Whit Walk. The newspaper reported that Corpus Christi walked along Manchester Road, which was lined with spectators, behind a new banner, led by the Manchester Pipe Band, and with

1,000 people in its procession. The Whit Walks in Oldham and district continued in strength into the 1960s and 1970s. The 'Oldham Evening Chronicle' reported in May 1975: 'Sunshine boosts Whit Walks as hundreds join in United Processions'. The 'Evening Chronicle' listed the churches in the district which had joined in the processions;

St Ambrose, Watersheddings;
St Mark's, Glodwick;
St Agnes, Lees;
St Thomas, Lees;
Holy Trinity, Coldhurst;
St John Hey;
St Cuthbert's, Fitton Hill;
St Thomas, Moorside;
St Hugh, Holts;
St James, Barry Street;
St Barnabas, Greenacres;
Oldham Parish Church;
Glodwick Baptist Church;
Watersheddings Methodist Church;
The Gospel Mission;
Northmoor Methodist Church;
Holy Trinity, Bardsley;
Keb Lane Methodist Church;
Greenacres Congregational Church;
Moorside Methodist Church;
Holy Trinity, Waterhead;
Smith Street Methodist Church;
Oldham Town Mission.

Altar boys of Holy Family RC Church, Hollinwood, Oldham, prepare for their late 1950s Whit Walk. Photograph courtesy of M.E.N.

In the districts, the report stated that a United Service had been held outside Chadderton Town Hall and that 600 people from five churches had walked in processions through Chadderton, whilst there were also Whit Walks in other parts of Chadderton. In Lees, the newspaper reported that 1,000 people had met, and led by Boarshurst Band walked to Leesfield Memorial Gardens where hymns were sung; the procession then walked to County End, calling at the homes of senior citizens for hymn singing. In Royton, 1,000 people combined in a Whit Walk led by Royton ATC Band with St Paul's, St Anne's and Trinity Methodist Church. In the town centre the 'Evening Chronicle' stated that Oldham Parish Church had been led by 'a traditional pipe band' in its procession.

Walking On!

Whit Walks are still carried on in the Oldham Metropolitan Borough area, by individual churches and there are some united walks. The tradition has lost support since the 1970s, but memories remain strong, especially amongst the members of the older generation. We recall some of those memories, of the bygone Whitsuns here.

The History and Memories of the Whit Walks

St Paul's Oldham in a 21st century Whit Walk with band and banner.

Roy Potts, now living in Failsworth, has a memory of Walking in Oldham with St James' Church: 'I walked in the 1950s with St James', Barry Street, Oldham. We formed-up outside the church with each section getting into its place in the order of procession. We then walked along Huddersfield Road, and around Derker, watched by many by-standers. Our "big" banner of St James' Church was preceeded in the Walk by the altar servers with the processional cross, the choir and the vicar the Reverend Chisholm, with Mr Southern, the organist. All of the parish groups were present in the procession.'

Eileen Tyson, now of Royton, tells of her childhood days walking in Crompton:
'Times were hard in the 1920s, but Whit Friday was the highlight of my childhood years. I lived in High Crompton, where two churches, St Mary's and Greenhill Methodist Church, walked on Whit Friday, but in those days, not together. I attended St Mary's Church. The excitement for a child began to build-up the week before Whitsun, when mothers took their children's baskets and crooks to be decorated with flowers for Whit Friday. On Whit Friday Eve, all of the children of St Mary's Church had to meet outside the school to practice their walking for the following day. The Sunday School teachers, who worked in the cotton mills, came directly from their work to receive the children. We were assembled in the order which we would be in on Whit Friday, and then marched to the vicarage, where on the lawn we were given instructions for the following day. When I arrived home, I was bathed and in honour of the Whit Walk, I had my hair put in "rags". These were uncomfortable in bed, but worth bearing for the curls the next day. Early on Whit Friday, the local greengrocer returned from Smithfield Market in Manchester, with flowers for the children in the procession, and with boxes of oranges for them afterwards.

Excitement grew as the children collected their flowers and awaited the arrival of the band which came by 'char-a-banc' from Buxton. We took our places in the procession and we watched as the men raised the "big" banner. The band "struck-up" and we walked to the vicarage lawn, where the vicar and his family welcomed us. A hymn was sung, a prayer said, and our Walk began. Our procession walked along one way and it was passed by the Methodist Church going in the opposite direction. As the band played, the horses and the cows in the fields "danced" and galloped about. Carrying and controlling the "big" banner wasn't easy, especially on a windy day!

The girls of St. Paul's Methodist Church, Shaw, Oldham, prepare for their 1960s Whit Walk. Photograph courtesy of M.E.N.

Our procession would stop at some of the large houses in the parish, and the children would sing hymns on the lawns. As our Sunday School went by our family's house, towards the end of the Walk, my mother would take my flowers and give me a cup for the drink with a bun, and an orange which I received, with the other children, when the procession was finished. The band members received a full lunch. After refreshments, the children changed clothes and went to a farmer's field for games, whilst the band entertained the adults.

On Trinity Sunday the children took their Walking Day baskets of flowers to their family graves in the local cemetery. Later the baskets were collected and put away for the next Whit Friday. On our Whit Walk we sang the hymn, 'Breathe On Me Breath of God'. Whenever I hear it sung, it reminds me of Whit Friday'.

Eileen adds later adult memories of Walking in Oldham:
'Later in life I moved home to Oldham and there I attended King Street Independent Methodist Church. This church walked on Whit Sunday afternoon, with Ross Street Methodist Church. We assembled on the church car park and the marshall put each section of the procession into its place. The "big" banner, the Boys' and Girls' Brigades; the primary; the junior and the adults. The procession stopped to sing hymns outside the Oldham Royal Infirmary, on West Street and Union Street, and it returned to King Street, along Copershill Road, where the final hymn was sung. By the 1970s the procession had become ecumenical, and eventually all the churches met at the Hulme Grammar School car park for a united act of worship. The thrill, as an adult, was far removed from the magical qualities of my childhood memories, but it was still thrilling, witnessing outside the church buildings to the Gift of the Holy Spirit at Whitsun'.

Eileen Tyson's Whit memories reveal some of the practices which were observed around the Whitsun festival, and the Whit Walks in former times. These involved the whole community and they brought people together. Each area had its own Whitsun traditions. These often saw churches walking to the local hospital, or to the vicarage, the manse or the presbytery, to sing hymns. Eileen Tyson records that the children's baskets of flowers were taken to the graves of departed family members in the local cemetery so that they were not forgotten at the Whitsun festival which they had once been a part of. She concludes her memories of Crompton Whitsuns, with the observation that they had 'magical qualities.'

All the churches in Oldham and surrounding districts had their Whit processions.

Brenda Horrocks, now of Mossley, remembers:
'I was involved happily in the Royton Whit Walks in the 1950s. My friend and I were 13 and 14 at the time. We readily attended church, at St Paul's, Royton. We were chosen to carry the ribbons on the large church banner and we were very pleased to be asked to do this. At Whitsun, in those times, the people pulled together to make it a very special part of the year. All the children had new clothes for the occasion, and everybody made sure that their doorsteps and window sills had been mopped, and donkey-stoned. The Whit Walks brought the community together in a way that doesn't sadly happen today. The happy memories remain with us.'

The History and Memories of the Whit Walks

St. James', Oldham, 1956. The Whitsun Walk in the parish, in the Derker district of Oldham, moves along Huddersfield Road, with altar servers, choir and banner in the lead. Photograph courtesy of R. Potts

Failsworth Walks

Failsworth in Oldham Metropolitan Borough had its Whit Walks on Whit Friday. The churches taking part included: St James'; St John's; Holy Trinity and the Methodist and the United Reformed Churches. The *'Evening Chronicle'* reported that, 'Failsworth Youth Band, Buxton and Parr Band and Burbage Silver Band led the 1974 Whit Processions.'

Whitsuntide in Lees, in the 1940s

A Whitsun Personal Memory from Peter Dyson.

'These stories are based on what to me is the best day of the year WHIT FRIDAY: the Friday after Whit Sunday. My first memories of Whitsuntide in the late 1940s just after the Second World War, were of brass; shiny silver brass; not the kind that you blow, march to and listen to, but the stuff that you spend. It was a local tradition that new clothes were purchased at Whitsuntide for "Sunday best" and for use in the Whit Walks. Children were, on Whit Sunday paraded to nearby relatives and friends who would provide the anxious child with a coin; hopefully silver; a tanner (2 ½p), a bob (5p), two bob (10p) or half a crown (12 ½p), which was usually popped into the top pocket of my new suit jacket. It was quite a profitable venture as my mum was the youngest of seven children so there were plenty of aunts and uncles to visit. My dad's family were all from the same village and although he only had one sister the extended family of extra aunts, uncles and other relatives was quite large. I was also the only child who lived on a street of eight terraced houses, so there were more benefactors to visit. As I was a Roman Catholic starting school was my first introduction to the ecclesiastical side of Whitsun. I went to St Edward's School, Lees. Lees is a village on the eastern outskirts of Oldham in Lancashire, although I lived in the next village of Springhead part of Saddleworth in the West Riding of Yorkshire. The boundary changes of 1974 has now put both villages in Greater Manchester, much to the discontent of the locals at the time.

On the first Sunday in May a statue of the Virgin Mary was placed at the front of the altar in church; this was crowned with lilies of the valley by an infant girl from the school. She had a retinue of four girl attendants holding posies of flowers and four boy attendants acting as train bearers and a cushion bearer who carried the crown on a satin cushion. On Whit Sunday; which was between three and six weeks later, dependent on when the feast of Easter fell, there would be a procession of witness of the parish of which this group was part. The congregation would walk in procession around the parish led by the parish priest and a brass band. In 1949 when I was seven years old and the church held the first procession of witness after the Second World War, I was chosen to be the cushion bearer for the procession and Patricia Smith was the girl chosen to crown the statue of the Virgin Mary.

The procession started at about ten o'clock on Whit Friday morning from St Edward's Church into the village and onto the High Street past the crowds of non-churchgoers who were standing on the pavements lining the streets. The procession comprised of the parish priest, who was preceeded by the head altar boy who carried a golden crucifix held aloft upon along polished wooden pole. The priest was followed by the other altar boys all dressed in the garment in which they served at Mass. The church banner was carried upon high by two men holding poles with four girls holding strings to steady the banner if the wind blew. A brass band which was hired for the day were next in line; then the May queen followed by her retinue carrying her train and her page boys. The school boys wearing grey trousers, white shirts, ties and red sashes trimmed with a gold fringe came behind. The school girls followed dressed in white frocks, blue silk sashes trimmed in white, white gloves and head-dresses with veils. They were followed by more senior girls known as the "Children of Mary". Each of these groups were in neat orderly files. The rest of the parishioners came behind in a reverent fashion. The brass band was there to play marches and hymns to keep the massed congregation moving along.'

'The procession walked through the village to the Lancashire/Yorkshire boundary at County End and up the hill through the village of Springhead and on to Grotton which was the eastern parish boundary. The procession then turned round and walked back towards Lees. We then walked through the village and instead of returning to church as I thought would happen we set off towards Oldham up the hill at Salem. The route then took us along the western parish boundary. The whole journey seemed to take forever and had taken about three hours to complete what was a five to six mile trip. This was not to be the end of the proceedings, as we then returned to church for Benediction. The whole event from start to finish took about three hours; quite a feat of endurance for a seven year old child!'

A Whit Walk through the terraced streets in the 1890s. Photograph courtesy of Oldham Libraries.

A Nineteenth Century Lees Procession

Walking Days in Lees date back into the nineteenth century. It is recorded that in 1897, the year of Queen Victoria's Diamond Jubilee, the Church of England, and Non-Conformist Sunday Schools united in a June procession through the village. Hey Church led the Walk, and Leesfield Church brought up its rear. This was said to have been the largest procession ever seen in Lees. After the Walk the schools gave their children, a free tea, and a field afternoon was held. The day ended with a torchlight procession to honour Queen Victoria! The numbers in the procession were:-

Hey Church and Sunday School	870
Springhead Congregational Sunday School	700
Salem Moravian Sunday School	370
Zion Methodist Sunday School	500
Primitive Methodist Sunday School	150
Christian Brethren Sunday School	170
Roundthorn Methodist New Connexion Sunday School	200
Leesfield Church and Sunday School	1320

This record of the procession in Leesfield gives a fascinating look at a nineteenth century Walking Day and an indication of the impact of these events in communities in other parts of Lancashire. We are left with the thought that the children, and the entire community, must have enjoyed quite a day in Lees in June 1897!

The Ashton Under Lyne Whit Walks.

The Walks in Ashton-under-Lyne can be traced back to 1873, and probably they began earlier. The 'Albion Church Magazine' reported: 'On Whit Friday, 1873, the Albion schools were joined by the Charlestown and Hurst Nook branches, and proceeded down Stamford Street, before returning to fields at the 'Firs' where buns and lemonade were distributed.'

Mary Whitehead, of Ashton's Albion Church, includes a section on the town's Whit Walks in her book about the Sunday School Movement: 'What Happened in and What Happened to Sunday Schools in Ashton-Under-Lyne.' She writes: 'The Walks were an event of the year when all the town turned out to take part, or to watch, with crowds of people lining the pavements to see the magnificent colourful processions making their way around the wide main streets of the town.'

In 1873 the Albion schools were led in the procession on Whit Friday, by the Alderley Edge and Macclesfield Militia Brass Bands.

Banner girls, informally dressed, in a 21st century Ashton-under-Lyne walking day.

1000 children joined the Walk and new banners were carried; to be much admired by the spectators. In the first years of Ashton's Walks the churches toured their own areas before entering the main streets of the town. On an occasion, in those times, when interdenominational relations were less than satisfactory, the Church of England churches were passing one-way along Stamford Street, and the Roman Catholics walking in the other direction. At one point both processions refused to give way before the Walk continued! We are not told how the matter was resolved.

In her book about Ashton's Sunday Schools, Mary Whitehead conducted a number of interviews with former participants in the Walks; we include some of the memories here.

INTERVIEWS

An Ashton man has memories of the Walks in the 1930s:
'We always got new clothes. I still can't understand how my parents ever 'rigged' us out for Whitsuntide. I can remember going to a shop in Ashton just before Whitsun for them. On Whit Sunday you put them on and that's when you'd go round and you'd visit all your relatives and they used to give you coppers. Now we had a lot of relatives, so you'd get all these coppers and we'd all come back with these coppers you see, we used to put them on the table and then my mother would say "here's two pence for you, two pence for you, and all the rest went into the kitty, so it was a way of supplementing the budget – but you only had to wear those clothes for Sunday from then on, the rest of the week they were put away, you weren't allowed to put them on unless there was really, really, something special.'

A memory of the 1950s at Whitsun recalled by an Ashton lady who attended Christ Church:
'We used to go then in the parish church ground for the service. I remember all the banners being up against the wall, where the Registry Office was, anyway then we all went round the back and we used to have a service held there and then when we were coming out in our turns the parish bells would be ringing, I've always remembered that, that's stuck in my mind, that, the bells ringing as we set off down Stamford Street. Our band was always requested to play 'Onward Christian Soldiers'. We used to go back to Sunday School and have a bun and a drink of milk. Whit Friday morning all the girls had white dresses, little boys with white shirts. We had ribbons and it always seemed to be sunny, it never seemed to rain on Whit Walks' day. I remember carrying a basket of flowers, they used to be the ones with the long handle and every time we stopped I put my basket down and then they set off and then somebody would come running "whose is this" and it used to be mine! This is how I went round Ashton like that, forgetting my basket. As we walked down Stamford Street there used to be crowds ten deep watching us. The following Saturday we would go on the trip to Southport on a double-decker bus.'

Catholic Buns and Pop!

Another Ashton memory is of a group of lads from the Albion Church who would watch the Roman Catholic Procession on Trinity Sunday, and follow everyone into the local Catholic Church for buns and pop. The lads thought they were being clever, but one of them now admits, that the Catholics probably knew what they were doing!

The Ashton-Under-Lyne *'Reporter'* newspaper published details of the Whit Walks, the Order of Procession and the churches taking part – a full page of the *'Reporter'* would be given over to this. In the rural areas around Ashton the churches and the chapels would walk around the farms singing hymns. In one of these districts the Whit Walk took four-and-a-half hours to complete, ending with 'raspberry buns, milk and games'.

The tradition of Ashton's Walks remained strong through the years. A lady from Charlestown recalled her youth in the 1950s processions:
'I was on the banner which meant girls chosen to hold one of about ten ribbons coming down from the banner other than the four ropes which the men would hold because they had to steady the banner for the carriers.' In those days she says "there never seemed to be any shortage of people who would carry the big banner, because I think they felt it was an honour." She remembers her young days in the 1950s when all the non-conformist churches in the area met on Whit Friday morning on the market ground. It was during this time that each church began to take its turn to lead the procession. She remembers that on their walk around the market area, the length of Stamford Street and then up Katherine Street, there would be "lots and lots of people watching and there was a custom of people running out to give money to the people who were walking."

Change and Decline

In the 1960s Ashton churches began to walk together on Whit Sunday rather than on the traditional Whit Friday. In 1971 the Hurst area held its twenty-sixth annual United Procession. These Walks, in due course, were to be discontinued, and a clergyman supported the decision saying: 'There is no longer a desire by the local community to turn-out to watch the Walk. It is a Walk of Witness, but who are we witnessing to? In Ashton they now walk along Stamford Street, witnessing to an empty street, shops and shutters'. The Ashton Walks still takes place, but in the words of one who joins in them: 'The Walk is a shadow of its former greatness, and it hasn't been helped by the change of the date with the council and the police asking that the Walk should happen now on Father's Day each year.'

The Halcyon Days Remembered

The Church of England and the Free Churches now meet to sing hymns on the car park in the town centre, and then with the traditional bands and banners they walk along Stamford Street. Mary Whitehead in her book on Sunday Schools, concludes with this comment: 'As the churches meet for the Walk, the nearby outdoor Market is busy with disinterested people. Very few line the route to attempt to support and enjoy the tradition of the Walks, but many of us still remember those past halcyon days'. Churches walking in the Ashton Procession,

now held on Father's Day each year, have included:
Ashton Parish Church of St Michael;
St Peter's;
St Gabriel's;
St James';
Holy Trinity;
Christ Church, and its Sunday Schools;
The Albion Church;
The Ashton Free Churches.

Mossley

In Mossley, a part of Tameside Metropolitan Borough, the tradition of walking on Whit Friday has continued. The churches process from 'Top' and from 'Bottom' Mossley, into Manchester Road, which is lined with spectators. The Mossley Walk remains well-supported, maintaining a tradition going back to the nineteenth century, and it involves all the local churches, including the Roman Catholic Church. A newcomer to the area, expressing his surprise at Whit Friday being a holiday, and his business being closed for the day, was told that 'Whit Friday was more important than Christmas in Mossley!'

All Saints', Micklehurst, Mossley, take part in their Whit Walk on the traditional Whit Friday.

The churches taking part in Mossley include:
St George's Parish Church;
St John's, Roughtown;
All Saints', Micklehurst;
St Joseph's R.C. Church;
and Mossley's Free Churches.

Stalybridge

In Stalybridge in Tameside, the Whit Friday tradition has given way to a Whit Sunday Procession. The various churches meet in, and walk around, the town centre. A participant has observed in conversation with the Author: 'We still have Whit Walks, but its not now like Whit Friday used to be'.

Mossley Methodist Sunday School walk in the town's Whit Friday Procession.

The Saddleworth Villages Whit Walks in Greater Manchester but across the Yorkshire border!

Though Saddleworth and its villages are administratively a part of Oldham Metropolitan Borough, and Greater Manchester, historically, they are in the West Riding of Yorkshire. Nonetheless, as with the other areas of Oldham Metropolitan Borough, Saddleworth has had a long tradition of Whit Walks taking place on Whit Friday. The 'Oldham Evening Chronicle' reported that mill workers in the districts around the town, were asked in 1952, which holidays they would like to be observed. The vote was unanimously in favour of Whit Friday, the traditional day of the Whit Walks. The Saddleworth author and poet Ammon Wrigley stated in 1918, that the Saddleworth villages first celebrated Whitsun with Whit Processions in 1849. Saddleworth's villages have resolutely held to their Whit Friday tradition of processions, despite the day no longer being a public holiday, and despite a number of other obstacles being put in their path. The Whit Friday tradition in Saddleworth remains strongly rooted in the community, and the Author, in his retirement, was happy to be a part of it, with Dobcross Parish Church in 2012. The Village Square in Dobcross was thronged with a 1,000 people for a service prior to the Walk beginning. The two village bands led the Dobcross procession to Uppermill for a United Service with the other churches, and the general procession of all the churches through Uppermill, was watched by hundreds of people lining the main street. Speaking at the United Service, the Author stated that the Whit Walks were witnessing to faith, bringing people together in community, expressing remembrance for those who took part in former times and upholding tradition.

On Whit Friday, 1,000 people and two bands gathered in Dobcross Square, Saddleworth for a service. Holy Trinity then walked into Uppermill village centre to join nine other churches in a colourful ecumenical procession watched by thousands of people on their traditional day for the Whit Walk. Holy Trinity's banner is a new banner, emphasising continuing commitment and enthusiasm for the Whit Walks.
Photograph courtesy of Beverley Wooding

Michael and Peter Fox have written the long story of Saddleworth processions in the book: 'A Saddleworth Whitsun'. In the preface to the book, the then Vicar of St Chad, Saddleworth, the Reverend Philip Stevens, wrote: 'What a wonderful tradition Whit Friday is. At Whitsun we celebrate the coming of the Holy Spirit upon the early Church. Our prayer for Whit Friday is that the Holy Spirit would be at work in our lives and in our community to enrich all that is wholesome and good'.

A Poet's Memories of Whit Friday in Saddleworth

In 1918, Ammon Wrigley, the local Poet and Author, penned his memories of Saddleworth Whit Fridays in his childhood. He remembered: 'I heard the bands playing merrily through the village streets. I saw little girls running down the fields to the school. I saw the procession of scholars winding through the fields, and the great silken banner of St Thomas, Delph, swaying in the wind. The roadway is thronged with people; women talking and laughing, as light-hearted as the children. The procession is nearing the Church gates. The vicar, wardens, and sidesmen walk beneath the great banner – they are stately and dignified. The church bell is ringing merrily, and all eyes scan the little ones in their new clothes. As I lean against a wall, a woman comes up and says: "It wouldn't be Whitsun if I didn't see the children walk." Ammon Wrigley concluded: 'Whit Friday was the happiest day of the year to children. The day of school feasts, of new clothes, processions, banners, brass bands, massed singing in the village streets and romping on the playing fields.'

In 'A Saddleworth Whitsun' Michael and Peter Fox write: 'Adults too, many of them nurtured on such pleasant memories, gained much enjoyment from the activities at Whitsun. Whitsuntide was an oasis in the dreary monotony of everyday life, and one of the brightest highlights of the Saddleworth year.'

When the Whit Walk tradition began at the end of 1840s, the processions were held at different times of Whit Week, but beyond 1850 'Whit Friday' became synonymous with the festivities. In 2013 the churches taking part in the Saddleworth villages' walks were:

Saddleworth Whit Friday Walk in 1900s. Towered over by St. Chad's Church, the scholars of St. Chad's and Kiln Green Sunday Schools form the procession that the band in the background will lead down to Uppermill Village, now the morning service is over. Photograph courtesy of Michael and Peter Fox.

In the Uppermill United Procession:
St Anne, Lydgate;
Christ Church, Friezland;
Ebenezer Church, Uppermill;
Uppermill Methodist Church;
St Chad, Saddleworth;
Kilngreen Mission Church in St Chad's Parish, Diggle;
Sacred Heart and St William Roman Catholic Church;

Dobcross Community Church;
Holy Trinity, Dobcross *and*
St Paul, Scouthead.
In addition to the United Procession into Uppermill, there are Walks in the other Saddleworth villages of Greenfield, Delph and Denshaw.

Greenfield - *The Procession has included:*
St Mary's Parish Church;
Greenfield Methodist Church and Boarshurst Church.

Delph - *The churches are:*
St Thomas Parish Church;
Delph Methodist Church.

Denshaw
In the out-lying village of Denshaw the parish church of Christ Church process around the village.

Band Contests

The Whit Friday celebrations in the Saddleworth villages (and adjacent areas) include village band contests when brass, silver and military bands from all part of the country converge for the several contests, organised by each village. This is a fitting way to end Saddleworth's Whit Friday, with celebrations into the late evening! In 'A Saddleworth Whitsun' the author points out that brass bands were an essential part of the Whit Friday Processions, and that some bands travelled into the villages by train, to be escorted from the station by enthusiastic children. Each village continues to have its own silver band with the youth and junior sections. The Walks in Saddleworth began, as they did elsewhere, as denominational events. In 'A Saddleworth Whitsun' Michael and Peter Fox tell of an element of competition between the different denominations at Whitsun, in former times. The various churches only 'reluctantly crossing the divide'. They record that a spirit of unity, began to develop as early as the 1920s, when: 'Whit Friday was made noteworthy by a pleasing innovation at Greenfield. The three Sunday Schools, St Mary's, the Wesleyan Church and Boarshurst, had a United Procession.' The experiment was voted a success: the vicar of Greenfield reminding everybody that as with the apostles at Whitsun, they 'should be of one mind.'

As the years progressed the Saddleworth Walks became inter-denominational, and eventually included the Roman Catholic Church. The Whit Friday Walk is maintained in Saddleworth by the churches with commitment and with enthusiasm.

Margaret Hardy, of Diggle, in St Chad's Saddleworth Parish, remembers past Whitsuntides in the villages:

Whit Sunday

'On Whit Sunday we were allowed to wear our new clothes. These we showed off to the family and friends who sometimes gave us money which we saved or spent on sweets. We went to Sunday School and practised our hymns for Whit Friday, which the Sunday School superintendent, had us singing, for what seemed weeks beforehand so we could sing louder and be prouder than the other Sunday Schools.'

Whit Friday

'Things started much earlier at Sunday School then, and as a little girl I used to get very excited and listen to bands arriving at the various churches. I always remember our band at St Chad's, marching up Court Street and onto Lee Street playing 'Hail Smiling Morn'. That was at 7.45 a.m. They were then given a good breakfast to prepare for the day's Walks. I would dash off to get my Whit basket of flowers, which had been duly made up at Spencers or Ashleys or perhaps Daniels, these being the three main green-grocers and florists in Uppermill. They also filled the big baskets with flowers – we still use two of these today, rimmed with ribbons, for the "tinies" to hold. We also had crooks filled with flowers which we still use yet. One had to have a good record of attendance to carry ribbons or baskets and especially the banner. We always set off from the old school at nine o'clock to go up to church for a short service with Kiln Green. We would really dash up Church Road to see if we could be in church before Kiln Green and a great cheer would go up when we spotted their banner and their red, white and blue sashes walking across the hills from Diggle for our United Service.

Then we all processed down for a service with all the other local churches held in the Square at 11.00 a.m. Dobcross – Wrigley Mill – Ebenezer – The Methodist – Friezland – Oh what a sight! We then all processed to the viaduct and back to our own respective Sunday Schools in time for lunch. Even the parents could buy a good solid lunch for half a crown. In the afternoon the children had sports in the field by Dam Head (now Walkers Close) and the band played. After tea everybody made for the band contest in the park to listen to top brass. The following Monday everyone would crowd around the wireless shop window to see if their photograph of walking in the Whit Walks was displayed and if you were lucky you could order a copy for about one shilling. As old as I am I still enjoy Whit Friday, having progressed through the years from basket, banner, ribbons and teaching in Sunday School to making food for all. I'm still going strong but I stop and wonder if children still get that same elated feeling as I did when in our church Procession of Witness, a feeling I still get today.'

The Walks And The Joy They Brought

The tradition of Whit Friday Walks lives on strongly in Saddleworth, but no longer in other parts of Oldham Metropolitan Borough. The *'Oldham Evening Chronicle'* featured an article in the 1960s remembering the Whit Friday tradition in the area, and lamenting its demise. It was entitled, with a banner headline: 'Whit Friday Walks and the Joy They Brought Around the Oldham Area'. *The anonymous contributor wrote:* 'It was a lovely morning, and when I woke and saw that it was only 5.30am I wondered why I was awake so soon and why I felt so disappointed. Then I remembered, and somehow the brightness of the morning seemed to dim. It was Whit Friday – and we were not walking round. Well, it was no use getting up early now, there was nothing to look forward to, or to hurry for so I stayed where I was, and as I was too wide awake to go back to sleep, I passed the time thinking back over other Whit Fridays, regretting what we have lost, and like many other people, wondering "Why?" There were so many good years to remember too. For the last fifteen years all the Whit Fridays had been good ones, and even before that there had been all kinds of Whit Fridays, some good, some not so good, but none just plain FLAT as they are now.' *The article ended with the writer's lament:* 'I wonder if those who carelessly let Whit Fridays be "voted away" realised how long the tradition had survived.' The article emphasised what the Whit Friday Walks and holiday had meant to people in Oldham, and the surrounding districts, and the prominence given to it by the *'Oldham Evening Chronicle'* justified the writer's memories and lament, at its passing.

The Rochdale Whit Walks

The Whit Walks in Rochdale were traditionally held on Whit Friday. Their origin lay in the mid-19th century with the Sunday School movement. The vicar of Rochdale at this time was Dr Molesworth, an influential figure in the town, and a priest who gained some notoriety for his support of the then existing Church Rates system, which levied a rate on the town's people for church building, and repairs. This was a cause of religious and political division, the non-conformists being adamantly against the levy. The Church Rates were made optional in 1857 and abolished in 1894. Dr Molesworth's defence of the Church Rates led to violent protests in Rochdale and to the reading of the Riot Act in the town.

St. John the Baptist girls Rochdale start their 1960s Whit Walk in traditional dress. Photograph courtesy of M.E.N.

Five Pounds to Send the Vicar to Hell!

Dr Molesworth's critics produced a poster which offered 'Five Pounds Reward to anyone who will send the present vicar to Hell, and bring the old one back!' Dr Molesworth was undeterred from holding his position that Church Rates were the only way to finance England's parish churches, but his cause was to be ultimately lost. This was a priest whose great energy would have been behind the Established Church and its Sunday Schools in Rochdale, and who would have presided over the early Rochdale Whit Walks. The Whit Friday Walk, like those in other towns and villages, was only abandoned in Rochdale during the two World Wars. It eventually became an ecumenical procession with the Church of England and the Free Churches joining together. Those taking part in the town centre Walk, processed from their churches to the Town Hall Square, where the vicar of Rochdale led a service, which included the singing of hymns led by the bands. To have been present at a service led by Dr Molesworth during the Church Rates dispute, would have been interesting!

A member of St Peter's, Newbold, Audrey Carr, described the Whit Fridays in Rochdale in former times:
'The crowds of spectators in the centre of Rochdale were dense, and the day of the Whit Walks brought great excitement to everybody, but especially to the children who would be dressed in their new Whitsun finery. We walked from Newbold to the town centre, as did the other churches. At St Peter's we had our own St Peter's Church Lads' Brigade Band which proudly accompanied the procession in their smart uniforms. The sight of the Town Hall Square full of banners, bands and children was inspiring. The spectators who lined the route of the Walk, joined enthusiastically in the spirit of the day.'

The churches taking part, in the Rochdale Whit Walks included:
Rochdale Parish Church;
St Mary's in the Baum;
St James;
St Mary's, Balderstone;
St Peter's, Newbold;
St Luke's, Deeplish;
The Good Shepherd Church;
St Alban's Rochdale;
St Ann's, Belfield;
The Salvation Army and the Free Churches.

After the Walks the children would enjoy a Field Afternoon, with buns and milk. The Church of England, the Free Churches and the Roman Catholic Churches were all part of the Whitsun tradition in Rochdale and to the surrounding districts of Littleborough, Smallbridge, Shore, Milnrow, Wardle and Whitworth. The long history of the processions in Rochdale centre, was brought to an end in the late 1960s with the then government's decision to replace Whitsun as a public holiday, with a new Spring Bank Holiday. This affected traditional Whit Walks days in many of the towns and villages of Lancashire, and was part of the changes in life in the 1960s and 1970s which led to the demise of the Whitsun Festival as a community event of considerable significance.

Whitsun in Union Square, Bury

The Whit Walks in Bury originated in the mid-nineteenth century with the growth of the Sunday Schools in the town. The Church of England, Free Church and Roman Catholic processions were part of the life of the community from the 1860s, only being interrupted by the two World Wars, and even then not being completely abandoned.

The Whit Walks in the centre of Bury had traditionally taken place on Whit Friday, when the churches gathered in Union Square. After the Second World War this custom continued, and the processions were supported in strong numbers by walkers and spectators, throughout the 1950s and in the early 1960s. *'The Bury Times'* featured a description of Whit Friday in May 1964, indicating that the Whitsun Festival remained a significant part of the community's life, but speculating as to whether the walkers had gathered in Union Square for the last time. It headlined: 'Last Service in Union Square'. *The report continued:* 'Few of the thousands of spectators who thronged vantage viewpoints along the route chosen for the annual Whit Friday

All Saints Elton, Bury process with their banner in a 1970s Bury Whit Walk. Photograph courtesy of Bury Library

procession this year realised that history was being made in Bury. It was a historic occasion for the 2,000 members of Bury's Anglican Churches and the 2,500 members of the Non-Conformist Churches because the services which took place in Union Square could well be the last to be held on the traditional site.'

'As the Anglican Churches moved off from Union Square their places were taken by the members of 19 Non-Conformist Churches who took part in a combined service. Referring to the changes that were taking place in the area, the speaker, in a short address, told the 2,500 Non-Conformists and spectators: "This could be, I don't say it is, but it could be the last time we shall meet in this Square. What will happen next year is in the hands of the good people who plan for us. This could be a very historic occasion."

In and around Manchester

The *'Bury Times'* report of the 1964 procession gave a picture of a strong continuing tradition – but times were about to change. In 1967 the end of the Whitsun Bank Holiday in favour of the Spring Bank Holiday, presented the organisers of the Bury Whit Friday Walks with a difficult decision; added difficulties had to be faced with increased traffic in the town centre. It was decided to end the long tradition of Whit Friday processions, and hold future Walks on Whit Sunday. The *'Bury Times'* in February 1967, had the banner headline: 'The Last Whit Friday Walks'. It reported that the Church of England and the Free Churches would hold their processions on Sundays in the future, because the new Spring Band Holiday 'will cancel Whit Friday as a holiday for thousands of Bury workers'. The Bury clergy were assured that local companies would grant a holiday on Whit Friday 1967, but that this would be for the last time. In the last Whit Friday Walk the Church of England and the Free Churches walked together for only the second time, and 30 churches took part. The secretary of Bury Chamber of Commerce stated: 'We are recommending firms to observe the traditional holiday, but next year the Chamber will advise them to switch to the new Spring Holiday date.' 1967 saw the last Whit Friday Walk, and the switch to Sunday took place in the following year.

To Walk or Not to Walk – That is the Question!

Young Walkers take part in a 1970s Whit Walk in Bury.

From the outset of the new Sunday Walk, the question of its continuance was debated annually. In 1968 11 Church of England Churches and 15 Free Churches joined the procession, but over the next five years that number went down to five Church of England, and three Free Churches. In 1971 the Roman Catholic Churches decided not to continue with their annual procession. The churches normally involved, St Bede's, St Marie's, St Joseph's and the Guardian Angels, had walked with 6,000 people in their procession. The churches had discussed the problem of police supervision of the Walks before making the decision. The 'Bury Times' reported: 'Catholics not to hold Walks on police advice'. The 'Bury Times' stated that the rector of Bury, the Reverend J.R. Smith had observed 'that it had become increasingly difficult to hold the processions over the years because of road and traffic concerns, but that the Church of England would continue with the Whit Walks.' The Free Churches decided to continue their united Walk with the Church of England. Over the following six years the Church of England and Free Church Procession followed a modified route in their Whit Walk. It eventually took place on Whit Sunday, when the Roman Catholic Churches no longer walked on that day. In

1977 the 'Bury Times' headlined: 'Century old tradition fades out – No Whit Walks decision by churches.' The newspaper reported that a meeting of Free Church and Church of England representatives had decided to discontinue the Walks. Lack of support, increased traffic and police difficulty in marshalling the Walks were given as the reasons for the decision.

The report concluded: 'Only family photos are left to remind us of Bury's great Whit Fridays of the past, never to be forgotten, by those who shared the warmth and splendour of it all.'

The decision to end the time-honoured tradition of the Bury Whit Walks, produced a lively response in the Readers' Viewpoint Page of the 'Bury Times' in 1977. Some of the letters expressing opinions are quoted here. The Viewpoint column was headed: 'They Want to Continue the Walks.'

The first response was from a local clergyman:
'Your editorial in Tuesday's issue about the Whit Walks is the most balanced statement on the subject so far, but it still implies that the ending of the Walks is a universal decision made by all the churches. Surely it should be recorded that many churches wish to continue, and that there is strong feeling that the apathy and negative attitudes of some should not be taken as the feelings of the whole. If people wish to withdraw let them do so. No-one should be compelled to walk, neither should they be compelled not to walk.

From a Bury resident hoping that 'the decision might be reversed:
'I find myself at odds with the decision by church authorities to discontinue the Whitsuntide processions for by any measurement the Walks of 1976 were well supported by participating churches. The decline of public interest, which must be accepted, is not a valid reason for cancellation as spectator involvement is surely not the main purpose of the event. Granted movement of population in certain parts of the town has considerably reduced church attendance but the reverse is true in other areas, and surely smaller Sunday School classes are a good reason for holding a Procession of Witness rather than giving up this grand tradition in the face of apparent apathy in some places. Let us hope, therefore, that it is not too late to reverse the decision.'

A letter expressed the regret of a Bury Church member:
'May I express my deep regret at the passing of yet another of our well loved traditions, namely the annual Whit Walks. The decision to stop the Walks was not by any means unanimous; indeed a vote was not taken at the meeting on Friday, February, 25th which was "called with a view to establishing a permanent organising committee charged with the responsibility of continuing on an annual basis a United Procession of Witness." The traffic hazards have been given as the reason for not holding the Walks, yet, I have never felt there has been any danger at all; the police have always looked after us magnificently. There are two questions I would like to have answered for me, which were never answered at the meeting: Why can the streets be closed and the traffic stopped on a busy Saturday, without apparently any bother at all, for the carnival? Why are we told we are witnessing to our faith on Good Friday night,

when not more than 40 or 50 of us walk through some of the main streets of the town mainly deserted, and yet we are told we are not witnessing to anything or anyone when we have a joyous procession with hundreds of people taking part.'

Another reader stated that they were saddened at the end of a Tradition, and called for Christian discipleship:
'I was saddened to read of the decision of the Bury churches no longer to hold the Procession of Witness on Whit Sunday. Surely, in these days of diminishing congregations throughout the world, this is a time to stand up and be counted as Christians, not let another tradition fall by the wayside. It is a good thing that Christ did not let the traffic problems on the road to Jerusalem stop him. Or the fact that he had no support in the Garden of Gethsemane, the reasons given for not continuing the Whit Walks being traffic and lack of support. I only hope that the few churches who hold Processions of Witness around their own parishes will not be influenced by the decisions of others, but continue to walk behind their banners and Witness to Christ as did the disciples on the Day of Pentecost.'

A reader did not think that the Walks should be ended, and expressed that opinion forcefully:
'Of the eight Churches which took part last year in the Whitsun Processions five or six still want to walk. Those who don't use the excuse that it is not a procession of witness because no-one is watching. Agreed the number is not the same as it used to be but it is increasing. Yet some of these will walk on Good Friday when there are fewer people around. There were fewer Christians in the early Church but they did not give up. So Christians of Bury unite and don't let them take from us one of the few traditions that is left.'

Walking Days and Whit Walks in Wigan and District

Christine Ross, of Wigan Museum, traces the Walking Day tradition in the town, back to the 1870s and 1880s. She states: 'These were the times of the cotton mills and cotton was available for the dresses of the girls who took part in what was originally the "Beating of the Bounds" by the various churches.' The Beating of the Bounds was a custom whereby parish churches processed around the boundaries of the parishes which they served. This annual observance evolved into Whit Walks and Walking Days in Wigan and surrounding districts. As elsewhere, the Church Sunday Schools became the major participants, and the clergy of the late nineteenth century were instrumental in their growth and in the development of the Walks. *Christine*

The Sacred heart RC Procession in a Wigan Walking Day.

Ross states: 'The clergy, and especially the rector of Wigan, were figures of authority and influence to whom people deferred.' In Wigan and district the Church of England and the Free Churches held their own individual processions; usually in late June or early July. These were known as "Walking Days". The Roman Catholic Church had its processions on Whit Monday, which were described as "Whit Walks". In the Church of England, over the decades, the churches involved were:-

The Parish Church, All Saints;
St George;
St Catherine (Scholes);
St Thomas;
St James (Poolstock);
Christ Church (Ince);
St Andrew;
St Michael and All Angels;
St Mark (Newtown);
St Mary (Ince);
St Stephen (Whelley);
St Anne (Beech Hill).

Over a wider part of the area, churches held Walking Days at: Abram, Platt Bridge, Ashton-in-Makerfield, Pemberton, Haigh, Hindley, Aspull, Shevington, Up Holland, New Springs, Billinge and Standish. Many of the churches had more than one procession each year. Some of the churches walked on consecutive days; others had processions on three successive days.

Christine Ross relates the time in her childhood when she was due, with full Sunday School attendance marks, to 'Lead Out' in front of the main banner at Platt Bridge. She remembers: 'I fell sick with scarlet fever, but my parents raised me to the front window of our house on pillows, to watch the procession pass by. I had a great Walking Day because St Nathaniel's stopped for me, and the members of the church gave me gifts of money!'

St. Luke's Orrell, Walking Day.

Christine Ross observed: 'In the Wigan area, people would bring chairs out from their houses for folk watching the processions to sit on – a strong community spirit prevailed in those days.' In 1980 the Church of England parishes in the Wigan Deanery met at the Market Square, and processed through the town centre of Wigan in a United Walking Day.

Whit Monday Wigan R.C. Procession

The Wigan Roman Catholic Churches held a United Whit Walk on Whit Monday each year. The churches taking part in an impressive procession through the town centre included:-

St John's;
St Mary's;
St Joseph's;
St Patrick's.
Roman Catholic Walks were also held in Hindley, Orrell, Billinge, Standish, Aspull and Ashton-in-Makerfield.

The Free Churches

The Free Churches in and around Wigan held their own Walking Days. These contributed to the tradition of Whit Walks and Walking Days, established more than one hundred years ago. The town centre Walks have been discontinued, but processions still take place in some of the surrounding communities, though without the numbers, and the support of former times.

Bolton and District Walking Days

The 'Bolton Chronicle' newspaper of June 1829, reported that a procession of churches had taken place in Bolton town centre, and that a lunch had been provided for the children afterwards. The article in the newspaper called for all the schools in Bolton to join in an annual procession, to combat Kersal Moor a 'place of vicious resort'. Kersal Moor was the venue of Manchester Races, and they were considered by the churches, to be one of the evils of the time. A churchman stated: 'Kersal Moor is a place where Youth cannot go without coming away with a loss of that moral and religious feeling which it is the province of the Sunday Schools to instill.' The Bolton churches and their Sunday Schools responded to Kersal Races, and the other temptations of the day, with Walking Day processions. In 1838 12,391 Sunday School children walked in Bolton processions. It is recorded that by the 1870s processions had become an annual tradition in Bolton. In 1876 the Roman Catholic churches of the town walked on Trinity Sunday, with 16,000 children.

Sunday Schools' Centenary Celebrations

In the booklet 'Bolton Church of England Sunday Schools' Centenary Celebrations' there is an account of the Celebration Procession, held in Bolton town centre on July 3rd, 1880:
'The schools gathered in the Town Hall Square, and processed through the main streets of the town. They carried many glittering banners, of tasteful, rich, beautiful and bewildering brilliance. Bunting decorated the route, with slogans such as "Success to the churches" hanging from private and public buildings. As the 7,000 children walked along Deansgate to Chorley New Road, the bells of all the churches pealed in glorious unison.' *The report concluded:* The day was somewhat marred by a sudden heavy shower as the procession came to its end.'

The churches taking part were:-
The Parish Church – St Peter;
All Saints';
St George;
Holy Trinity;
St Mark;
St James;
St Luke;
St Paul, Deansgate;
Emmanuel Church;
All Souls';
St Paul, Halliwell;
St Paul, Astley Bridge;
St Matthew;
St Bartholomew;
St George the Martyr;
Christ Church;
Walmsley Church;
Eagley Mills Mission.

The Bolton Church Sunday Schools gather in the Town Hall Square to celebrate the Sunday Schools Centenary in 1880.
Photograph courtesy of Bolton Library.

As the churches prepared to leave the Town Hall Square, thousands of young voices joined in the 'Old Hundreth' led by Ringley Band. Bolton Parish Church led the 1880 procession with 1,800 children in its Sunday School. The Free Churches had their own 1880 centenary celebrations and procession, with 12,820 children walking through Bolton centre; an indication of the strength of non-conformity in nineteenth century Bolton. The Church of England Sunday Schools ended their centenary celebration of the Sunday School movement with a United Service in St George's Church attended by St Mark's, St Matthew's and 3,000 children. The vicar of St Mark's, Bolton, the Reverend J.G. Doman ended the service with these words: 'With the Blessing of God, good results will surely come from our Centenary Celebration Procession.' The congregation sang the hymn: 'Crown Him with Many Crowns' and the organist played, as a voluntary, the 'Hallelujah Chorus!'

A Defence of The Processions

In his own Church of St Mark, the Reverend Doman, a priest who believed in the beauty of holiness, and who was an Anglo Catholic or 'High Churchman' defended the children's processions against the objections of some church people. The critics alleged that the Centenary Walking Day gave a false impression of Church commitment. That the bands played 'worldly' tunes; the processions displayed 'political overtones' and that the 'moral behaviour' of some in the procession could be questionable! The Reverend Doman countered that: 'The Sunday Schools were a mighty force for good and that the processions were a worthy way of celebrating them. 'He stated that: 'The Centenary Celebration had included solemn worship and prayer, but that the children, who were not governed by adult logic, needed to participate, and the processions helped them to do so with a thrill of joy.' Whit Walks and Walking Days have always had their critics, and likewise they have had their defenders, such as the Reverend Doman. The war years saw the Bolton processions discontinued. After the Second World War they were re-started in the late 1940s and they continued into the 1970s. The Roman Catholic Procession, on Trinity Sunday, came to an end in 1974, and many of the Church of England, and of the Free Church Walks have been discontinued. Difficulties with traffic, the cost of the bands and the general change in society, with lack of community involvement, are cited as the reasons for the tradition's demise.

Walking Days between Wigan and Bolton

In many of the towns and villages between Wigan and Bolton there has been a tradition of annual Walking Days. Some continue, others have come to an end. Wigan Museum has a record of all the villages and towns which held Walking Days, and of the churches which took part in them. In former times they would have been major community events, dating back into the nineteenth century. Where they continue, they have usually become ecumenical processions with all the churches walking together.

Leigh Area Walks

In Leigh, churches in the Walks included:-
St Mary's Parish Church;
St Bartholomew's Church;
Christ Church, Pennington;
St John's Church;
St Peter's, Westleigh;
St Paul's, Westleigh;
St Thomas, Bedford;
Bethesda Free Church;
Leigh Wesleyean Church;
Our Lady of the Rosary R.C. Church;
St Joseph's, Bedford R.C. Church;
The Apostles, Westleigh.
St Stephen, Astley;

St George, Tyldsley;
St John, Hindley Green;
St John, Mosley Common;
St Paul, Little Hulton;
St Thomas, Golborne;
Hindley Presbyterian Church;
New Jerusalem Church, Tyldsley;
The Top Chapel, Tyldsley
and Lamberhead Green Wesleyan Church.

Such traditional Walking Days in the Bolton and Wigan areas, would have been replicated in every town and village.

The town of Atherton, half-way between Bolton and Wigan had a long tradition of processions. The three Church of England churches – Atherton Parish Church, and its mission churches, St George's and St Philip's – the Free Churches and the Roman Catholic Church, took part in Walking Day processions through the centre of the town. There were Walking Days in the neighbouring villages of Hindsford and of Howe Bridge.

Atherton, Hindsford and Howe Bridge Processions

Walking Days in Atherton were, by tradition, held on the third weekend of June each year. On the Saturday of that weekend, the Free Churches had their procession, and on the Sunday, Atherton Parish Church, and its two mission churches walked. St Richard's Roman Catholic Church had its own procession. The separate Anglican, and Free Church Walks were impressive events. The processions walked along Atherton's main Market Street, which would be lined with spectators. The Anglican Procession, had three bands, with many banners, and it included the children of Atherton's three Church of England schools:- St Georges Primary School; St Philip's Primary School; and Hesketh Fletcher Secondary School. In the late 1960s, St Richard's Roman Catholic Church ended its Walking Day. The Anglicans and the Free Churches joined together in an ecumenical procession in 1976. This was held, on police advice on the Sunday, when the churches were informed that if they walked together on the same day, they could have the town 'without constraint'.

St. George's Church, Atherton, walk through the town in a 1980s Walking Day.
Photograph courtesy of J. Bunting.

The churches walking in the United Procession were:-
Atherton Parish Church – St John's;
St George's;
St Philip's;
Bag Lane Methodist Church;
Atherton Independent Methodist Church;
Central Methodist Church;
Alma Street Methodist Church;
The Atherton Salvation Army Citadel;
Atherton Baptist Church;
Atherton Unitarian Church.

At first, the three Anglican Churches walked as one group, but in 1978 they dispersed throughout the procession. The format was introduced of a different church leading the Walk each year. In 1994 the Church of the Nazarene joined in the procession, but thereafter all of the Free Church, with the exception of Bag Lane Methodist Church, decided not to join in the Walking Day. The last 'traditional' Walking Day in Atherton ended in 1999. It was then decided that all of the Atherton Churches would join in a Millennium Celebration procession. This event was held in September of that year. A new format was adopted. There were no individual church banners. One, 'Churches Together' banner, and one band, led an informal Walk with people taking a place anywhere in the procession. This new style of outdoor witness ended after three years.

It seems that wherever the traditional Walks are changed, the end result is their demise. In Atherton, one church, Bag Lane Methodist, has kept to the Walking Day tradition, processing on its own through the town centre with banner and band. Those who fear the disappearance of the Walking Day, and Whit Walk tradition, walk with them in spirit!

Jim Bunting, a Churchwarden at St George's Mission Church in Atherton, comments:
'In 2012 St George's Church celebrated its centenary with a traditional procession around the lower Hag Fold part of Atherton, which St George's Church serves.'

Howe Bridge Village Walks Remembered

In the booklet 'Howe Bridge Remembered' Edna Aspden-Lee wrote:
'Walking Day was a very special time in the life of the village. St Michael's Church and Sunday School walked, along a fixed route as an act of faith. We processed along the Wigan Road as far as the Punch Bowl Public House, and then down Leigh Road to the school room. At the school we had a tea party of sandwiches, jelly and cakes. One of the Sunday School teachers owned a coal cart. It was huge, and it was drawn by a large horse. The cart was decorated and the little children and elderly folk rode on it. After our Walking Day tea, we went in family groups to the cricket field next to the vicarage. The band that had led the procession came into the field, and some people danced to the music it provided. The small shops in the village provided toy and ice cream stalls. Children joined in the games, including one of their own, devising called 'Pull over the stick', a very popular game. The

church wardens at that time arranged sporting events on the field, including races, in which the children took part. If the weather was unkind, and we were unfortunate we would carry on the celebrations in the school hall. The band would come into the hall and entertain us. Everyone wore their best clothes for the Walking Day, no matter how poor the family was. Children were turned-out in very pretty clothes for this day. I was a Brownie, and later a Girl Guide, and so I wore a uniform. The Sunday School football team members joined in the Walk. It was a very special day for everyone in the village, and the town. All the streets on the route were lined with spectators and some houses hung out Union flags.'

Hindsford Walking Day

Douglas Fairhurst, who now lives in Oxfordshire, writes about the village of Hindsford, and its Walking Days in his youth:

'The parish of St Anne, Hindsford, lies exactly between the two townships of Atherton and Tyldesley in South Lancashire and is part of the Diocese of Manchester. It is an ecclesiastical district and, as such, does not appear on any official maps. The original church was a small brick built mission and served the mining community from about the 1860s until it was decided that a more substantial building was needed at the end of the 1890s. A design by the firm of Austin and Paley was chosen and work started in clearing the site on Tyldesley Road in 1898. The foundation stone was laid in 1899 and the church was completed and dedicated in June 1901. From the start it was a very popular parish and had strong ties with Hindsford Church of England Infant and Junior School situated in Green Street. This school opened in 1899 and was used by many organisations in the village for various social activities.'

'I was born in 1942 and my memories of Walking Days date from 1949. I attended the school and, when I was seven years old, I became a member of the church choir. As well as singing the morning and evening services, we played a major part in the procession. Walking Day was always on the last Sunday in June, which coincided with the end of the school year and the start of the annual Wakes holidays. A great deal of preparation was done in the weeks before the big day. Meetings were held by the various groups, such as the Sunday School, Cubs and Boy Scouts, Mothers' Union and the Church of England Mens' Society. All were given a specific part in the procession and in the case of the Sunday School, a decision had to be made as to the colour of the dress material to be used. An important part of the procession, was the appearance of brass bands. There were many local bands in the surrounding districts, but they had to be paid for. The money needed for this was raised by voluntary contributions from members of the village. For many years, my mother was treasurer for the Mothers' Union and she volunteered to do this task. She would start the collection street by street each

St. Anne's Hindsford Walking Day in the 1950s. Photograph courtesy of D. Fairhurst

week from the beginning of May and of course took me with her, as my father would be at work in the local mine, Chanters Colliery. Everyone was very generous, including the members of the Roman Catholic Church. This collection was important as the amount raised decided whether we had one or two bands.'

St. Anne's Hindsford Walking Day in the 1950s. Douglas Fairhurst is the second chorister on the left.

'Come the big day and we all assembled. After a prayer the procession set off. Heading the procession would be two Walk marshalls, and for many years my father was one of these before he became verger. Following them would be the first of the brass bands. This was usually Tyldesley Prize Band, led for many years by a drum major who was a relative of my grandmother. He was a great attraction as he used to swing his drum major's staff and also throw it up in the air. There was a trolley bus route through the village which ran between Leigh and Swinton and all the people watching always hoped that his staff would get caught in the overhead wires, but it never did. After the band came the main banner, which had a picture of the church on the front and was hooked onto two large poles. It was carried by a team of four men and they always hoped for a fine day with little wind. They always had a tricky time turning round at either end of the boundaries. The streamers attached to the banner were held by those who had been confirmed that year and was seen as a great honour. Next came the church choir, lay reader and the vicar with his two church wardens carrying their staffs of office, followed by the kindergarten with their small banner and then senior Sunday School. The second brass band lead the Mothers' Union and then the Cubs and Boy Scouts, the Church of England Mens' Society brought up the rear. As well as going round the streets, the procession went along the main Tyldesley Road. As the event was on a Sunday afternoon, the police closed this road to traffic, for about an hour and a half. One of the traditions of the Walk was that people watching would give money to the children taking part. In the austere years in the 1940s and 1950s this generous gift was very welcome and was also appreciated by the local corner shops, especially those that sold sweets.

The Walk finished on a field belonging to a local farmer. After a welcome meal of sandwiches, cakes, tea and pop games were organised. It always seemed that we had a sunny day for the Walking Day. Sadly, with the advent of television and more people having cars, this event became less and less popular and because the police were no longer able to close the main road, the event ended.'

Walks in Cheshire

Just outside the Lancashire boundary in the towns and districts of Hyde and Stockport, there were traditional Whit Walks. In some parishes Walks go on in these areas across the county border in Cheshire, but in others they have been discontinued.

Other Walks and Walking Days

These happen in many Lancashire towns and villages outside the Manchester area, for example, Chorley, Warrington, Accrington, Nelson, Colne, Padiham, Croston, and Tarleton.

Many of these Walks are now ecumenical witnessing to the unity of Christians.

Having looked at the origin and development of Whit Walks and the memories of them, we now consider their future. The most impressive of these retain the traditional dates and format for Walks and are ecumenical.

Chapter 9 - Epilogue

Whit Walks And Walking Days
– Have They A Future?

In chapter one we traced the first Whit Walk back to Manchester on Whit Monday 1801. This Church of England procession became the forerunner of, and the model for, other Whit Walks in the Manchester area, and for Walking Days throughout Lancashire. Whit Monday 1801 began a tradition which continues in Manchester city centre at Whitsun and in parts of Greater Manchester on other dates. As we have noted the Walks no longer take place in some of the areas where there had been a tradition of processions. Where the Walks go on, they have usually declined in pageantry, and in the numbers taking part, since their heyday. The Walks began in different communities, at different times in the nineteenth century. That many of them survived into the 1980s and 1990s – and that some still go on today, is a testimony to the strength of this tradition, and its impact on people's lives, as expressed in the numerous memories of the Walks recalled in this book.

Why have the Walks, generally declined? Twenty-first century society is different from that of the nineteenth century era, which gave birth to the Whit Walks, and different from the first half of the twentieth century which sustained them. In our own times, churches, through their Sunday Schools, are no longer the sole providers of education, welfare and leisure. The Sunday Schools, where they remain part of church life, now attract only a minority of children. Priority in the use of the roads is given to un-interrupted traffic flow, and some processions have had to be re-routed, or ended. In the inner-areas of cities and towns, once the strongest communities involved in the Walks, there has been population movement with re-housing. This has resulted in the closure of many churches and chapels. In the past fifty years the growth of materialism has weakened faith commitment, and community spirit. These factors have conspired together against the tradition of the Whit Walks.

A spectator at a recent procession lamented this saying: 'In the old days we had nothing in material terms, but in Church life, and Community Spirit, we had everything!'

In her book about Sunday Schools in Ashton-under-Lyne, Mary Whitehead writes:
'Victorian values perceived the poorer classes as sinners who could be "saved" by instilling in them Christian moral values.' In the early nineteenth century, Industrialists supported the Sunday Schools in the expectation, that they would teach their workers, discipline, honesty and punctuality. In those days when the French Revolution was still fresh in memory, some in the governing establishment were not in favour of the Sunday Schools educating workers and their children, fearing that this would lead to demands for improvement in their condition. That the Sunday School movement accepted the challenge of educating the poor, along with providing welfare and leisure, made it a real force for good, in times when State education, and welfare was non-existent.'

In 1867 Sir James Kay Shuttleworth stated: 'Long before enlightened statesmen, and leaders of public opinion, called for the education of the people, the congregation of the churches, through their Sunday Schools, began it.'

From Pilgrimage to Celebration!

What was the Whit Walk in its origin? It was, first of all, the child of the Sunday School movement. The first 1801 Manchester Whit Walk could be described as a pilgrimage. A 'pilgrimage' is a 'journey to a holy place'. The first Whit Walk was a journey (a walk) to a holy place to worship, at Manchester's ancient Collegiate Church – now its Cathedral. Pilgrimages are probably thought to be solemn events. Pilgrimages in medieval England were lively affairs. The Whit Walks, with their martial bands, were not solemn acts of witness, but they ended with worship at a holy place. Later they came to be regarded as occasions for remembering the life, and the achievement of the Sunday School movement. The Whit Walks were processions of lively, Christian witness, expressed through colour and pageantry. Banners were carried; bands played; the spectators applauded (this was unique to Manchester's Walks) and thousands of smiling faces were to be seen in the processions, and along their route. The Whit Walks, were for many, a fitting celebration of God's life – giving Holy Spirit, which the Festival of Whitsun commemorates!

Were the Walks an Effective Witness?

Over the history of the Walks, some have questioned if they were effective acts of Christian Witness. In 1880, the then vicar of St Mark's, Bolton, answered the critics, by defending the processions, and their unique form of celebratory and colourful witness. Others have shared his opinion, including amongst their number, no less a figure than Archbishop William Temple, when he was the Bishop of Manchester. Some may say that silent, and solemn outdoor processions are more effective acts of witness. There is no evidence to support such a claim.

Church Outreach Today?

Is there a place for outdoor church processions, like the Whit Walks, in the present times? Secular processions still attract crowds of spectators. There are pageants, parades, carnivals and fetes throughout the country. In Manchester city centre there are now parades on 'Manchester Day' and on other occasions. For two centuries the churches have been involved in outdoor processions in Manchester and elsewhere in Lancashire.

In a local booklet 'The History of Wythenshawe', the author records that Whit Walks set the pattern for community events in the newly built housing estate of Wythenshawe, outside Manchester. The author states: 'The churches have had a lot to teach communities about the beauty and pageantry of outdoor processions, and this was the case in early Wythenshawe.'

It would seem right for church processions to continue, along with the secular parades of today. Despite the difficulties that change has brought for the churches over the past fifty years, it remains their calling to reach out into their communities. Hanging from the walls of many Manchester churches are Whit Walks and Walking Day banners, which are no longer carried out into the community in church processions. The banners are a reminder of the Church's outreach in the past, and a challenge to its continuance in the present. Some churches now have different forms of outreach than the Whit Walks and Walking Days. Where the Walks still have a place in the annual calendar of events, they remain a strong tradition for the people whose lives they have been a part of. The keeping of tradition because it is 'tradition' should not be dismissed. The British Constitution, Monarchy and Parliament hold to many aspects of tradition, because they are 'tradition'. The Whit Walks and Walking Days continue in some places today, because they are traditional, but also in order to remember, and celebrate, the spiritual and social achievements of the Sunday School movement, and to witness to the Christian Faith which inspired it. Where Whit Walks are well presented; carried out in their traditional form, properly supported and organised with commitment and enthusiasm, they can continue to be a lively, joyful and colourful act of Christian Witness.

Manchester's "Whit Monday" Procession 1801 to -------?

In this book we began with the history and memories of Manchester's Whit Monday Procession, and those of other Whit Walks, which were inspired by it as the first Whit Walk. In Manchester the Roman Catholic Procession of Whit Friday ended in the 1980s. It would be the cause of sadness to many people if the Church of England Walk also came to an end. This would see the great Whit Walk tradition in the city disappear. There are formidable challenges to its continuation. Traffic will increase, and the planned extensions to the Metrolink tram service will close further city centre roads to processions and parades. It is unfortunate that pedestrianised streets are not available for processions because of their fixed furnishings. With moveable street furnishing 'pedestrian ways' could have been used for processions, and parades, without disrupting traffic and allowing Mancunians to take part in community celebrations in their city centre. In these changed times, the hope of a significant number of people would be that Manchester's unique Whit Walk tradition could be maintained and renewed.

Churches Together?

In some towns and villages where the Walks have been renewed they have become ecumenical 'Churches Together' events. This has given them the added purpose of expressing the unity of Christians. Saddleworth and Mossley and other processions are examples of all the churches walking together – Church of England, Free Church and Roman Catholic – along the same route, and on the same day. That this has not happened in the centre of Manchester is perhaps due to a past history of strong denominational loyalty on the part of the different churches. In these ecumenical times this is a cause of regret; a United Walk could revive the tradition. Earlier in this book we noted that Canon Stanley Meadows, writing in the 1970s, asked the question: 'Whither the Whit Walks?' and that he stated that he should 'hate to see such a great tradition simply fizzle out.' The hope would be, that if the Whit Walks in Manchester

At St. Paul's Bennett Street Sunday School, the children were taught by people "who were giants in their lives". On the closure of the Bennett Street Sunday School, its banner was placed behind the altar at St. Paul's Church, New Cross, which was itself closed in the 1970s.
Photograph courtesy of E. Cox.

city centre, ever came to an end, they would do so with a bang rather than with a whimper. This would fittingly remember all those who have been part of this great tradition since 1801, and it would commemorate those who gave of themselves in the Sunday School movement. The people who taught the children the Faith; who organised community events and excursions to the countryside, and the seaside, and who became significant figures in the memories of those whose lives they touched and moulded and to whom they gave education, and welfare.

When St Paul's Sunday School, Bennett Street in New Cross, closed its doors for the last time in the 1960s, a service was held in St Paul's Church to give thanks for the life and work of Bennett Street Sunday School. There was a full congregation, and the preacher at the service, the rector of St Paul's, the Reverend George Henshaw said: 'Those of you who attended Bennett Street Sunday School, were taught, and cared for in many ways, by people who were "Giants in your lives!" Many former Sunday School children remember the 'Giants in their lives', with Thanks to God.

Imagine the Heyday Again!

The Saddleworth poet, Ammon Wrigley, wrote in his later years, that sometimes as he walked in the villages, and on the hills of Saddleworth, he imagined again the great Whit Walks of his moorland childhood.

Should Manchester's city centre Whit Walks sadly one day reach a final end, many Mancunians, and Salfordians, may imagine as they pass through the city, that they see again the be-ribboned banners dipping in the breeze. Hear again the hymns resounding around Albert Square from thousands of young voices; and thrill again to the marches of the many bands.

They may imagine, that they are Walking again, with Banners and Bands!

Appendix 1

The General Arrangements and Instructions for Whit Monday

1. It is suggested that no child under the age of seven years be allowed to walk in the procession, and that not less than one teacher be appointed to every twenty-four scholars. The scholars must be formed six abreast by the Superintendent and teachers on leaving their respective schools, this order being maintained throughout the procession, but they must not occupy the whole of the carriageway. A clear space of at least a yard should be available between the spectators on the footpath and the outer flanks of the procession to allow for free passage of Ambulance workers and Police Officers. Uniformed Youth Organisations may walk four abreast.
No school to arrive in Albert Square before 8.00 a.m.

2. Each school must enter Albert Square by the street set opposite it's name on the Procession Order, and upon arrival will be directed to it's position by one of the Marshalls. Schools will face the Town Hall. Scholars must not wander aimlessly about the Square.

3. Bands must cease playing before entering Albert Square, and then be formed close to, but not upon the footpath in front of the Town Hall, at the heads of the column in which their schools are placed.

4. Singing in the Square. All schools are to reach Albert Square not later than 9 a.m. At 9.10 a.m. the usual singing will commence and will include Onward Christian Soldiers, The Church's One Foundation, All People that on Earth do Dwell, the National Anthem will conclude the singing, after Prayers and the Blessing. The singing will be led from a raised platform at the front of the Town Hall, using a white flag as a baton. A sustained chord will be played by the bands appointed and the singing must begin at the following beat of the baton.

5. The Procession will leave the Square at 9.30 a.m. by the usual route to the Cathedral. Divine Service in the Cathedral will commence at 10.15 a.m., and conclude at 11 a.m. It is requested that bands cease playing when passing the Cathedral during the Service.

6. These are a precise statement of the Arrangements and Instructions for the Walk. The streets used by the various churches to enter the Square, as directed by the Organising Committee, were Cross Street, South Street and Brazennose Street.

Appendix 2

Whit Sunday District Processions

In Openshaw:
St Barnabas;
St Clement, Higher Openshaw;
Openshaw Salvation Army Citadel.
In Audenshaw:
St Stephen;
St Hilda;
Bridge Street Congregational Church.
In Clayton:
St Cross;
North Road Methodist Church;
St Matthew, Seymour Road;
Carver Hall Manchester City Mission Church.
In Harpurhey:
St Stephen's;
Christ Church.
In Newton Heath and Failsworth:
All Saint's;
St Wilfrid's;
St Mary's R.C. Church;
St John's;
Culcheth Methodist Church;
Newton Heath Methodist Church;
Newton Heath Evangelical Church.
In Denton and Reddish:
Christ Church, Denton;
St Mary's R.C. Church, Denton;
Manchester Road Methodist Church;
Wilton Street Chapel;
St Agnes, Reddish;
St Elisabeth, Reddish.
In Salford and District:
St Mark's R.C. Church, Swinton;
Irlam Congregational Church;
Barton Methodist Church;
Patricroft Methodist Church;
St John's, Pendlebury;
St John's Mission, Irlams-o-th-Height;
Charlestown Congregational Church;
St Patrick's R.C. Church.

In Gorton:
St George, Abbey Hey;
St Philip;
St James;
All Saints;
St Mark's.
In Dukinfield:
Crescent Road Congregational Church;
St Mary's Roman Catholic Church;
Wellington Street Methodist Church;
St Mark's;
Foundry Street Methodist Church.
In Longsight:
St Clement's;
North Road Methodist Church.
In Levenshulme:
St Peter's;
St Andrew's;
St Mark's.
In the Edge Lane area of Droylsden:
St Andrew's;
Edge Lane Methodist Church.
In Hyde:
Rosemount Methodist Church;
Flowery Field Church;
Talbot Road Methodist Church.
In Ashton Under Lyne:
St Mary's R.C. Church;
St John's Church;
St Ann's R.C. Church.
In Farnworth and Walkden:
Ellesmere Street Methodist Church;
Albert Road Congregational Church;
New Jerusalem Sunday School;
Walkden Congregational Church.
In Rochdale:
St John the Baptist;
St Vincent's R.C. Church;
St Stephen's, Swinton.

In Crumpsall and Heaton Park:
St Thomas, Crumpsall;
St Margaret's, Heaton Park;
Besses O-th-Barn New Church;
Heaton Park Congregational Church;
Besses-O-th-Barn Congregational Church.
In Oldham and Chadderton:
Chadderton Congregational Church;
St Mary's R.C. Church;

Pitt Street East Baptist Church;
Union Street Methodist Church;
Church of the Nazarene, York Street;
Sacred Heart R.C. Church, Derker;
St James, Derker;
St Paul's;
St Mark's, Glodwick;
St Barnabas;
St Luke's Chadderton;
Holy Trinity, Bardsley.
In Royton and Shaw:
St Paul's Methodist Church;
Oldham Road Baptist Church;
All Saints' Church.

In Bury:
St Bede's R.C. Church;
Our Lady's R.C. Church;
St Joseph's R.C. Church.
In the Langley Estate, Middleton:
All Saints' and Martyrs Church.
In Wythenshawe:
St Luke's, Benchill;
St John's and St Thomas R.C. Church, Benchill;

Roundthorn Hall Sunday School;
Benchill Congregational Church;
St Aidan's R.C. Church, Northern Moor;
Brownley Green Methodist Church.
In Hulme:
St Philip.
In Hollinwood:
Corpus Christ R.C. Church;
Holy Family R.C. Church.
In Heywood:
St James;
St Margaret, Darnhill.

Appendix 3

Whit Friday Procession Arrangements
April 22nd, 1904

'The Marshalls of the Procession beg you will submit to our Congregations on the next two Sundays the following regulations for the greater good of all concerned. They have been agreed to by the rectors at their meeting:-

1. That children under six years of age are not to take part in the Procession.
2. That only the Crossbearer, and four Acolytes accompanying may wear Cassocks and Cottas.
3. That the time scheduled for entering the Square is to be strictly observed.
4. That no persons are to leave the ranks in which they enter the Square until the Hymn 'Faith of our Fathers' has been sung. It is requested that this law be absolutely kept.
5. That care be taken to watch the Conductor after the bugles have sounded and maintain silence. The air of the Hymn will be played through once by the Bands, after which all will join in the singing, men and boys with heads uncovered.

6. The Marshalls, both in Albert Square and along the route, will wear a silver star.
7. The direction as to marching four deep along the tram-lines needs to be insisted on.

The Procession Marshalls.

Appendix 4

The Churches of the Whit Friday Procession

St John's Cathedral Church, Chapel Street, Salford.
School numbers (1965) 293
Bands: Little Hulton Pipe Band
           Gravel Lane Band
           British Rail Manchester Band.

St Boniface, Whit Lane, Lower Broughton.
School numbers (1965) 450
Band: Cheetham Hill Prize Band.

St Peter's, Greengate, Salford.
School numbers (1965) 104
Band: Prestwich Borough Band.
St Peter's has now been closed.

St Sebastian, Pendleton.
School numbers (1965) 325
Bands: St Sebastian's Pipe Band
           Wigan Boys' Band.

Mother of God and St James, Ellor Street, Salford.
School numbers (1965) 800
Bands: Burnage Prize Band
           Lofthouse Colliery Band.

St Joseph's, Ellesmere Street, Salford.
School numbers (1965) 500
Bands: Irlam Public Band
           St Joseph's Fife Band.

Mount Carmel, Ordsall Lane, Salford.
School numbers (1965) 250
Bands: 123 Field Regiment T.A.
           Our Lady's Pipe Band.
Mount Carmel Church is now closed.

In and around Manchester

St Thomas, Higher Broughton.
School numbers (1965) 1,565
Bands: St Thomas Pipe Band
            St Thomas Boys' Band
            Banks Brass Band

St Chad's, Cheetham Hill Road.
School numbers (1965) 410
Band: Lindley Band.
St Chad's originally stood in Rook Street off Piccadilly. It was rebuilt in Cheetham.

Ukrainian Society, Bury Old Road.
'Band':   Ukrainian Male Choir.

St Edmund, Miles Platting.
School numbers (1965) 400
Bands: Middleton Band
            Kearsley Silver Prize Band.
St Edmund's is now closed.

St Patrick, Livesey Street, Collyhurst.
School numbers (1965) 700
Bands: Terrence McSweeney Pipe Band
            Blackley Prize Band
            St Patrick's Girls' Band

St Malachy, Rochdale Road, Collyhurst.
School numbers (1965) 500
Bands: Thornleigh Bolton Salesian Band
            Beswick Prize Band
            St Malachy's Pipe Band.

Corpus Christi, Varley Street, Miles Platting.
School numbers (1965) 490
Bands: Corpus Christi Drum and Fife Band
            Manchester Central Band.
Corpus Christi is now closed.

St Vincent, Ashton Old Road, Openshaw.
School numbers (1965) 200
Bands: All Souls' Ancoats Band
            St John's Oldham Pipe Band.
St Vincent is now closed.

St Willibrord, North Road, Clayton.
School numbers (1965) 400
Bands: New Mills Old Prize Band
           Droylsden District Band.

St Brigid's, Mill Street, Bradford.
School numbers (1965) 240
Bands: Oldham Band
           Pointon Band.
St Brigid's has been re-built on Grey Mare Lane, Bradford.

St Anne's Carruthers Street, Ancoats.
School numbers (1965) 750
Bands: St Anne's Pipe Band
           St Anne's Brass Band.
St Anne's has been re-built on the same site.

St Aloysius, Ardwick Green.
School numbers (1965) 503
Bands: Ardwick Silver Band
           Hollingworth Prize Band
           Rose Fletcher Pipe Band
           Scots' Guards Association Band.
St Aloysius is now closed.

Holy Name, Oxford Road.
School numbers (1965) 800
Bands: Wythenshawe Prize Band
           Prince Charles Edward Pipe Band

Our Lady's, Moss Side.
School numbers (1965) 100
Band: New Mills Prize Band

St Wilfrid, Hulme.
School numbers (1965) 609
Bands: Central Manchester Band
           Duke of Lancaster's Own Yeomann Band
St Wilfrid is now closed.

St Augustine's, Granby Row; York Street and All Saints, Chorlton on Medlock.
School numbers (1965) 180
Bands: St Anthony's, Woodhouse Park Pipe Band
           Black Dyke Junior Band.
St Augustine's originally stood in Granby Row. It was re-built in York Street, but destroyed by enemy action in the Second World War. A third St Augustine's replaced the Holy Family Church at All Saints, Chorlton on Medlock.

The Polish Society, Church of Divine Mercy, Moss Side.
Band: Brian Boru Pipe Band.

St Anne's, Adelphi, Salford.
Church closed.

St Alban, Fawcett Street, Ancoats.
St Alban's stood just off Great Ancoats Street.
It was closed and demolished in the 1960s.

St Michael's George, Leigh Street, Ancoats.
School numbers (1965) 153
Bands: The Kerry Pipers Band.
St Michael is now closed.

The Italian Society.
Originating in part of Ancoats, known as 'Little Italy'.
Joined St Michael's, Ancoats, in the Procession. The Italian Society with St Michael's held a second procession through part of the city centre and Ancoats on Trinity Sunday evenings.

St William, Simpson Street, Angel Meadow.
Church closed in the 1930s.
School numbers in 1840 - 1050.

St Casimir, Pilling Street, Collyhurst.
The church closed in the 1920s.

St Joseph's Industrial School, Longsight.
Now closed.

St Mary's, Mulberry Street, Manchester.
'The Hidden Gem'.
St Mary's was given the name 'The Hidden Gem' by Cardinal Vaughan, then Bishop of Salford. The Bishop, standing in the church said:
'Everywhere you look you behold a Hidden Gem'.

St Mary's was built in 1794, serving a slum district which suffered outbreaks of Cholera, and Typhus. The church opened Manchester's first Roman Catholic cemetery in 1816. St Mary's took part in the Whit Friday Walk from its beginning, until it lost its parish population and its Schools with re-housing of residents. The Church Guide Book states: 'St Mary's stands sentinel over the destinies of Roman Catholic and of non-Roman Catholics in Manchester'.

Corpus Christi Miles Platting in a 1920s Whit Friday R.C Walk.

Corpus Christi Miles Platting in a 1960s Whit Friday R.C Walk.

In and around Manchester

*The Author with Canon Roy Chow, the organiser of the Church of England Procession in Manchester City Centre.
They are walking with St Cuthbert's Miles Platting in a 1980s Procession.*

Acknowledgements

The Author's Thanks are extended to:

Julie Hurst for word-processing the manuscript of this book.

Beverley Wooding for preparing the book for publishing.

Simon Burns for assistance with photographs.

The Bishop of Manchester 2002-2012 for his Foreword.

Harold Hawksworth for reproducing some of the photographs.

The Manchester Evening News for permission to reproduce photographs, and quote extracts from the Evening News, and the Manchester Evening Chronicle.

The Oldham Evening Chronicle.
The Bury Times.
The Bolton News.

The, Bolton, Bury, Oldham, and Ashton-under-Lyne libraries.
The Wigan Museum.

Mary Whitehead, Author of 'What Happened in, and What Happened to, Sunday Schools in Ashton-under-Lyne.

Michael and Peter Fox, Authors of 'A Saddleworth Whitsuntide.'

The Author of 'Howe Bridge Remembered.'

Father Lannon of the Salford Diocesan Archives and the Diocese of Salford, for assistance with the Manchester Roman Catholic Whit Friday Procession.

James Stanhope Brown for permission to use extracts from his book 'Angels from the Meadow.'

Beverley Wooding for her great assistance with the photographs and revising parts of the text.

Manchester Library for various photographs.

Iris Burns for her assistance with the book.

And – to all those who have recalled their memories of the Whit Walks and loaned or given photographs of them.